# a Time to Live Anew

## A PRACTICAL GUIDE TO MANAGING YOUR RETIREMENT

### Harry W. Hepner

PROFESSOR EMERITUS, PSYCHOLOGY, SYRACUSE UNIVERSITY
AND MANAGEMENT CONSULTANT

McGRAW-HILL BOOK COMPANY

New York    St. Louis    San Francisco
London    Sydney    Toronto    Mexico    Panama

RETIREMENT—A TIME TO LIVE ANEW

# Author to Reader—A Personal Note

IF YOU HAVE RETIRED, or expect to do so in the near future, you doubtless have found it especially instructive to observe how people react as they approach the time for retirement, as well as what they do during the years that follow. You probably do this kind of observing without being especially aware of it, because retirement involves more adjustments than most of us realize. This habit of observing and talking with retirees in order to learn from them is a likely characteristic of the mentally alert person as he grows older.

Seeing, talking with, and reading about retirees can become profoundly enlightening. My observations have indicated that only an outstanding few have learned to think of retirement as an opportunity to enrich their lives, a time when they can add to and complement the sense of self-worth which they achieved in their work life. These men want to round out the best that has been developing within themselves through the previous years. Their spirits are high. Their outlook toward the future is an inspiration to me as well as to others who associate with them.

In contrast with these admired few, I have also met prospective retirees in the business world who held positions of important responsibility in their companies but who became emotionally aroused when they talked about their imminent retirement. Some even reviled in abusive language the company and the retirement policies of management. I was nonplussed, because I knew that these men had been well-treated by their management. I also knew that they had really enjoyed their work, as proved by the years of selfless devotion they had given to the company and their careers. I did not, at first, realize that many managerial, professional, and other trained men who give years of devotion to their work concentrate so hard on doing their job that they do not learn how to think of retirement as an opportunity—a time to move ahead into a new stage of life.

One of the early discoveries from my observations of retirees was that formal education does not always prepare men for retirement. Some very well-educated men in the academic world, as well as certain ones in business, do not adjust happily to retirement. The most striking example occurred when I was having lunch in the university cafeteria with a faculty friend whom we shall call Bill S. He had been retired several years. Previous to retirement, he was one of those rare personalities that every campus needs. Not only was he popular as a classroom teacher, but he took a personal interest in his students, particularly those from foreign countries. Whenever one of his foreign-born students ran out of funds and needed food and a place to live, he usually went to Bill's house. Sometimes his home resembled a crowded dormitory more than a home. At various times, ten or more students might be temporarily staying at Bill's house. Through the years, he had befriended many students to help them get an education.

I knew that Bill had not saved any money for retirement, and I wanted him to know that I respected the value choices he had made. As we were having lunch I mentioned several kindnesses he had done for others at his expense and congratulated him for his chosen values. Surprisingly, he became very angry, angry with himself because he considered his own life to have been one of failure. (See also page 214.)

The reactions of Bill and other retirees challenged me. I began to search for explanations as to why so many fine men who had led worthy work lives went through unnecessary tribulations in their retirement.

Of course my interest in the problems of retirees became accentuated when I, too, underwent mandatory retirement from university teaching. Now that I have been retired for ten years from teaching industrial psychology, I want to review some of the interpretations I have made on the basis of observations as a consultant in industry, as a student of applied psychology, and as an inquisitive retiree. Of the various kinds of adjustment to retirement that I observed, six are mentioned in the brief descriptions that follow.

When I talked with retirees and asked an individual how he was reacting to his retirement, the most frequent answer was "I'm happy. If I am happy, that's all that matters." On further discussion, I might find that he was neither very happy nor very unhappy— *he had merely adapted himself to the monotony of a life of nothingness* and had accepted that as happiness.

A different group of retirees, not especially conscious of how happy they are, consists of *those who continue to do the same kinds of work as previously but in another setting.* The different setting may be with another employer or for a community or other service organization. One of the distinctive characteristics of these men is their adaptability. Most of them enjoyed their career and are happy in their retirement because they have found other ways to gain the same satisfactions they enjoyed in their former employment.

A somewhat related group of men, not especially adaptable, go through no special adjustment process when they reach the usual age of retirement. *These men, whose careers call for creative talents* —artists, composers, musicians, writers, inventors, research specialists, philosophers, and many others—continue to do "what comes naturally." They never really retire. They simply continue to utilize the knowledge, skills, and judgment they developed through the years.

In contrast, the members of a different but very large group are *those who find it very difficult to utilize the knowledge, skills, and judgment they developed through the years.* These are the men who retire from the more responsible positions of modern business. Through the years they learned to develop and use their work potentials within the company type of business organization. When retirement forces them to function in an organizational setup that is unfamiliar to them, many feel uncertain, "shelved," or at the least, a bit confused. They have to learn how to adapt themselves to a new stage in life that may be more trying than the adjustment they made when they left school and took a regular job for the first time. The adjustment to retirement is more difficult because work habits and ways of thinking have been firmly established.

Most of my observations of retirees have been with men of business. I have worked and associated with them for several decades. I like them and enjoy their friendship. The one business group that requires a clarifying explanation consists of *those who insist emphatically that they enjoy retirement.* The pattern of adjustment of a member of this group usually discloses that when he had to retire because he had reached the mandatory age for it, he knew that he still had a lot of good potential that could be used by someone somewhere. He also knew that the management of his company did not want him to continue to work there. As a result, his feelings were hurt, and he became resentful. He felt as do many retirees but he adjusted differently—to overcome his feelings of rejection, he made up his mind to enjoy retirement to the utmost— he pursued his recreational activities with a ferocity that belied his claimed happiness.

Many different interpretations of happiness and patterns of adjustment to retirement were found, but one especially successful retirement group consisted of those whose occupational status, position in the community, education, health, or recreational activity followed no special pattern. They were, however, enjoying a kind of happiness favorable to peace and wisdom—*they were living in terms of a sustaining framework of thinking* that gave purpose to their lives. They had facial expressions of outward calm and, more importantly, their whole manner portrayed an inner serenity, a serenity which indicated that they had learned to enjoy the gift of living. They were happy, and yet they had not sought happiness as such. Happiness came to them, as it must to all men, not as an end in itself but as a by-product or side effect. It came to them because they had somehow learned to live in terms of a continuing interest, a theme, a code of ethics, or a goal that gave a lasting feeling of self-fulfillment. They lived for something more important than the attainment of personal happiness.

Of course most of the retirees whom I interviewed had high ethical standards and achievement goals before retirement. In their retirement they were interested in discussing ideas which might be of value to them. Questions they asked were likely to be expressed in phrasings which meant: "How can my life in retirement become more significant, not necessarily in a full-time job but in some way that gives purpose, other than rest, to the day when I wake up in the morning?" and "How can I stretch my mind occasionally in meaningful ways that will enable me to honestly feel that I have kept on growing as a person *all* the years of my life?" They realized that the retirement years should be very happy but that happiness for the intelligent retiree must have deeper meanings than mere self-entertainment. Their questions and interest stimulated me to collect and write the findings which have been of help to me and may be to others as well.

This book has been written for the recent or prospective retiree who

1. Is in good health.

2. Has income adequate for his needs.

3. Has worked hard and liked his work and the people with whom he worked.

4. Wants to know what other retirees and researchers have learned about retirement; wants ideas that may stimulate his thinking.

5. Intends to enjoy a mentally active retirement, one that will enable him to say to himself: "I have found greater satisfactions in retirement than I imagined possible in my youth."

The typical retiree does not know at the time of retirement what he wants to do to enjoy the future available to him, but he realizes that his retirement offers time to think and freedom to choose. In most cases, he is not very certain of what to think about, nor does he try to evaluate many of the choices available to him. His next step may be to get away as far as possible from his old work environment and go some place where he can play a little and think a lot.

If you have reached the age of personal interest in retirement, you know that you have learned so much through the years of work and your other experiences that you are proud of your inner resources. You probably are ready to review the total picture in order to build on the past and move ahead to even greater satisfactions than were possible while you were working full time. This special time to live anew can offer you finer meanings of Browning's thought: "The best is yet to be/The last of life, for which the first was made. . . ."

It is the purpose of this book to show how some men of business and the professions, men who have enjoyed their work, can reinterpret and assimilate their knowledge about retirement in relation to themselves. The effect on the outlook of the individual reader should be of an optimistic tone.

Of course this book will not give you all the answers, but it may stimulate thinking on your part that will lead you to develop answers for yourself.

*Harry W. Hepner*

# Acknowledgments

HUNDREDS OF individuals have shaped the content of this book. Certain business leaders made indirect contributions when they gave me assignments as a management consultant, assignments that happened to improve my understanding of retirees and their problems. These working relationships not only sharpened my insight into the influences that motivate retirees but also stimulated me to develop constructive approaches to the better utilization of the unappreciated potential within many men who retire from business and the professions.

One of my faculty colleagues, Raymond G. Kuhlen, frequently enriched my thinking through our discussions of current problems and researches in gerontology and related fields. Professor Rolf H. Monge suggested many enlightening research reports for my reading.

Warren Cobb, Elvyn S. Cowgill, Roy H. deBrauwere, John H. Harrigan, Hyman Hirsch, Leslie P. Moyer, Walter A. Papworth, Delmont K. Pfeffer, Sidney L. and Alice D. Pressey, Robert B. Robinson, Warren A. Rolph, and William D. Stansil made substantive recommendations. My secretary, Gladys K. Kennedy, not only typed the manuscript in its several stages but also made numerous inspections to ensure accuracy.

xi

Acknowledgments to authors and publishers for use of their published materials are given in the references. In addition to the mentioned sources, I am grateful to the following individuals for the special information or assistance they gave me in improving my knowledge of retirees and their thinking:

Walter F. Arnold, E. J. Boroughs, Sr., Donald P. Boyer, Jr., Charles and Kay Burlingham, R. H. Chadwick, Frances and John A. Clark III, James A. Close, Martin Coniff, John L. Crawford, John Cronk, Harry Devlin, Dudley P. Diggs, M. J. Donnelly, Fred and Kathryn Dudley, Clyde Ellis, William J. Eschenfelder, Bert J. Fuller, Harry S. Ganders, Nina E. Hepner, Ray Holcombe, Herschel Hollopeter, Alice Kline, Endicott R. Lovell, James R. Mailler, L. P. Marks, Herman S. Marshall, Luther L. Mays, Albert Mendelsohn, John K. Menzies, Percy Miller, Robert C. Mixter, Don S. More, James V. O'Leary, Gardner Putney, John A. Riddick, H. Rodriquez, Loyd W. Rowland, E. A. Soderstrom, Charles S. Venable, Howard Vescelius, John Von Pischke, Dean Warren, Elmer Winter, Joan L. Winter, Frank Wolford, Abraham Wolfson, and A. H. Wohlrab.

# Contents

xiii

*Retirement—a Time to Live Anew*

# PART ONE

# Attitudes and Intentions

CHAPTER ONE

# Your First Reactions
# to Retirement

*"For age is opportunity no less*
*Than youth itself, though in another dress."*
　　—HENRY WADSWORTH LONGFELLOW

IF YOU HAVE NOT been the "honored guest" at a retirement party
or even attended one, you should find it an interesting experience.
These parties differ markedly. In a large corporation, the "higher-
ups" in the managerial hierarchy are likely to be given a pleasant
send-off when they retire: cocktails, dinner, speeches seasoned with
humorous anecdotes about the retiree, and one fairly good speech
by the retiree—perhaps written by an able ghost-writer of the
company's public relations department.

When a member of the middle management echelon or a technical specialist retires, there may be less formality and less of the
plush. The retiree's speech is likely to be unwritten, but it is his own
and sincere. The general atmosphere is convivial. The girls of the
office attend, and they are dressed in their frilliest prettiest gowns
because some of the eligible bachelor salesmen are likely to be
present. Invariably, the retiree gets kissed by each of the girls. And
he usually enjoys it!

3

In the university world where I have enjoyed many happy years as a faculty member, the parties for retirees are likely to be on the sedate side, less humor and more of the serious stiffness that is characteristic of introverted scientists. On some occasions the men are attired in the black tuxedos they bought when they were freshmen in college. The few women present are mostly bookish Ph.D. spinsters, and so there is little conviviality and certainly no kissing of the retiree by the girls. But the paper carefully prepared and read by the retiree is likely to be worth hearing.

Two elements are evident but never mentioned openly in any retirement party, regardless of whether it is conducted for a member of a corporate family or someone in the academic world: (1) the younger men in the group, particularly those who worked for or with the retiree, are glad to see the "old man" go—the chances of their moving ahead have increased and now they will have more opportunity to do their own work without his influence; (2) the retiree himself is sure within himself that no one, absolutely no one, can ever really fill his place! In spite of his convictions about the lack of ability of his successor, he is so conscious of the party and the felicitations of friends that he talks about the possible benefits of retirement during the party. This emphasis on the pleasures usually lasts for a month or two after the retirement date. (See pages 77 to 80 for some later thoughts and feelings.)

### First thoughts on possible benefits

If you will ask prospective or recent retirees in the early stages of their retirement what benefits they expect to enjoy or have, the first answers are likely to include ideas such as the following, stated by nineteen individuals:

1. *A sense of release from pressures.* Examples:
   "After forty-five years of getting out in the morning and going to work on time, it's a BIG BONANZA to be able to roll over and take another snooze followed by a leisurely shave, shower, breakfast, and reading the morning paper."

"When you are working on a regular job, the requirements and routines of the job must be performed, but when you retire, you are released from drudgery. Now I am free to do anything at any time that I wish—not as the job requires."

"Now that I've struggled through putting the children through college and they are on their own, I can begin to enjoy life with a sense of completion about my responsibilities."

"My first reaction to retirement was a new feeling of freedom. I was free from bothersome obligations, from commitments, from competition. I could do whatever I wanted. But now I am having a second reaction from the first. It is the sobering discovery that the freedom of retirement also brings with it the very important need to have worthwhile wants."

"I'm released from obeying certain social conventions that were part of my job. I do not have to visit anyone socially in order to advance myself or the company's interests. I can decline or accept invitations as I wish and I can seek the friendships of people whom I choose."

"I do not have to please certain supervisors, customers, clients, or colleagues. I am free from all organization pressures of deadlines and budgets. Some of these I enjoyed but some I would have preferred to ignore or be without."

One release from inner pressure that will be mentioned, but only in confidence, by a few retirees is their belief that almost every man has one or two secret feelings about certain situational requirements in his work life when he was not quite as loyal to his principles as he thought he should be. He let expediency overrule his best ideals. Retirement means that he need not go through that kind of conflict within himself again.

2. *Opportunities to enjoy the self-chosen activities and hobbies.* Examples:

"I want to work in the garden and the yard even though the crabgrass grows right back again. The house, yard, and garden will keep me busy for the next few years. After that, I'll think of something else that ought to be done to keep me out of doors.

"My home workshop and do-it-yourself tools have not been used enough to keep them from getting rusty. My workshop and tools are extensions of my fingers and arms—'cutting off their use,' as by moving into an apartment, would be something like cutting off a hand."

"I want to be able to sit down and read the books I've intended to read for years but never got around to. Maybe I'll even take an evening course or two and, hopefully, discover that the old brain 'ain't' as bad as my kids claimed years ago."

"When I was a boy, I was interested in music—thought I could be a great pianist some day. Obviously, I never made it but I'd like to refurbish what I once knew and could do."

"Like most busy men, I have been promising myself for years that come retirement with its leisure time, I would do something 'worthwhile.' Even though I enjoyed my daily work, I found that some of the bright ideas that intruded into my work mind had to be shunted aside for a more favorable time in the future. Retirement is the one last opportunity I will have to put actual effort into the implementing of those good intentions."

3. *Improving relations with family and friends.* Examples:

"I want to sort of compensate my wife for all the thousands of times I pursued my business interests regardless of how unfair the situation was to her. I neglected her over weekends, holidays, and in the evenings for many years, and on many occasions when I let her remain alone or to shift for herself in order to further my career. Of course I always rationalized it by telling her I was doing it for both of us and eventually it would pay off and I'd devote myself to her when I retired. Well, the time is here and I am looking forward to the companionship we shall have together. Perhaps I can make up to some extent for her quiet acceptance of the situations I imposed on her more often than she deserved."

"The children have grown up, married, and left home. I am not going to try to live with any one of them, but I do want to be with each family to know them better and show them that I am available if they should need me. That won't take more than a month or two each year but I can plan the year's activities with that purpose as a starting point."

"Now that the children have left home, my wife and I have gotten acquainted with the children of the neighborhood. They visit our house and we plan ahead to have candies, toys, and games ready for their calls. I plan my conversations with them. As a result, we have learned to feel optimistic about the future generation. I really don't see how the world can go all bad, ever, when there are so many nice children who will take our place. I might, in my retirement, even try to arrange to help out in one of the nearby orphanages."

4. *Travel plans.* Examples:

"My wife and I have traveled a great deal in this country but not in Europe or South America. We are looking forward to seeing London, Paris, Rome, Istanbul, Hawaii, Rio de Janeiro, and a dozen other places. After several jaunts to the tourist spots, we shall have some new places in mind for later trips."

"I've had a yen for years to own a cruising ketch and take off for parts unknown. Retirement will give me the opportunity until the wife rebels."

5. *Move to a new area.* Examples:

"I'm fed up with the harsh climate where I have had to live most of my life. Now that we can move to almost any place we choose, we are on our way, someplace, soon."

"I suppose every person who retires likes to think that a lot of other places must be more attractive: better climate, lower taxes, more friendly people, and lower living costs. I do not know where they are but my wife and I are starting off in a small mobile home and we are going to look at a lot of towns and areas we have read about. We'll take our time and eventually make up our minds."

"I'm going to some retirement spot where I can play golf every day and attend a cocktail party every evening if I want!"

## Rationalizations

As a retiree in the early stage of retirement, you will enjoy hearing the usual rationalizations about retirement. An example is the comment of some other retiree who tells you about a conversation between a man of seventy and a youth of twenty. When the youth pointed out the difference between their ages, he said: "Ah, that means I'm fifty years to the good in comparison with you." To which the older man replied: "Not necessarily, I'm sure of my fifty years but you are not!"

A common type of rationalization deals with the lessening of one's urges as he grows older, as in "The best thing about getting older is that all the things I couldn't have when I was young, I no longer want."

One of the frequent rationalizations in which we indulge deals with definitions of old age. Years are not especially significant in defining old age. Some persons seem old at forty. Others seem young at eighty. Oliver Wendell Holmes expressed this when he said, "To be seventy years young is sometimes more cheerful and hopeful than to be forty years old."

As Jonathan Swift put it: "Every man desires to live long but no man would be old."

We all know that some people become old while young, whereas others remain young even though they have lived many years. And we change our definitions, as Bernard M. Baruch stated: "To me, old age is always fifteen years older than I am." Perhaps this recognition has given rise to the humorous description of the three stages in a man's life as first, youth; second, middle age; and third, the oft-used greeting given the older person: "My, but you're looking well!"

Concepts and definitions of aging vary widely. A man may be as old as his friends think him to be, as his arteries, or as he feels. To most persons, it lies in the eye of the beholder. To a child of seven, the adolescent is old. To the adolescent, people in their forties are old. To the man in the sixties, the octogenarian is old.

Those of us who have reached the sixties have known some adolescents who seemed to be old and worn-out before they attained adulthood!

Today the normal man at sixty-five feels younger than his ancestors did at forty-five.

Now that science and technology have added more years to our lives, it is up to you and to me to add more life to our years. We can forget about definitions of old age and concentrate instead on squeezing as much pleasure as possible from our remaining years. As a possible aid in the "squeezing" we should become acquainted with definitions of the sciences that deal with aging.

*Gerontology* is the science of aging. The word is derived from the Greek *geron,* meaning *old man,* and *ology,* the *study of.*

*Geriatrics* is the field of medical practice which is concerned with the physiologic and disease problems of those in later maturity and of the elderly. Geriatrics deals with the health of the aged.

*Aging* is a process that occurs in all persons, regardless of chronological age. Strictly speaking, we should use "the aged" when we refer to older people, but the common practice has developed of referring to "the aging" rather than to "the aged"—many people who are past middle age dislike to think of themselves as "aged."

You and I should be delighted that children born in the United States enjoy increasingly longer life expectancies. In 1789, the expectancy was thirty-five years. Currently, it is about double that figure. Of course the fact that the average person today is living longer and enjoying the benefits of our modern technological developments means that men can retire earlier. Many of us who now retire at the age of sixty or thereabout have an extra quarter of a lifetime or more to use as we please.

But all these scientific studies and evaluations, helpful as they may be, will not be enough to satisfy you. A longer life is not enough —breadth and depth are more important. You will need not only rationalizations about the past and the present, but personal convictions that will sustain you through the years ahead, whatever their number may be. During retirement, the perspectives gained through your earlier years should enable you to move ahead to the optimum enjoyment of living at its very best.

## Reassurances regarding the stage ahead

Adjustment to retirement by many healthy, mentally alert men is not easy. Instead, it is stressful. The stresses brought about by retirement are somewhat similar to those of adolescence, but adulthood gives us certain advantages we did not have during adolescence. We have acquired some perspectives of life and learned how to deal with some stresses. We have learned some proved procedures that were not available to us in our adolescence. Rightly treated, aging can be made more satisfying, even more thrilling than youth. W. Somerset Maugham phrased the prospect beautifully for us:

For the complete life, the perfect pattern, includes old age as well as youth and maturity. The beauty of the morning and the radiance of noon are good, but it would be a very silly person who drew the curtains and turned on the light in order to shut out the tranquility of the evening.[1]

An important approach to dealing with the stresses when you enter retirement should be to utilize the same positive adjustment patterns you learned in your years before retirement. Throughout your earlier years, when you met the usual problems of illness, bereavement, or loss of job, you didn't throw up your hands or go into an emotional tailspin. Instead, you dealt with each situation as intelligently and constructively as you could. You kept your emotional balance. The same attitude applies to the problems and adjustments of retirement.

Aging is not a burden that has been placed upon you and all others by a cruel Nature. Far from it. It will bring its own rewards to you if you will train yourself to see and appreciate them.

The old satisfactions from work, achievement, and success must evolve into new ways of life that bring about a sense of growth as a person through appreciating some of the neglected enjoyments of living. Retirement at its best is not merely a matter of aging, but a challenge toward growth as a person.

We ought to enter old age in the same spirit that a good student enters the senior year in college—with a zestful anticipation toward a summing up of what has been learned in the previous stages of the program and expectations of new growth in previously neglected aspects of living.

Retirement *suddenly* offers you a great amount of time to use as you wish, not as a job requires. This is one of life's best opportunities to develop new and better ways of gaining self-expression and usefulness as a person. However, some of the criteria for ego satisfactions which were applied during early adulthood and middle age may not be appropriate to the retirement years. Previous to retirement you may have justified your existence by the possessions you owned, your status, or by the numbers of friends with whom you associated, but now you are moving into a way of life that becomes gratifying to you in terms of other, possibly finer enjoyments.[2] Instead of merely adding more things to your living, you now can concentrate on the meanings of things and ideas. You can seek new interpretations of the intrinsically worthwhile things in life. In this way your sense of growth as a person continues into new and more satisfying directions.

In times past, people who reached sixty had only two major phases in their lives: learning and earning. Now there is a third: one in which to harvest the just rewards of the first two—the *interpreting*. Instead of looking upon retirement with fear and doubt, you can learn to regard it as a challenge to interpret your experiences, both old and new. Interpreting here means perceiving them in their proper perspectives and gaining pleasure from their significance. Chapters 11 to 14 deal with this important phase of life.

The fact that you could adapt yourself to the stress situations of your youth indicates that you have the inner resources to adapt yourself satisfactorily to the stresses and opportunities of your later years. If you do not make intelligent adaptations as you grow older, you run the risk of developing senile characteristics even though there are no organic causes of senility. You might become cranky, loquacious, boastful about real or imagined past achievements, follow some fad of the time, or become ultraconservative and find fault with modern customs, particularly those of the younger generation.

When you were young you may have hoped to become financially able to retire and enjoy life. Well, now you've reached it. At least you are retired. Why not, therefore, think of retirement not as a catastrophe, but as an opportunity for learning new aspects of living?

## Research studies of how well others adjusted to retirement

Reports of research studies are of some value in deciding whether you are likely to learn to enjoy retirement, but the usual sociologists' surveys tell you what happened among numbers of people! What happens to most or certain classifications of people does not tell you what will happen to *you*. As an example, statistics of one survey indicated that in the sixty-five to seventy-four age group, 12 percent have some limitation of physical mobility. Data of that kind have interest for the scientists but they say nothing about you as an individual. You may be either in the 12 percent group that has some physical limitations in getting around or you may be one of the 88 percent that does not have the problem.

However, data of research studies are of value because they suggest probabilities. You are likely to gain some reassurance for yourself from excerpts [3] of several especially significant reports presented here:

1. One extensive study of some 4,000 people approximately seventy years of age and over, from many income and occupational strata, resulted in hopeful findings for prospective retirees, regardless of health and economic status: "Overall, the data suggest quite emphatically that a high proportion of retirees possess a degree of role flexibility which enables them readily to adapt to a greatly reduced income and to a new life situation. Although the influence of health and economic factors is clear, the picture is largely one of successful adjustment, even for those whose health and economic situation are poor." [4]

2. When 500 men over sixty were asked whether they thought of themselves as middle-aged, elderly, old, or what, those who regarded themselves as younger or who denied that they were old had higher morale than those who admitted to being old or elderly. [5] Most of those who still perceived themselves as young or middle-aged were from the high-status groups. Generally, those who claim to be or imagine that they are younger are not only in a higher category of the socioeconomic scale, but are also more optimistic about their health and are more often employed than those who say they are old.

3. The findings of another study of eighty-seven older men suggested "that at least among older men who are not suffering from ill health or economic deprivation, there are psychological gains in old age that compensate for its losses." [6] According to this study, the new satisfactions can be in the forms of reconciling goals to achieve-

ments, decreased need for achievement, enjoying friendships, and other pleasurable activities that were not as readily available before retirement. The achievements in the retirement years can be self-selected and directed toward growth as a person.

4. A comprehensive study was made of the needs of older people of the Kips Bay–Yorkville Health District of New York City. The venture was cooperatively conducted by the Department of Health of New York City, Cornell University Medical College, Cornell University Social Science Research Center, and the Russell Sage Foundation. The sample selection procedure was purposely drawn to represent the lower economic stratum—59 percent of the 500 were drawn from that stratum. Only 11 percent were well-to-do, and 30 percent were from the middle economic class. The sample dealt with predominantly foreign-born groups in an urban setting.

One of the most significant findings was the following: "When economic and social status groups are compared on the question of satisfaction with retirement, we find that 59 per cent of the high status group have found retirement better than expected, but only 24 per cent of the low status group have found it so." [7]

5. A systematic study of forty-seven elderly men who were physically and mentally healthy and representative of the aging who continue to function adequately in the community showed that many of them, though sixty-one to ninety-one years of age, considered their "aging" changes to be increases, not deficits, for living. They thought of the changes associated with advancing age as positive and of their other limiting changes as modifiable in the direction of the positive. This means that if you start your retirement years not in an anxious but in a positive frame of thinking, you are likely to discover that advancing age can lead to not only acceptable, but happy, reactions for you. [8]

6. One study in a midwestern city, using a statistically balanced sample of 100 men and 100 women, sixty-five years of age and over, showed that those over eighty were just about as happy and well-adjusted as the sixty-five-year-olds. [9] Generally, the people who felt unhappy and wretched after eighty were wretched and miserable before they were sixty-five.

### "Retirement shock"

To many an able man, mandatory retirement is a kind of condemnation to a reduced state of existence. In the years on his job, a man becomes a member of a network of pleasant human relations in an organization. Retirement demolishes them. As a result, he feels that he has become a less important member of society. Small wonder that the thought of retirement is like an approaching dark cloud in his life and that some refer to the effects of the event as "retirement shock." In some cases, the dark-cloud effects last so long that the retiree fails to discover the positive benefits of retirement.

Harold R. Hall, professor of research in business administration, Graduate School of Business Administration, Harvard University, after thirty years in active business, resigned his position to devote full time to the study of executive retirement. The primary method of obtaining information was by means of personal interviews. He obtained interview data from 125 retired executives and 300 active executives of companies. In addition, about fifty interviews were held with professional men. He was especially interested in the activity programming and financial programming by retirees before retirement. Interestingly, he found that the omission of activity programming in preparation for retirement is likely to cause the retiree more trouble than does inadequate financial programming. The test of the benefits of activity programming comes in the crucial first year of retirement.[10]

Hall's study of the approximate degree and range of retirement shock of executives indicated that "Perhaps one-half of the retired executives experienced adjustment trouble after they left their companies." The following two paragraphs were written by an executive who stated that he had experienced great retirement shock:

Although any realistic executive can foresee the financial problems and readjustments that will accompany retirement, it is my belief that few of them foresee what retirement will mean to them psychologically. Certainly I had no such foresight. On the last day of a given year the retiring executive is a respected and honored member of an important business group. *One day later he is—nobody.* Unwanted, unneeded, with no established place in the business community, his world has shrunk to the dimensions of his insignificant and unplaced self. This sudden change, inadequately realized in advance, has been rightly identified as "retirement shock." Only those who have experienced it can have any concept of the force of its impact.

I am aware that some retiring executives escape this shock. They retire happily to active and long-anticipated participation in other well-established interests. Or their retirement frees them from certain unhappy environmental conditions in their business careers. Most retiring executives, however, are in neither of these two classes. For them no lately adopted hobbies or other avocational interests can possibly substitute for the happiness of achievement and of established standing in a successful and respected business position. *Life goes on, but its zest is gone.*[11]

Hall's study of executives compared the attitudes toward retirement on the part of younger executives, thirty-five to fifty years of age, with the attitudes of older executives, sixty to sixty-five years of age. The findings indicated that the majority of younger executives thought that they would want to leave their companies at normal retirement age. Most of them expressed the feeling, "I'll welcome retirement, just give me a chance to get away from this business pressure."

In contrast, the majority of older executives wanted to continue with their companies because the alternative of retirement did not appeal to them. Of the older men, 65 percent wanted to stay on full time with their companies; only 15 percent of the younger men thought they would want to stay on full time. To the older men, those near retirement, the disadvantages of pressure all but disappeared from their thinking. Overall, the executives who said that they wanted to continue with their companies looked with disfavor on "retirement from" and lacked a concept of "retirement to."

In the case of some executives who wanted to continue with the company, the wife was an important influence. She objected to having the husband around the house, to a cutback in the standard of living that would come from a reduced salary, or she wanted to keep the prestige of being married to an active executive.

In general, when the wishes of executives were considered *at or*

*near the normal age of their retirement*, about 90 percent would
have liked to continue active and productive assignments with their
companies, with a new business firm, or with some public-service
activity.[12] Approximately three-fourths of the executives wanted to
continue with their old organizations, full time or part time. Generally, increasing age tends to be accompanied by increasing appre-
hension over the prospect of retirement. In many instances, the
closer the individual comes to retirement age, the more likely he is
to repress the whole idea.[13]

### Socioeconomic-level differences

Changes in mental outlook at the time of retirement may be
seriously discomforting or they may be taken in stride, even welcomed. The likelihood of shock or pleasure varies decidedly with
retirees from different socioeconomic levels.

A questionnaire survey of 301 older employees of the Standard
Oil Company of differences in attitudes toward aging and retirement
at various occupational levels indicated that retirement-planning
programs should be designed for at least two occupational levels:
one program should meet the needs of upper-level occupational
groups, who seem to have relatively favorable attitudes and plans
for their old age but who may need the opportunity to reinterpret
and assimilate their knowledge; a second program should be designed for the manual worker, who although he may have favorable
abstract concepts of retirement and old age, cannot find in those
abstractions the promise of a meaningful and well-rounded life for
himself.[14]

In the lower occupational levels and in rural areas the desire to
continue to work in a paying job is far lower than among executives
and professional men. A study by Dr. J. H. Jones of the Louisiana
Agricultural Extension Service, Caldwell Parish, during the summer
of 1966 covered 950 persons; 883 did not want to work and only 40
were employed. Another 27 wanted to work but were not employed
because of health reasons. Interestingly, only 58 claimed that the
meeting of expenses was never a serious problem! And yet, about

one-half of the 950 mentioned finances as always being a problem, serious or mild.[15] Apparently the problem was not serious enough to cause most of these 475 to want to go to work—they could make do with what little they had!

A third study of retired men, one that probably dealt with individuals somewhere between those of the occupational levels of the Hall study and those of Caldwell Parish, was sponsored by the Institute of Life Insurance and conducted by an independent research organization. All the 429 male retirees surveyed were fifty-five or older, taken from a total sample of approximately 7,000 households. Three out of four had been skilled or semiskilled workers before retirement. About one out of five had been a white-collar worker, professional or business proprietor; 3 percent had been unskilled workers.

Only 44 percent of the retirees stated that they had retired voluntarily. The rest retired largely because of company regulations or due to health or disability problems. (Even though these reported figures indicate that less than half the retired men in the United States really wanted to retire, it is quite probable that some who said they had retired for nonvoluntary reasons were glad to do so.)

Less than a third gave much thought to retirement before it took place. Before they retired, only 28 percent had given "quite a bit of thought" to retirement, and only 6 percent had made detailed plans such as moving to a smaller residence, saving money, or making investments for retirement needs. This 6 percent figure suggests that if you look to most of your retired friends to give you guidance in planning your own retirement, you are not likely to get very much help. Most retirees just gravitate into retirement—few do intelligent thinking or planning for it. Two-thirds of the group sampled had to live on much smaller incomes after retirement, but few considered finances their greatest problem. And most felt that finding things to do in retirement was "no problem at all."

Only 17 percent rated their finances as "a big problem." Half of them said finances were "no problem at all."

About one out of seven of the retirees was still earning some money by working at least part time.[16]

Generally, when income differences in relation to adjustment to retirement are considered, the studies indicate that those with high incomes and those with low incomes tend to find it easier to cope with retirement than those in the middle-income ranges.

The problems of retirement for many individuals appear to be most severe just before retirement but the anxieties tend to recede as the retiree develops ways of adjustment to the new conditions.

Most retirees do adapt themselves to retirement after a few months, but the adaptation may be one of dullness, not zestful living. Many who claim they are happy realize, in a limited way, that their lives have become as dulled to worthy living as those of the feebleminded who are happy when they are physically comfortable. The Arabs sense the difference when they say, "Time is life"; not "Time is money."

Your ability to go happily through all the stages of adjustment to retirement and to enjoy being a retiree can be facilitated to a great extent by the preparation you give yourself for your new role. A large part of the preparation is in your attitudes. If you have developed favorable attitudes toward the problems involved, you should be able to make the adjustments more easily.

When you accept retirement in a meek, unconcerned spirit, you are doing far more psychologically than leaving the world of work; you are, in a way, resigning yourself to an inactive, dull existence. That is why many normal, healthy men "fight" retirement. They refuse to quit active living that easily. They plan for retirement, but those who set up "nice-looking" plans that have little meaning for them will not achieve an easy way of retired life. The preretirement attitude, not the plan, is a determining factor. This favorable preretirement attitude must include a recognition of the problems of retirement.

## REFERENCES

1. From *The Summing Up* by W. Somerset Maugham, by permission of Doubleday & Company, Inc., and A. P. Watt & Son, London, authorized by the Literary Executors of W. Somerset Maugham and William Heinmann Ltd., outside the United States.
2. This view of aging is part of the "disengagement theory," as contrasted

with the "activity theory." See E. Cumming and W. E. Henry, *Growing Old*, New York: Basic Books, 1961, and Robert J. Havighurst, Bernice L. Neugarten, and Sheldon S. Tobin, "Disengagement, Personality and Life Satisfaction in the Later Years," in *Age With A Future*, from Hansen (ed.), Philadelphia: F. A. Davis Co., 1964, pp. 419–425.

3. The author recognizes that these excerpts are taken out of context. A book of this kind could not include all that some researchers might like to see. However, those readers who wish to know the context may use the listed references.

4. Gordon F. Streib, Wayne E. Thompson, and E. A. Suchman, "The Cornell Study of Occupational Retirement," *The Journal of Social Issues*, vol. 14, no. 2, p. 13, 1958.

5. Bernard Kutner, David Fanshel, Alice M. Togo, and Thomas S. Langner, *Five Hundred over Sixty*, New York: Russell Sage Foundation, 1956, p. 98.

6. See Suzanne Kate Reichard, Florine Livson, and Paul G. Petersen of the Institute of Industrial Relations, University of California, Berkeley, in *Aging and Personality*, New York, John Wiley & Sons, Inc., 1962, p. 168.

7. Kutner et al., *op. cit.*, p. 87.

8. See James E. Birren et al. (eds.), *Human Aging*, Public Health Service Publication no. 986, 1963, chap. 11.

9. See Robert J. Havighurst and Ruth Albrecht, *Older People*, New York: Longmans, Green and Co., Inc., 1953, p. 53.

10. Harold R. Hall, *Some Observations on Executive Retirement*, Boston: Harvard University, Graduate School of Business Administration, Division of Research, 1953, p. 10.

11. *Ibid.*, pp. 94–95.

12. *Ibid.*, pp. 87–91.

13. G. H. Crook and M. Heinsten, *The Older Worker in Industry*, Berkeley: University of California, Institute of Industrial Relations, 1958.

14. Ernest W. Burgess, Lawrence G. Corey, Peter C. Pineo, and Richard T. Thornbury, "Occupational Differences in Attitudes toward Aging and Retirement," *Journal of Gerontology*, vol. 13, no. 2, pp. 203–206, April, 1958.

15. C. L. Mondart, Sr., "Vocational Education for the Aged," presented at the Sixth Annual Conference of the Louisiana State Advisory Committee on Aging, Oct. 26, 1967.

16. "Some Data on Life Insurance and Related Characteristics of the Older Population," Nov., 1964, Institute of Life Insurance, 277 Park Ave., New York, N.Y. 10017.

## CHAPTER TWO

# Anticipating Your Retirement Problems

*"To quit and sit back and let the world go by, is the equivalent of introducing dry rot into the tree of life."*

—EDWARD J. STEIGLITZ [1]

IN INDUSTRY when you reach the company's mandatory retirement age, you will become a *former* executive who no longer holds his position of personal leadership and responsibility, a *former* accountant who has no accounting to do, a *former* marketing man who has nothing to sell and no prospects on whom to call, or some other *former* careerist. The same kind of changed situation can occur to a retiree from the professions as well as from business.

The years you gave to your vocation were given with a realization that you did your work as a result of self-development and under conditions that involved competitive effort. You knew that if you didn't do your job in an acceptable manner you would be replaced. But you did your work, day after day, and year after year. You achieved a certain way of life for yourself. It became a comfortable, reassuring pattern of living each day and each year. Then, suddenly, that way of life was shifted. The event—retirement!

The problems that you see ahead for yourself probably have been mentioned by other retirees. They usually mention:

1. Life without work would be empty. (He has not as yet found another job or developed interests as satisfying as his previous occupation, but that problem can be solved.)

2. The income will be less and the reduction comes at a time when a man's potential for increasing his income have been lessened. (He may be unduly apprehensive or does not give proper weight to the lessened expenses in relation to his retirement income.)

3. He fears loneliness. (He has not as yet discovered that lots of interesting people can be found almost anywhere if he will look for them. Besides, many fellow retirees are interesting conversationalists and often become delightful friends.)

4. He conjures specters of poor health and an early death. (Retirement does not speed one's death. Many assume that it does because they see instances of retirees who die within a few years after they retire. Available evidence indicates that most of these were in poor health *before* they retired. In some instances, the retirement, per se, probably prolonged rather than shortened their life.)

Small wonder that some very fine men are embittered when they retire—they have not prepared themselves mentally for retirement. This kind of neglect of preparation can be recognized by observers as shown by the revelatory Kips Bay–Yorkville, New York, study, *Five Hundred over Sixty*. A negative evaluation of retirement is found among those: "(1) whose self-image (reflecting feelings of deprivation) is also negative, (2) who are relatively isolated socially, (3) who tended to dislike the idea of retirement in the first place, and (4) who had to give up their jobs because of poor health." [2]

As you can see, these characteristics can be recognized by the prospective retiree *before* retirement. Of the above list, what is the key factor that you and I as retirees must face up to?

I think it is in the "feelings of deprivation." Of what does (or will) retirement deprive you? What pleasures will it take away from you and what "insults of life" will it involve for you?

Some feelings of deprivation are likely to arise on the part of retirees who have earned a relatively high salary. The psychological needs differ somewhat from those of men who earned low salaries. Most men from the low-income strata have learned how to accept a static level of achievement and purchasing power. The higher-income retirees still have their strong urges to advance, to improve their income and their social status. Their inner needs for a sense of ongoingness at the time of mandatory retirement is likely to be exceedingly strong. This fundamental motive of life has been called the drive for continued "expansion." Those who, before retirement, have attained a high level of achievement are almost certain to want to continue to be active in retirement. When activity stops abruptly, contentment is likely to stop.

This effect was succinctly stated by President Elliot of Harvard when at the age of sixty he wrote to William James: "We have a sense of growth and increased capacity for useful service. We find our lives enriched and amplified from year to year. So long as this enlarging process goes on, we shall be content. If it stops suddenly, we shall be content to that date."

A first step in your dealing with the problems is to recognize and prepare yourself mentally for them. To help you do this is the purpose of this chapter.

## YOU, only YOU, can make your retirement successful

If your retirement turns out to be successful, it will be an achievement on your part, not a happenstance. It will be the product of your thoughtful efforts, initiative, and determination. Admittedly, you may have a friend or an employer give you an unasked-for job, but employment is only one aspect of successful retirement. The more difficult aspects are your morale, your self-esteem, your attitude toward the future, and continuing growth as a person.

New self-images and objectives in living are not acquired overnight. Time and conscious effort by an individual who has good inner resources are needed. The process, however, can be expedited through a systematic program as indicated by an experiment con-

ducted by Ruth Andrus who, using eleven college graduates, aged
sixty and over, directed a program designed to test the hypothesis
that appreciable and significant changes would occur in older persons who are in a cooperative, stimulating, and supportive environment. Through a program of lectures and discussions, creative writing, work in gardens, art, etc., positive psychological changes were
effected. These changes included greater alertness, more vigor,
higher self-esteem, and the development of a more hopeful attitude
toward the future. For these men the image of "old age" was shat-
tered and in its place was substituted a picture of the more nearly
normal functioning man.[3]

Note that in this experiment someone provided the stimulation to
the oldsters. *In your case, you should realize that no one will provide
the stimulation for you—you will have to do it for yourself.* You are
responsible for your happiness in retirement. This has been true
throughout your life, but when you retire, you may have a tendency
to let down, to say to yourself: "I'm tired of looking after others—let
somebody else look after me now."

One way to bring yourself back to the attitude that you will look
after yourself in a more determined manner than ever is to visit a
place where retirees do their loafing. There you will see a lot of old
folks sitting around waiting for someone to wait on them. They gave
up long ago. Now they are existing in their own boredom. (I visited
such a place before I retired and the effects of the visit made it easy
for me to keep busy ever since!)

The big difference between those who achieve genuine happiness
in retirement and those who are defeated by it is not in the degree or
intensity of their feelings of frustration when they retire but in their
refusal to accept defeat and to continue persistently in the quest for
active, meaningful living. Research studies have shown that those
who get "highly favorable adjustment" scores in regard to attitudes
toward their aging tend to think of themselves as "middle-aged"
regardless of their calendar age.

When Booth Tarkington was seventy-five, someone asked him
whether old people feel old in spirit. He answered, "I don't know.
Why don't you ask some of them?"

Let us consider some of the common problems that are associated with a retiree's willingness to give up. How he counteracts the effects of these will be helpful in bringing about an effective self-image and an urge to adopt more zestful living.

## What has status meant to you?

As mentioned above, one of the most painful effects of retirement to men of achievement in business is the loss of job status. Top- and middle-management executives are likely to be men whose ego needs demand a title. Once they attain it, they protect it assiduously. And when they lose it, they deeply resent the loss. After retirement, they feel they have become a "nobody." Kindhearted associates in the company may try to prevent or alleviate these negative reactions. They may allow the prospective retiree in the company to keep his regular title, but they change the organizational structure to make place for training a younger man. In spite of the intended kindness, the older man is likely to feel shunted aside, downgraded, especially when the number of his subordinates has been decreased. Many a man in business and government measures his status by the number of his subordinates, and any shift in the organizational structure that decreases the number of his subordinates is often a traumatic event for him.

This way of thinking even takes place among research men in industry. I have seen group leaders in an industrial laboratory become angry merely because one of their men was shifted to another research project. Too many able research men and engineers in industry have "sold" their potentials for doing creative work by going into a relatively ordinary administrative job that happened to have a title.

Of course many fine men in the professional world are not concerned about administrative types of status—they do their work because of its intrinsic values. A great scientist does not need a title. A great teacher does not need a title. None of the great teachers whom I ever had needed a title. All were dedicated to teaching, to helping youth develop youth's best potentials.

A teacher who loves to teach practices teaching methods, likes his students, and is not concerned about getting status by becoming a dean, a school principal, or a city superintendent. He has chosen his values, lives by them, and is likely to be happy in retirement. Some superior businessmen, as well as scientists, are not concerned about status. They do their work because of its intrinsic values for the social benefits: by raising the standard of living through marketing new and better products and services to more people, by producing goods at lower costs in order to contribute to the benefits of mass production and consumption, and by organizing and directing the efforts of employees in ways that strengthen their characters and utilize their potentials for personal growth.

Isn't this a rather idealistic way to perceive the socioeconomic thinking of businessmen? Yes, it is, but it is easy to find idealistic businessmen, as exemplified by the records of the International Executive Service Corps. These men are not youngsters of the Peace Corps. Instead, they are mature industrialists who work for nothing or very little remuneration in foreign countries. Most are retirees, practical men over sixty years of age. They volunteer to go abroad to help businessmen in the developing countries who need their expert counsel. At this writing, more than 300 have gone to some thirty countries to share the benefits of their know-how with their counterparts abroad. In addition to those who have already made their contributions, IESC receives about 200 inquiries a month from executives, preretired as well as retired, most of whom are willing to go whenever or wherever they are needed. (See also Chapter 8.)

## *How will you react when some people think of you as "old"?*

Retirement shock, if it does occur, does not usually take place because of the suddenness of retirement. Almost all men know when they will retire. Psychological effects often attributed to shock are accentuated when the retired individual realizes that others refer to him as an "old-timer" or use an appellation even less complimentary, such as "a has-been." Sooner or later, you too will discover that you occasionally are treated as an aging person. Younger men will refer to you as "Mr. Obsolete," "Old Out-of-Phase," or say that you are "too old to participate in certain functions."

Some older people also resent members of the younger generation. The young people who perceive that certain older persons resent them will have a tendency to avoid them. Fortunately, some older persons have caused the young to develop pleasant feelings toward them. This favorable reaction is commonly found among those who in childhood felt that they were given love and understanding in the company of grandpa and grandma. A research study indicated that, in general, young people saw old people negatively in regard to their energy, health, strength, happiness, and tempo of behavior. On the positive side, young people perceived them as "wise" and "kind." [4]

You may, at times, get an impression that certain younger people treat you courteously as an obligation on their part. Instead of letting it bother you emotionally, use the attitude of any effective salesman. When he calls on a prospect and the prospect acts in a coldly polite rather than in a warm friendly manner, the salesman does not go into a mood of depression—he tries to think of an approach that will arouse the prospect's interest. Of course, when you try to "sell" the well-meaning young person in regard to the worth of your ideas, you will have some difficulty in adopting the salesman's positive attitude, but you can do it. Perhaps the first question you should ask yourself is "Do I expect young people to defer to me because I am older or do I really plan to reach the young person in terms of his interests?" Most young people will respond warmly when we think with them in terms of their interests.

## Your personal appearance in retirement

At first you may prefer to think that the reactions of others can be attributed to your facial appearance, especially the lines added since youth. Instead of feeling sorry for the way your face is lined, you should take pride in the fact that life wrote the lines. Those lines tell a story to the intelligent observer. They are likely to be meaningful to the perceptive person. Remember the statement of the Hollywood cameraman who said that a face too smooth at maturity reminds him of an undecorated china plate—it lacks character.

However, it might be well to note any tendency to become slovenly in appearance after you retire. If you have always paid very little attention to your attire and general appearance, you will probably continue to follow that pattern after you retire. The important question is whether you shift from good grooming before retirement to slovenliness after you retire. The slovenliness in itself is not important, but the attitude of contempt for the rest of society that it suggests is important. Its psychological significance is related to that indicated by the long hair and dirty clothing of the rebel who deliberately shows his disdain for society by his unkempt appearance. Whenever I visit retirement centers in the South and see the many men and women who seem to live for weeks, even months, in a minimum change of clothing, I wonder whether life wouldn't improve for them if they just wore their best wardrobes more often. These slovenly retirees are not of the usual rebel or beatnik types— they do not disdain society, but they do seem to neglect the psychological benefits of "dressing up" occasionally. Perhaps they should remind themselves of the maxim: "Beautiful young people are the products of heredity and parental care. Beautiful old people are created by themselves."

And when you find that your face is getting a lot of big moles of the aging variety, go to a specialist and have him remove them. It is a simple office procedure. In your conceptions of yourself, believe that others will consider you old only insofar as you think of yourself as old. If some people do think of you as old, hope that they will say: "You're the youngest older man I know." That's a compliment.

How should you answer the question when others ask you how old you are: should you dodge their question, answer it, or brag about your age? Most men answer it, but they avoid bragging about it because they recognize that to some people bragging indicates a subconscious desire for pity.

## What about your wife's attitude toward your retirement?

Many a retiree discovers the importance of his self-image when he remains around the house more than when he was fully employed. In most American families the husband leaves home and returns at specific hours on scheduled days. When the husband retires and "hangs around the house all day," the wife's daily routine is disrupted. Also, the higher-status wife may feel that once her husband retires, she loses not only in family income but also in social status, or at least will have to establish some relationships in social groups new to her. The wife's image of herself and her role in the home and the community has developed over the years. She wants to maintain it.

When a husband remains at home all day, he gets in the way of the vacuum cleaner and on his wife's nerves. And if he takes over some of the home responsibilities he may become more of a nuisance to his wife than a helper. The typical wife is willing to let him do some of the housework, but she wants to be the decision maker, the supervisor, and the planner. She cannot easily accept the husband's "hanging around the house and bossing her." If he decides to ease the friction by deferring to her decision making, he may feel that he regresses to a weakened position in the domestic scene. Thus, the husband who has lost his supervisory role in industry also loses his authority-figure role in the home. If he thinks of his place in the home in this way, he is likely to rebel—he does not like his self-image. The wife wants to keep the home atmosphere pleasant but does not know how to resolve the situation.

Dr. John Briggs, internist, St. Paul, Minnesota, has described the "ired wife in a retired life" syndrome. The wife is in good health when, suddenly, the retired husband is around the house every day. He interferes with her routines. Eventually she becomes upset, frustrated, antagonistic to her husband, and she develops hypochondriacal adjustment mechanisms. She complains to her physician of aches, pains, and other disorders. Dr. Briggs found that if she finds somebody who listens to her problem, helps her face it, and she and her husband work out mutually satisfactory agreements about his retirement, the symptoms are likely to disappear.[5]

The oft-heard expression among wives of retirees: "For better or for worse but not for lunch" was invented by a woman who wanted to emphasize the importance of giving the wife an occasional respite from the chore of feeding her retiree husband every meal. Usually it is not the chore of getting his lunch that bothers her—it is more likely to be the fact that his being "under her feet" constantly becomes fatiguing, especially when he hangs around in an aimless, useless manner.

The retired husband who feels "lost" because he can no longer enjoy the companionship of his old work associates each day may become especially attentive to his wife. At first she is pleased. Later, when he becomes more and more bored by lack of a worthwhile responsibility in retirement, he "discovers" that her health is so poor that he must stay home all day every day in order to take care of her! The retiree who makes this kind of adjustment is not so exceptional as one might think. This tension-reducing "discovery" has also been noted on the part of retirees who at first enjoy retirement by playing golf every day. After several months of it, golf palls on some of them and they then like to imagine that the wife's health condition requires the husband's constant attention. That, at least to the husband, is more important than golf but not very appropriate for either one.

How well can you and the wife "endure" each other twenty-four hours a day, seven days a week? Only you and your wife can answer that question, but one helpful recommendation is that you recognize the possibility of this kind of stress situation *before* you retire. Decide how you are going to cope with it *before* retirement. Maybe you will decide to take a part-time job.

When the wife of an acquaintance found her recently retired husband at seven o'clock in the morning down in the basement doing the family laundry, she said: "Get out of here—that's my job. The fact that you no longer have your job does not mean that you can take mine. Get out of the house and find your own job." He did. He got a part-time job in a neighborhood hardware store where he is enjoying himself as the neighborhood's Mr. Fixit of the broken appliances that the housewives bring in to have repaired.

Another common answer is to isolate yourself in a home workshop or study in order that you will be in the living quarters only during scheduled hours of each day. Or you may plan to do more mutually enjoyable activities together. Some couples do a lot of traveling, practice a hobby together, or participate in community service organizations. Many become better grandparents.

The role of the grandparents has changed to some extent in the last few generations as a result of the increased life span, the earlier marriages, and the earlier pregnancies of young couples. Parents are becoming grandparents earlier and remaining in the grandparent role more years than in previous eras. These factors indicate that we shall have increased numbers of four-generation families. The retired male will therefore become increasingly present in inter-generational family relationships. One researcher surveyed 291 families regarding retirement of the father in the familial relationships. He included the question: *Do you feel that retirement has brought your father closer to his immediate family?* Sixty-eight percent said there had been no change, thirty percent said it had brought him closer to his family, and two percent said it had made him feel less close.[6]

## Prepare to find yourself increasingly in a world of women

Statistically, the older you get, the more you are likely to associate with women. Of the over-sixty-five ages, for every 100 men there are 120 women. The relative number of women increases with the ages of men; after age seventy-five, there are 130 women for each 100 men.

When a man is working he gains most of his social satisfactions during the day from his relationships with other men and women who are working with and around him. The social relationships with women are, however, only incidental. The primary relationships are structured around the work. The occupational structure supplies psychological relationships for each member of the work group. This kind of environmental situation insofar as it applied to you in your work situation means that when you retire, you will lose the social relationships and identity in a group that your job provided.

Assuming that you are married and that your wife has the usual social ties of the married woman of her age and economic status, you will find that you have to spend more time with your wife and her companions. Too, as you grow older, more and more of your wife's friends will be widows. You will discover that you are having more social relationships in a female world. But, it will not give you the ego-satisfactions that the women get from it nor the kind of social relationships that you enjoyed in the business world.

Whatever relationships you have with your wife's social groups, your dominant social relations should be masculine and not merely those which a man has when he happens to be present at a social affair just because he's an available male.

The best way to control the situation for your benefit, that of your wife, and of her friends is for you to pursue your own chosen activities systematically: have definite places to work, work definite hours, and talk about your work in ways that male associates will enjoy. Make a definite effort to have some male friends unless you, of course, prefer to have more women than men as friends.

The answer must be found in your having a definite interest of your own. It may be a special project of a business nature, a community service, a hobby of the home-workshop variety, growing and breeding plants, painting, sculpturing, or research in a field that fuels enthusiasm for you. It should be purposeful to you, such as a challenging project of your own. (See Chapters 5 to 10.) To protect yourself from spur-of-the-moment interruptions by your wife, you may want to consider what men in certain retirement communities do—they have a "Honeydew" day or claim membership in the "Gopher" Club. When the wife says: "Honey, do this for me" or "Go for that," the husband says: "I'll do it on my regular "Honeydew" day, or "I can't go for that until my Gopher day—the club rules don't permit it!"

The self-protection of your masculine prerogatives does not, of course, prevent you from developing a more companionable relationship with your wife. After all, you probably feel some guilt about the way you treated her during the many hours, days, and weeks that you devoted to advancement in your career while your wife and the children were left to find their recreation without your company.

## You'll associate with other retirees

You will not have any problems in associating with the emotionally well-adjusted retirees, but occasionally you will deal with a few of those who call themselves "unemployed" or "retired," but should be called the "disemployed." They have passed the mandatory retirement age and are pensioners or annuitants but cannot get jobs because of their age and other limitations. Some think of themselves as "available for work," simply because they do not accept the role of the retiree. They resent their reduced income and the changes in their lifelong habits. They continue to think of themselves as "unemployed" rather than "retired." They feel frustrated, mistreated.

Most of the retirees who feel sorry for themselves have not been damaged by mandatory retirement—they felt sorry for themselves for many years but now they have more time to talk about it. And since you too are retired, they assume that you have plenty of time to listen to their endless recitals of their ailments (called "organ recitals" by some listeners), the way people ignore and mistreat them, the bills they have to pay, and so on ad nauseum. What can you do about it?

One answer is: "Locate people whose interests are similar to yours and develop friendships with those." This is possible and sensible, but you will find it necessary to associate with some older people whose interests differ from yours.

The easiest answer is to be polite and ignore or avoid them. But if you want to get a bit of stimulation from them, listen for cues about how they got that way: their early adjustment history, the problems they had, and how they dealt with them. You may find it necessary to adopt the role of the strong, helpful friend to some of these poorly adjusted persons with whom you have to associate. If you do, you should not try to do it as a trained specialist, but in the spirit of a friend. You may not feel especially competent in this role, but you will do the best you can simply because it is necessary. This is really not a burden but a normal responsibility which the strong have always had to perform for their associates and will have to continue to perform in every generation.

### Expect to sense some effects of decreased income

If, as a retiree, you will have less income than before retirement, you may experience certain immediate effects on your morale. You may feel depressed, mainly because you previously measured your value to the world in terms of dollars. Your feelings of depression are likely to induce increased attention to your health. You may develop more complaints about your physical well-being than you had prior to retirement. This type of reaction is fairly common but you should bear in mind that as you become accustomed to your reduced income, your morale will improve and, insofar as this adjustment was a factor, your health is also likely to improve. Bear in mind that demoralization as a phase of aging is likely to be quite short-lived.

The best available research study on the effects on morale of reduced incomes on retirees is reported in the Kutner study:

> Although it might have been predicted otherwise, it is of particular import to note that income at retirement and one's present income are *not* factors in determining the individual's attitude toward retirement. In fact, there are about equal numbers receiving Old Age Assistance and Old Age and Survivors Insurance, or being assisted by relatives in each of the groups evaluating their retirement as "better" or "worse" than expected. *This would indicate that of all the values involved in adjustment to retirement, the feeling of being useful and wanted is paramount.* It would seem that the maintenance of good social relationships and the discovery of self-fulfilling activities would contribute to adjustment during retirement. . . .
> Since retirement forces many persons out of a lifelong routine into

unwanted leisure, it is understandable that resistance to retirement should be so great. Further, it appears that it is not lack of money but lack of a significant role that is one of the main sources of deprivation in retirement. The blow to the ego signified by retirement in our society is due to the fact that retirement tends to imply uselessness, which is reinforced by the behavior of others toward the retirees.[7]

## What about the intellectual changes with aging?

If you were to examine the literature on aging, you would be able to find many volumes and articles that report hundreds of studies on this question., However, most of the studies deal with abilities that are relatively unimportant in living the good life. One problem in studying the mental capacities of the aging is that they are likely to be resistant to being probed when they are in the seventies. At that age, they are not interested in analyzing their present situation. When, however, they are in their eighties, the resistance is likely to be less.[8] Measurements at various ages indicate that you can benefit more by using whatever mental capacities you have than by worrying about abilities now reduced in extent.

Researchers in the field, the psychologists who specialize in studies of the aging and the gerontologists, have found that older people are more likely to suffer from "atrophy of disuse" than from formidable incapacities. When they take part in an organized learning program, they learn slowly at first and do poorly on formal tests, but once they get "into the swing" of a study program, they progress quite satisfactorily.

Some memory losses for recent events bother many of the elderly, but vocabulary comprehension usually remains strong with most of the aging. The older person may need more time to make a choice between a number of possible responses to a situation but, given enough time, he arrives at a correct decision as readily as the younger person. Studies of the psychological effects of aging indicate that in the case of adults who have kept themselves mentally alert the decrement in intellectual performance is less than previously supposed, and the fall in many cases is so small that it is difficult to measure. Lots of cases are on record to show that retirees have done some outstanding mental work after they retired.

The story of Dr. Benjamin Minge Duggar's achievements has become a classic in retirement literature. He had been professor of mycology at the University of Wisconsin until age seventy-one, when state law made his retirement mandatory. At about that time the Lederle Laboratories Division of American Cyanamid Company was initiating a special antibiotic research program. Dr. Duggar was hired. After two years of hard work he isolated a golden mold which in the laboratory controlled over fifty disease organisms. Called Aureomycin, it was the first broad-spectrum antibiotic available for clinical use. It was also destined to be the father of the tetracycline antibiotic group which includes Achromycin, a widely prescribed drug.

Dr. Duggar was ever the young man. Even after his eightieth birthday he continued to fish, bowl, and play golf with associates at Lederle. On the golf course he regularly broke 90.

He had an insatiable curiosity about things of a scientific nature. Even after his discovery of Aureomycin he continued screening soil samples in hopes of developing a better drug. While on automobile vacation trips, he would stop periodically to collect soil samples, which he immediately dispatched to the laboratories. Some of his best materials came from cemeteries, he once cheerfully remarked. (The undisturbed soil there is conducive to growth of pure strains of microorganisms.)

His day at the laboratory began at 8 A.M. and ran well past 5 P.M. Saturdays and Sundays often found him back in the lab to check over the data of the past week's work and to plan for the next week. His philosophy was "Keep active, mentally and physically."

The minds of most retirees who wish to do mental work function very well. Many continue to have mental clarity as long as they live regardless of the fact that they live into the nineties. If loss in mental functioning does take place in the last years, it usually comes very slowly. The retiree who fears that this may happen to him will probably fare better if he assumes that he can function quite effectively when necessary. This is often demonstrated when you see how aging individuals think in times of emergencies that require clarity of thinking. Even the common belief that we lose our memories for recent events as we grow older is likely to be the result of a lack of interest in the event. If we really want to remember something, we usually can.

You can rest assured that unless you have had some exceptional limiting influence of the serious ailment type, you will have plenty of capacity to take advantage of your retirement opportunities in the form of added time for new projects, leisure, hobbies, closer relations with family members, renewal of neglected friendships, and to develop a personal philosophy in terms of the perspectives that the years have given you.

Perhaps you will have some unexpected problems as a retiree. These may be in living arrangements, or other matters, but you have had and have overcome similar problems in the past. Whatever your special problems were years ago, real or imagined, you must have developed the inner resources to handle them; otherwise, you wouldn't have reached your present stage. If you managed somehow to rise above a serious problem or two in the past, you should be able to do it again. If you do have to do it again and again, you can achieve that strength of character, too. As the old saying goes, "The test of a soldier is not what he does in battle but what he does in a siege."

## REFERENCES

1. From *The Second Forty Years*, Philadelphia, Pa.: J. B. Lippincott Company, 1952, p. 86.
2. Bernard Kutner, David Fanshel, Alice M. Togo, and Thomas S. Langner, *Five Hundred over Sixty*, New York: Russell Sage Foundation, 1956, p. 89.
3. See Ruth Andrus, "Personality Changes in an Older Age Group," *Geriatrics*, vol. 10, pp. 432–435.
4. M. K. Calhoun and L. E. Gottesman, "Stereotypes of Old Age in Two Samples," (mimeo), Division of Gerontology, University of Michigan.
5. See Bertram B. Moss, *Caring for the Aged*, Garden City, N.Y.: Doubleday & Company, Inc., 1966, p. 34. Rights to this book within the British Empire are held by McIntosh & Otis, New York.

6. Gordon F. Streib, "Intergenerational Relations: Perspectives of the Two Generations on the Older Parent," *Journal of Marriage and the Family*, November, 1965, p. 475.
7. Kutner et al., *op. cit.*, pp. 89–90.
8. See Richard H. Williams and Claudine C. Wirths, *Lives through the Years— Styles of Life and Successful Aging*, New York: Atherton Press, 1965, p. 196.

## CHAPTER THREE

# "I Welcome Retirement"

*"Absence of occupation is not a rest,*
*A mind quite vacant is a mind distressed."*
—WILLIAM COWPER

YES, CERTAIN MEN do welcome retirement. Some welcome it because they think of it as a getting away from their occupational problems; they look forward to it as a kind of heaven on earth. Others welcome it because of health problems, organic or functional. Let us take a look at several different classifications of those who long for retirement.

## The "passive dependents"

These can be seen in any community but they are especially well represented on the park benches where retirees congregate. Edwin A. Lahey, a newspaperman, described retirees of Bayfront Park in downtown Miami:

> There should be an air of euphoria ascending from the luxuriant vendure of this park. But, instead of a sense of well being, you feel loneliness and desolation. Retired people come here. They bring their restlessness, their sense of uselessness. They sit immobilized on the

39

benches before the band stand, on the benches scattered throughout
the park. Some of them gab about the past with others. Some of them
just sit, gazing into the distance.

Many of the above type of "relaxers" are the same fellows whose
hardest day at their place of work was the time they lost their seat
cushion! They are the individuals who were reluctant to shoulder
responsibilities when they were working. They also let the wife carry
many of the responsibilities of life as well as of the home. The wife
usually controls the budget. And when the wife dies, these men are
likely to marry shortly after her death. They need another woman on
whom they can lean.

These retirees offer dull evidence of the humorous saying on the
placard found in a few offices: "Who says you can't make a living
doing nothing—I've been doing it all my life!" Some of those who
live in certain retirement areas do exert themselves to take a sem-
blance of exercise—they fish! Even that may get tiresome, as indicated by the experience of a friend who was looking over Florida
retirement communities with the thought that he might want to live
there. In one of the areas he visited, he lived at a motel located near
a stream. He noted that an elderly retiree fished from a nearby
bridge each day. When he walked out to the retiree, he said: "It
must be nice to be able to fish every day." To which the retiree said:
"Yeh, but you know, you can get damn sick and tired of fishing
when you fish every day, 365 days of the year!" Fishing, though
appropriate for many retirees can, like any single activity, become
boresome after awhile.

Generally, many passive dependents are noted for a certain kind
of activity—they eat a lot, and some also drink more than needed
to participate in pleasant social occasions. They also tend to do some
petty gambling, which explains why we find dog racing and similar
types of sports in some of the larger retirement communities. Another
characteristic related to gambling is that the passive dependents are
poor handlers of money. They are likely to be extravagant and to
spend somewhat foolishly whatever extra money they happen to
have.

Of course not many of this "rocking chair" category [1] ever pursued a voluntary educational or self-development program. A few may have risen to a minor position in business but that came about as a result of years of service rather than drive, initiative, or a reaching out for more responsibility. Besides they did not like to work over-time. Work in itself offered few inner satisfactions. They worked because other people worked, but they looked forward to the day when they could "get away from it all." Men who do not really enjoy their work look forward to the extra time available in retirement. They differ from able, mature men who get so much pleasure from their work that they cannot imagine how play could ever possibly be as pleasurable as work. Work is their play. One writer on aging quoted a retiree who had gone to work again: "It ain't no fun to rest when you ain't tired."

Certainly, the prospective retiree who says he is just going to sit around the house and do nothing usually receives little respect. Apply the idea to a vacation. Tell someone you are not going to do anything on your vacation—just sit around the house. Your friends will wonder how you can be so stupid, so willing to waste time in so dull a manner.

A systematic research study of the meanings of work in relation to retirement indicated that work for an individual may have five func-tional meanings: providing income, regulating the worker's pattern of life-activity, identification as a person in his society, patterns of association in a group setting as in employer-employee relations, and meaningful life-experiences. It is one "place where the worker's store of life-experience is enriched through interaction with the world about him and where he receives new ideas, expresses his own ideas, and modifies his conception of the world and of himself in relation to it." The authors presented detailed statistical findings of occupational variations in reactions to work meanings. One impor-tant finding in regard to those who welcome retirement was that "the workers of lower skill and socioeconomic status are more likely to see their work as having no meaning other than that of earning money." As we would expect, those who found more than economic meanings in their work lives were more likely to be reluctant to retire at an arbitrarily set age.[2]

*Those disappointed in themselves*
*and the way things worked out*

Not all who welcome retirement do so because they liked to lean on others or never enjoyed their work. One group consists of men who liked to work and had worthy ambitions which they tried to fulfill, but somehow things never came out right for them. Other men were promoted. The company where they worked was merged with another company. Their superior in management underrated them or lived too long to make way for the advancement of his ambitious subordinate. In some instances, the almost-successful individual happened to be married to a wife who preferred to stay where they were rather than move to another area at the company's request. Or any one of numerous influences may have occurred. A major factor in the history of these men whose potentials in many cases were good is that this type of "underachiever" waits and waits for things to break in his favor instead of taking time by the forelock and determining his own future in the manner of the man who knows what he wants and goes after it somewhere else.

As a result of the big differences between the underachiever's self-image and his actual accomplishments, he welcomes retirement in a sad sort of way. He gives up. But the psychological effects are also sad—he is apt to retire to a "nothingness of bitterness," not to what the well-adjusted man seeks in retirement. The latter seeks new kinds of challenge, regardless of the possibilities of defeat.

Typically, these embittered retirees are rabid critics of business and of men who symbolize the successful. Indeed, one of the problems that the successful, active retiree faces in his personal relations with old friends who identify even mildly with the defeated is that he, too, is somewhat hated. The underachievers say to themselves: "He made it, but I didn't." Obviously, the envied retiree who senses this kind of reaction to himself tries all the harder to build up whatever self-respect the envious friend deserves for his worthwhile but unrecognized accomplishments.

*The wistful retirees* whom you meet are a subdivision of the underachievers, but they do not express their feelings of inadequacy by finding fault with the scheme of things or with the successful. Instead, they "stand around" in a pathetic manner and hope that someone will notice them and talk with them. The most frequent examples are noted among the lonely women who have lost their husbands or never had one. They talk endlessly with other lonesome wistful women. A two-hour telephone conversation is not unusual. These are the kinds of old ladies who are a problem to customer-contact employees of businesses, particularly banks. They expect tellers and officers to talk with them endlessly even though other customers are waiting. Some are well-to-do widows but they failed to live up to their self-image as they had defined themselves years ago. Now they feel just as defeated as men who had ambitions years ago but never attained them.

Consumer researchers who send interviewers out to interview representative consumers are likely to get too high a proportion of reports from old people, particularly the lonely, wistful ones. They like to be interviewed. Unfortunately, their answers are not especially significant for marketing because their emotional needs are so deep-seated that they tend to give answers which are likely to elicit sympathy rather than offer practical suggestions.

Interestingly, modern marketing by means of television offers satisfactions that the underachievers and wistful need. They enjoy entertainment that makes them feel superior without trying. Extra time, to them, does not lead to its use in discovering new opportunities that lead to further growth. Instead, it is treated as something to fill in an aimless manner for its tranquilizing, palliative extenuations.

The use of leisure time is a problem not only to retirees; as E. B. Weiss has stated, it is also a problem in our civilization: "Society has no greater challenge today than that of preparing for a lifetime devoted mostly to non-work." And Irwin Edman in his essay "On American Leisure" indicated our responsibility to ourselves as retirees when he said: "The best test of the quality of a civilization is the quality of its leisure. Not what the citizens of a commonwealth do when they are obliged to do something by necessity, but by what they do when they can do anything by choice, is the criterion of a people's life. One can tell much about a man by noting the objects and pastimes to which he spontaneously turns for joy." [3]

Surprisingly to them, retirement for many men in good health and vigor becomes a less happy state than they had imagined. One of the main reasons is the discovery that they really like to work. They soon tire of twiddling their thumbs while they watch others enjoy life through their work. The urge to do something, to get busy, to meet work associates, and to feel worthwhile again becomes overwhelming. They want to be useful. They want to have the satisfaction of knowing that they are still capable of earning their keep. That is what they have been doing most of the years of their life.

At the same time that they want to feel useful again they do not relish the idea of performing only "little jobs," jobs that do not utilize what they know and can do. They search for a challenge worthy of their abilities acquired through the years of worthy achievement. If they do not find challenging activities, they may keep busy by performing trivialities in an important manner.

### Those who are busy with routines of trivialities

Anyone who observes a wide variety of retirees is certain to note the behavioral pattern of the retiree who busies himself every day with trivialities. This type of individual, previous to retirement, worked at a normal daily pace. When he retired, he was unable to find work that satisfied his image of his abilities and status. Now that he is retired, he finds that his income is adequate to meet the standard of living he desires. He rationalizes himself into believing that he earned the privilege of taking it easy. He soon gets into a habit of thinking that the house and yard require so much attention that he ought to take good care of their requirements. He learns how to stretch out every little task he starts. When he decides that the lawn should be mowed, he starts the job but soon notes that the mower needs tightening of a screw. Next, his screwdriver doesn't quite do the job as well as he would like. That gives him a reason for driving to the hardware store. The wife decides to go along to do some shopping at a specialty shop near the hardware store. He also runs across a friend and they have a chat. When he and the wife return home it's lunch time. After lunch he takes a nap. After the nap, the sun is too hot for mowing the lawn. So he turns on the TV and watches a baseball game, even though he did not really care very much for baseball before he retired. And that's the end of a working day filled with trivialities that he would not have allowed to occur before he retired.

Strangest of all, the man who falls into this kind of routine claims vehemently that he's busy! If he needs any further justifications to himself that his routines do keep him busy, he can always find a good excuse—health problems won't allow him to work any harder. Or his wife's health requires him to be at home. (This is true in a few cases but not in nearly as many as claimed.)

Leisure, recreation, work, and "keeping busy" are defined in many different ways by retirees. Those who keep busy performing trivialities are only using the old ego-saving device of nursing a feeble feeling of self-importance in a world that has moved away from them. They are practicing the old art of "killing time." One man, seventy years of age, retired for five years, insisted that he was so busy that he had no time for leisure—he spent so much time watching television, helping his wife around the house, doing church work, and participating in the activities of a retirement club that he had no time for leisure!

Retirement as a reward for a well-spent lifetime of work is a pleasing idea to many men who worked hard, but it is not enough for the healthy man who knows that he could still make additional contributions to society and add to his own growth as a person. Ordinary leisure-time activities, though enjoyable, may not provide complete answers to the superior mind. The superior mind does not care for time fillers to fill the years unless they provide challenge, interpretation of life, or a sense of growth. That is why so many retirees claim they enjoy their trivial activities—they are throttling their natural desires to be doing something more purposeful. Their exaggerated "busyness" with trivialities is a way of saying: "If I can't be doing the important things I would really like to do, I'll do the unimportant in an 'important' manner!"

It is easy for many members of this group to become invalids prematurely. They have quit or resigned themselves to retirement rather than increase their resistance to being relegated to the sideline activities.

### Those who want to get away from pressures of the job

If you are acquainted with the pressures experienced by many workers of modern industry, you can understand why some men who reach retirement age are glad to retire. They want "to get out from under" they say. This kind of pressure varies with the job but it probably varies even more in relation to the characteristics of individuals who hold different kinds of jobs. This point of view would seem to be confirmed by a six-year study of 86,750 Du Pont Company executives and other employees. The researchers studied the annual heart-attack rates among men of four groups: (1) executives consisting of vice-presidents, plant managers, assistant plant managers, district sales managers, laboratory directors, division managers, and departmental general managers; (2) foremen, clerical supervisors, and other lower-level management personnel; (3) skilled, semiskilled and unskilled wage workers; and (4) lowest-level salaried workers, mostly clerical workers.

We would expect the annual heart-attack rates to be highest for the executives, those of group 1. Actually, their rate was the lowest of the four groups, 2.2 per thousand employees. It was highest for group 2, 4 per thousand employees. The rate among the lowest level salaried workers, group 4, was 3.7 per thousand employees. The group 3 rate was 3.2.

Apparently, the effects of stress vary not so much with the jobs as with the kinds of people who are in the jobs.[4] One possible explanation for the low heart-attack rate of executives is that men who have proved their stamina under stress are the men from whom top executives are chosen.

Some top executives who feel that they are under unpleasant stress retire before the company's mandatory retirement date. These are likely to be top-level men who must put into effect policies and practices with which they do not entirely agree. This occurs most commonly in companies which have brought influential newcomers into the board of directors or the president's office. The subordinate executives must adapt themselves to these new personalities, regardless of their own convictions about the appropriateness of the policies and practices that the newcomers demand. When these pressured executives can do so and are near the mandatory retirement age, they are likely to retire ahead of schedule. Later, many of these ahead-of-schedule retirees become very anxious to get a job or to be active in work that enables them to be useful again.

*"I've earned the reward of not working"* is a characteristic statement of a related group of employees who either feel that they are under excessive pressures or define their work situation as though it were a "sentence" to hard labor. These men are anxious to retire and give as their reason: "I've earned the reward of not working." Actually, some of these belong in the group who are disappointed in themselves and the way things worked out for them. The thought of continuing to work in a situation that will not develop favorably for them is so obnoxious that they want to get away from the job as soon as they can arrange a satisfactory retirement. Later, they too may want to become useful again.

The man who rationalizes his inactivity in retirement by arguing that he has earned the reward of not working is likely to suffer from frequent feelings of futility. He wakes up in the morning and says to himself: "Another day with nothing to do and nobody cares whether I do it." Such feelings, of course, have erosive effects on a man's self-respect.

It is this kind of inactivity that causes some writers to emphasize the hazards of boredom as in this example:

The most costly disease in America is not cancer or coronaries. The most costly disease is boredom—costly for both individual and society. . . . Retirement, supposed to be a chance to join the winner's circle, has turned out to be more dangerous than automobiles or LSD. Retirement for most people is literal consignment to no-man's land. It is the chance to do everything that leads to nothing.[5]

## Health factors

Of course some men who welcome retirement do so as a result of health problems, problems which are organic in nature, diagnosed as serious by a physician, and treated regularly and systematically. We are not, in this book, attempting to minimize these influences in causing the ill person to want to retire. Our concern here is with those retirees whose health problems are limited to functional ailments of the kind that cause the physician to say after his examination of the patient: "I can't find anything wrong on the basis of my examination and tests." Therapists in this field refer to certain reported ailments as "psychosomatic," commonly described as bodily symptoms which arise from mental states. The public usually refers to the condition as "hypochondria" or as "hypochondriasis," a pathological condition that is characterized by exaggerated anxiety about one's health and pessimistic interpretations of various mild discomforts about some organ or function.

Hypochondriasis is not a disease entity but a syndrome consisting of an anxious preoccupation with the body or a part of the body which the patient believes to be diseased or not functioning properly. These chronic complainers, in many instances, develop their complaints as a defense against failure or as atonement for feelings of guilt. Many hypochondriacs are difficult to live with.

The man who retires and has had no previous satisfying interest other than work is a likely candidate for hypochondriasis, especially when he tries to find a new job and is unsuccessful in getting the kind of position he considers worthy of his self-image. He remains at home until "a suitable opportunity presents itself." Soon the boredom of sitting around the house means that little pains, real or imagined, become big pains. Anxieties increase. Tensions mount.

The retiree develops feelings of neglect and persecution. The psychiatric investigators of one group of 332 people, all over sixty years old, had these findings in their report:

> Verbalized excessive hypochondriasis was invariably linked with depressive episodes, and feelings of neglect and persecution were found in close to 60 per cent. Defensive reactions were found among only 25 per cent of those who were working past the retired age. The individuals who continued to occupy their time by working had an excellent method of warding off depressive episodes; those who engaged in adequately planned actiivties fared equally well.[6]

Norman Cousins has pointed out some recognized relationships between positive outlook and health of the aged. He mentions findings of researchers who have reported striking connections between what a man thinks, what he does, and what happens to his vital body chemistry:

> The biological basis for this formulation may be found in the work of Hans Selye.[7] Selye has been tracking down changes produced in human chemistry by brain activity. In particular, he has studied the effects of anxiety, stress, and exhaustion on the adrenal glands. He reports a direct physiological connection between persistent tension and fear and the weakening of the total human organism. What happens, he finds, is that the supply of adrenalin runs dry and the body loses its chemical balance, or homeostasis, to use a term made medically famous by Walter Cannon. The effects of adrenal exhaustion vary all the way from physical crippling to heart disease. This does not mean, of course, that Selye hypothesizes a single cause of human disease that might be susceptible to a single answer. What he does is to establish the fact of chemical imbalance resulting from the negative emotions.
>
> Selye is primarily concerned with the *overworked* or exhausted adrenal glands. But what about the effects of the *underworked* adrenal glands? Adrenal insufficiency, whether from depletion or atrophy, is the key. Are we to assume no problems are created by constant boredom, inaction, or purposelessness if the body is thrown out of chemical balance? Does the body pay no price for emotional, mental, and physical lethargy and stupefaction?
>
> Why should we suppose that inactivity is invariably benevolent? There is the inactivity that restores, of course; but isn't there also the inactivity that destroys through withdrawal and decay? . . .
>
> What is most desirable in relaxation is the possibility for rejuvena-

# UNIVERSAL SYMBOL
## OF
## EMERGENCY MEDICAL IDENTIFICATION

The symbol below means that the person wearing it carries information about himself which should be known to anyone helping him during an accident or sudden illness. It was designed by the American Medical Association for universal use as an emergency medical identification symbol.

The symbol means: Look for the medical information that can protect life. The American Medical Association offers this symbol for universal use by all groups distributing cards and devices for emergency medical identification and by the manufacturers of such devices. The objective is universal use of an easily recognized symbol.

A universal symbol now offers worldwide protection to all who have health conditions requiring special care in an emegency.

The symbol indicates that there are vital medical facts on a personal health information card in the bearer's purse or wallet or on a wristlet, an anklet, or a medallion around the neck.

### WHO SHOULD WEAR THE IDENTIFICATION SYMBOL?

An easily observed signal device bearing the symbol and a few words of information should be worn continuously by persons having any of four broad classes of problems.

1. *Health conditions that can produce an emergency* warrant use of the symbol. Persons with periodic seizures can be saved much unnecessary hospitalization if they carry information identifying their problem. Heart patients, particularly those with coronary heart disease and subject to attacks of angina pectoris, often cause emergencies which can be handled more easily if suitable information is available. The diabetic who appears to be intoxicated while suffering an insulin reaction is a classic example of the need for immediate medical identification.

2. *Reactions to the medicines used in emergencies* warrant labeling of susceptible persons. Those allergic to horse serum often react violently to the tetanus antitoxin so frequently used prophylactically after an injury. Sedative drugs, including opium derivatives, can produce adverse reactions but are often used in emergencies unless there is a warning against their use.

3. *Failure to use needed medicines* following an emergency can be critical. People requiring regular doses of potent drugs may be unable to give information on their needs to doctors caring for them. . . . Everyone taking corticosteroid drugs should wear a signal device noting their need for this medication. The same reasoning applies to persons regularly taking insulin, thyroid, the anticoagulants or any of a number of biological or chemical preparations.

4. *Inability to communicate* is of itself a problem justifying a signal device and a note on one's identification card. Though rare, true aphasia occurs often enough to be noted. A person who speaks a language different from the one usually spoken in his neighborhood would be protected by a notation of the language he does speak.

A medical identification card can be carried by everyone, even though a signal device is not needed. The name of one's physician, whom to notify about one's injury or illness, the date of immunization for tetanus especially and the fact that one has no continuing health problem needing attention are valuable bits of information. Those who have health problems can use the card to present the needed information.

Many organizations and manufacturers sell durable signal devices for emergency medical identifications. The names of those reported to the AMA as having adopted the Universal Symbol for their emergency signal devices, can be obtained from the AMA.

An identification kit including this list of names, a pamphlet describing the symbol and its uses, and a copy of the AMA identification card may be obtained by sending a request to the American Medical Association, Department of Health Education, Box H, 535 North Dearborn Street, Chicago, Ill. 60610.

The above information was obtained from Donald A. Dukelow, M.D., of the AMA Department of Health Education, and from *The Cameo*, New York State Executive Department, Office for the Aging, 11 N. Pearl Street, Albany, N.Y. 12207.

tion. But this calls for a reasonable degree of purpose and buoyancy. . . . It is a perversion of rationalism to argue that words like "hope" or "faith" or "love" or "grace" are without physiological significance. The benevolent emotions are useful not just because they are pleasant but because they are regenerative. The will to live produces a responsive chemistry.

Our central point here is that retirement can be a disease if it produces a shutting-down instead of an opening-up. People who have been physically or mentally active and who are suddenly plunged into an existence in which they are not needed or are extraneous—an existence devoid of challenge or stimulation—have moved into a hazardous new arena. Conversely, a feeling of being needed and an active life of the mind confer limitless benefits in well-being.[8]

Would you like to have more evidence of the above findings from the medical director of a large nursing home? When Dr. S. H. May, medical director of the A. Holly Patterson Home in Nassau County, New York, spoke before a meeting of the Institute for Nursing Home Administrators at Cornell University, a report of his talk included the following statement: "The greatest revelation in the study of aging is that determination and motivation are more important in prolonging useful life than a person's physical condition." He spoke of a heart study made of 100 patients of more than 90 years of age. "It is commonly thought that those living to this age must have superb hearts," he said. "But tests showed that only three of the 100 have normal hearts." He also said that senility was another area of misconception. "About half of the so-called senility cases are caused primarily by emotional disturbances such as self pity and loss of trust, not by physical deterioration of body."[9]

Old age, in terms of years, does not result in chronic illness. Most disabilities that occur in old age are aspects of chronic degenerative diseases rather than inevitable effects of age per se.

Physicians tell us that no disease is caused by getting older. There are no specific diseases of old age, but certain disorders increase in frequency among the aging. As we all know, arteriosclerosis, high blood pressure, heart disease, diabetes mellitus, the arthrides, and certain types of cancer are associated with aging.

In terms of function, any one organ in a person's body may be relatively old while other organs are still young. Some organs and parts of the body may decline rapidly, others slowly, while in the same period of time certain ones do not seem to decline in any significant ways.

Any discussion of relationships between aging and health must recognize individual variations. Psychologically and functionally, there really is no typical aged person. The variations that are found among persons of any age bracket are likely to be greater and more significant than the similarities. However, we do need as working concepts the recognition of statistical probabilities in discussions of changes with aging.

A booklet, *A New Concept of Aging,* by the Committee on Aging, American Medical Association, offers a typical question of a statistical nature and gives the committee's answers:

> *Isn't it true that 81% of all non-institutionalized persons over 65 have some type of chronic disease or condition?*
>
> The fact is that of these 81% with some chronic condition, 40% have no limitation and another 26% have only some limitation— from mild to moderate—in their major activity. Less than 16% of persons in this age group are unable to carry on their major activity because of a chronic condition. This breakdown gives a more accurate picture of the health status of our senior group. The term "chronic" in itself refers only to the duration of a condition. It does not refer to its severity.

Interestingly, one study of illnesses of the aging showed that "with women each advance in years brought an increase in the percentage of those with a subnormal physical state. . . . With men, the same process took place up to 75 years, after which a change occurred." The researcher concluded that "men of extreme old age appear to be physically either in very good or very bad shape, whereas women tend to suffer from increasing degrees of decrepitude, though they possess a power of sheer survival that is denied to the male." [10] Another medical study of men over seventy-five showed that few of them were average in health; about one-half of them were in outstanding health and the other half in exceptionally bad shape. [11]

Men, on the average, tend to die earlier than women but some of those men who attain advanced ages are likely to be of exceedingly strong fiber and in very good physical health. However, women have a tenacious hold on life and often survive in spite of chronic ill-health in their advanced years.

A survey by the National Opinion Research Center, using a nationwide area probability sample of 1,734 people sixty-five years of age and older, showed that more than half of the respondents said their health was better than that of other people their age. Many of these older people took certain chronic illnesses for granted and continued to live a relatively normal life.[12]

Our continuous National Health Survey is giving us a wealth of information about the health conditions of people of all ages. These data show that of the 12,000 centenarians studied in the United States, those still alert and active seem to outnumber the other centenarians who lead an inert, passive existence. Apparently the busy hundred-year-olds are more likely to survive than the nonbusy ones.

Travelers have reported that in those parts of the world where the society honors the elderly, old people are believed to keep their mental abilities intact and to have few mental illnesses. A possible explanation for this finding by some investigators is that the few persons who are observed to survive to a very old age are exceptionally healthy members of their societies and therefore are not statistically comparable to the elderly in the United States.

Retirement in itself is not a cause of ill-health, but there is some relationship between health after retirement and attitude toward retirement. The attitude of a man's family toward the retirement of the individual is also significant. Generally, the health of those who do not object to retirement is better than the health of those who have a negative attitude toward retirement. Also, the health of those retirees whose families wanted them to retire is likely to be better than of those retirees whose families do not want the man to retire.

### WORK AND HEALTH ARE RELATED

Scientific researches do not show whether good health on the part of retirees who work is caused by the work or whether the healthy retirees are the ones who are likely to continue to work. The large percentage of men who are in excellent health are likely to need activity—work is still a stimulating activity to them.

To be happy, one's hands and mind should be busy. Sitting in front of the television set hour after hour, fishing every day, golfing, and similar time fillers offer no real challenges and are likely to result in frustration rather than happiness, especially when the individual has had a history of aggressive activity.

A systematic study of persons sixty years of age and older showed that people "who continue to work after the usual age of retirement have a higher intellectual capacity than those who do not, and the electro-encephalograph indicates that, physiologically, their brains are functioning in a manner which more closely resembles records of younger individuals." [13]

Researches also indicate that people sixty years of age and over who are occupationally active and think of themselves as in good health are, in the opinions of others, younger than people who have withdrawn from the world of work.

One of my business friends found that when his father had retired at seventy, the retiree developed all kinds of seemingly serious ailments. The son solved the problem by buying a rundown old apartment house and then told his father that he had to rebuild it, furnish the apartments, and rent them. The father enjoyed this kind of work so much that he continued with it for almost fifteen years before he died at age eighty-six.

## TO PREPARE YOURSELF MENTALLY

If you want to prepare yourself mentally in regard to the health aspect of the aging process, get acquainted with some very old people who are in poor organic health but are enjoying life nonetheless. I know several beyond eighty-five who are in constant pain, but they are mentally alert, cheerful, and they never complain. They have maintained lively interest in the contemporary world. They refuse to let pain and limited mobility shut out the privilege of enjoying life. One, for example, does not allow her wheelchair limitations to keep her at home when she wants to attend a social event—she goes and has a good time.

Clinicians who work with the aged report numerous cases of

patients who, in spite of serious afflictions, develop friendlier behavior and more positive attitudes in the course of psychotherapy.
Dr. Eugenia S. Shere, for example, has described some results of
group therapy with the elderly at Cushing Hospital, Framingham,
Massachusetts. One eighty-two-year-old woman patient, confined to
a special wheelchair, was diagnosed as afflicted with five conditions:
hypertensive cardiovascular disease, generalized arteriosclerosis,
osteoarthritis of the spine and hip joint, history of acute gastric
hemorrhages, and postoperative status for colectomy and appendec-
tomy. Imagine having this kind of medical history and still developing friendlier behavior, more tasteful dress, and a positive attitude
toward remarriage "regardless of age!" All this in spite of her emotional state in the initial contacts as described by quoting her self-
evaluation when asked how she felt: "Ugly." [14] After reading Dr.
Shere's reports on results with certain patients, one wonders
whether anyone with relatively mild ailments should ever complain!

As stated in the booklet, A New Concept of Aging, by the Committee on Aging of the American Medical Association: "What the
Committee feels is that the key to positive health lies in struggle
rather than retreat—in enjoyment rather than avoidance of the stress
of living. It might be said that the 'wounds of combat' are definitely
preferable to the decay of idleness, both from a biological and a
moral standpoint."

### Personal adjustments to retirement

Formal retirement usually takes place as of a specific date but
psychological retirement may or may not take place at all. As previously indicated, some men want to retire. Those who want to get
away from their job are exemplified by the passive dependents and
those who have a health problem. These men are the "From's."
They retire. Period. (See IA of table on page 57.)

However, of those who want to leave their regular work, an
important but small group want to retire to a more satisfying activity in order to pursue a well-established interest such as a business
of their own, a hobby, or a sport. These are the "To's." (See IB in
the table.)

# RETIREES CLASSIFIED IN REGARD TO THEIR DESIRE TO RETIRE

I. Those who *want to retire* consist of the two groups *A* and *B*:

    A. The "From's," who want to get away from their jobs because of unsatisfying situations. They are exemplified by the following, as described earlier in this chapter:

        1. The passive dependents.

        2. Those disappointed in themselves and the way things worked out.

        3. Those who can keep busy with trivialities.

        4. Men under considerable stress at work, particularly members of the foremen, clerical supervisors, and lower management personnel.

        5. Executives who disagree with the policies of new or recent newcomers into the management or financial controls of the firm.

        6. "I've earned the reward of not working."

        7. The health-problem people.

    B. The "To's" who want to go into a more satisfying activity. Exemplified by:

        1. Those who want to satisfy a childhood or long-term urge that could not be satisfied on the job. Example: a technically trained laboratory scientist who has had an urge to live in the wilderness. He is now retired and lives in a cabin on an island in the St. Lawrence River, his nearest neighbor one mile away. He and his wife get their meat supply by hunting and fishing.

        2. To satisfy an urge of symbolical origin. Example: a retired clergyman who has had no training in a biological science is spending his available time studying plant lice—a Freudian interpretation is applicable.

        3. To pursue a well-established interest as exemplified by the sports- and hobby-minded retirees.

II. The men who *do not want to retire*—they will continue to be active. Many of these think of retirement as an age of self-fulfillment.

    A. The creative men: artists, writers, research scientists, and inventors. They continue to work indefinitely in their own field of interest, regardless of whether they are or are not retired.

    B. The men who in their own minds are convinced that they are quite capable of being useful and are anxious to continue to use their best potentials.

    C. Those who have an urge to grow as individuals, to discover new meanings in living for themselves.

For aid in your thinking about your own adjustments to retirement, you may find the table on this page helpful. To which category do you think you now belong?

The content of the remainder of this book is organized in accordance with the several major adjustments to retirement as often found among men of the II*B* and II*C* categories. The several kinds of adjustments and the numbers of the chapters which deal with them follow:

    4. "I'll keep on working."

    5–7. Purposeful projects that *are related* to the retiree's former industry or current retirement interests.

    8–10. Volunteer services, hobbies, and special interests that *are not related* to the retiree's former industry or work.

    11–14. A challenging purpose throughout retirement—the quest for a personal philosophy, a framework of thinking that gives meaning to one's life.

In contrast to the above men who want to retire, several important groups consist of those who *do not want to retire*. They will continue or seek to continue to be active. They may be mostly creative workers who simply keep on doing, in some way or other, essentially the same work they enjoyed before formal retirement. (See IIA.)

Others who undergo mandatory retirement believe that they are still quite capable, perhaps more capable than ever, of being useful. They have an urge to do something that "counts," that offers a role that is meaningful to them. These men want to utilize the potentials developed in the previous years. They will search until they do find something to do, something that is challenging and gives a feeling of growth as a person.

The reflective, foresighted retiree will decide that since he cannot lengthen his life, he will increase the quality, the inner excellence, of his living. This is a period of adjustment, when the individual becomes especially eager to develop more fully a personal philosophy. (See IIC.)

## REFERENCES

1. For a report of a study of the "rocking chair category," see S. Reichard, F. Livson, and P. G. Peterson, *Aging and Personality*, New York: John Wiley & Sons, Inc., 1962.
2. See Eugene A. Friedmann, Robert J. Havighurst et al., *The Meaning of Work and Retirement*, Chicago: The University of Chicago Press, 1954, pp. 5, 170–186.
3. Irwin Edman, *Adam, the Baby, and the Man from Mars*, New York: Houghton Mifflin Company, 1929.
4. See Sidney Pell and C. Anthony D'Alonzo, "Acute Myocardial Infarction in a Large Industrial Population—Report of a Six-year Study," *Journal of The American Medical Association*, Sept. 14, 1964, pp. 831–838.
5. Norman Cousins, "Art, Adrenalin, and the Enjoyment of Living," *Saturday Review*, Apr. 20, 1968, p. 20. Copyright 1968, Saturday Review, Inc.
6. See E. W. Busse et al., "Studies in the Processes of Aging: The Strengths and Weaknesses of Psychic Functioning in the Aged," *American Journal of Psychiatry*, 111, 1955, pp. 896–912.
7. To become acquainted with the personality and some of the working concepts of Hans Selye, Director of the Institut et de Chirurgie experimentals, Université de Montreál, read his book, *The Story of the Adaptation Syndrome*, Montreal, Canada: Acta, Inc., 1952.

8. Norman Cousins, *op. cit.*, p. 21.
9. "Will to Live Important," *Herald-American*, Syracuse, N.Y., July 14, 1968, p. 17.
10. See studies by J. H. Sheldon summarized in James E. Birren (ed.), *Handbook of Aging and the Individual*, Chicago: The University of Chicago Press, 1960, p. 309.
11. See Sebastian DeGrazia, "The Uses of Time," chap. 5, in Robert W. Kleemeir, *Aging and Leisure*, New York: Oxford University Press, 1961, p. 139.
12. See report of Seminar on the Aging, Aspen, Colorado, Sept. 8–13, 1958, Council on Social Work Education, 345 E. 46th St., New York, p. 54.
13. E. W. Busse et al., "Studies in the Processes of Aging: The Strengths and Weaknesses of Psychic Functioning in the Aged," *American Journal of Psychiatry*, 111, 1955, pp. 896–912.
14. See Robert Kastenbaum, *New Thoughts on Old Age*, New York: Springer Publishing Company, Inc., 1964, p. 150.

## CHAPTER FOUR

# "I'll Keep on Working"

*"Growing old is no more than a bad habit
which a busy man has no time to form."*
—ANDRÉ MAUROIS

AMONG THE PEASANTS of the Andean regions of Ecuador, Peru, and Bolivia, "retirement" as a word is unknown. Healthy old people continue to labor in reduced form as long as they are physically able to do so. Of course their economy is technologically simple in comparison with ours. In the United States the trend has been in the direction of a reduced likelihood of working after sixty-five. In 1900, of persons sixty-five and over, two of every five were classified as gainfully employed. By 1960, this figure had changed to less than one in every five as still in the labor force. These statistics include persons of every occupational category, ranging from unskilled labor to the professional and most advanced managerial occupations.

Regardless of the above statistics, it is probable that the majority of the readers of this book will continue to perform some kind of productive work after sixty-five. Besides, statistics that apply to the general population should not be a determining guide for you, a specific individual, in planning your work future. Remember the man who firmly believed he would die around the age of seventy because all his immediate ancestors were members of an actuarial

61

classification, the majority of whom had died before that age. Accordingly, he spent all his savings by the time he was seventy-two. Well, he lived to be eighty-eight, but he had to depend on relatives to support him during the last sixteen years!

Most men who work enjoy working, as indicated by findings from a nationwide sample of employed who were asked: "If by some chance you inherited enough money to live comfortably without working, do you think you would work anyway or not?" Eighty percent replied that they would continue to work. But the proportion who thought they would go on working declined from 90 percent at ages twenty-one to thirty-four to 61 percent at ages fifty-five to sixty-four. As reasons for continuing to work, a high proportion of the white-collar workers mentioned "interest in their work" or "accomplishment" but the percentages of farmers and manual workers who would work for those reasons were small. The reason given by the manual workers was likely to be "to keep occupied." [1]

A questionnaire survey of retirees from the armed forces to which 519 responded included the question: *Is gainful employment necessary to contentment and health?*" The answer was "Yes" by 90 percent. Typical comments were:

> "To keep busy on a fairly full schedule of desirable activities is essential to contentment and good health but this need not be financially gainful employment."

> "Man needs to work, needs to produce, and needs the feeling of being useful."

> "Yes, by all means. If you want to die young, quit working and you will." [2]

One reason why so many retirees want to continue to work is that they realize Justice Oliver Wendell Holmes was right when he said: "To live is to function; to stop functioning is to stop living."

One study of executive retirees who followed full- or part-time work programs indicated that they were more alert than those who were doing no work. [3]

The percentage of the general population who work after age sixty-five is higher than some people assume. According to one

study, about 17 percent of the sixty-five-and-over group are working. However, the percentage reported in a second study was 23
percent. A third study, based on a sample survey, reported that the
percent of males age sixty-five and over who worked *full-time the
year round* was 15.6. Of those sixty-five to sixty-nine, the percent
who worked was 29.4; of those seventy to seventy-four, the percent
was 10.4 and of those seventy-five and older, the percent dropped
to 6.2. Of those who are working, one in three men and one in five
women are self-employed; one in twenty among the elderly in the
labor force are looking for a job. Persons over sixty-five represent
4 percent of the total labor force in the United States.[4]

Statistically, older workers in the higher-level occupations show
the least interest in retirement—their work gives them too many
intrinsic satisfactions which are greater than the nonwork state of
conventional retirement. They differ from those of the lower job
levels. When early retirement at age sixty-two became available
under Social Security, more than 700,000 men, or one-fourth of those
aged sixty-two to sixty-four, applied for the early benefits. However,
most of these were in the lower job levels, in poor health, or were
subject to imminent layoff.

Most of those who are highly successful participants in our economic life want to continue to work—and idleness does not appeal
to them. When forced to retire by mandatory regulations, some will
become active in a similar company or in a different field. Many of
these men want to work not because they need money to live comfortably, but to them it is the one way in which they meet their
psychological needs for gaining a sense of self-worth. They want
to continue to be active in a world which they have learned to enjoy
through their everyday activities. There is also a widespread belief
that activities in later life contribute to a "preservation of youth,"
that work has therapeutic effects regarding emotional problems.
Activity is believed to postpone physical deterioration. Scientific
evidence of this kind is difficult to obtain, but some researchers who
made studies of the human brain found evidence that exercise of
the brain cells delays the aging process.[5] Most able men of business
realize that having worthwhile challenges in the later years is

preferable to merely keeping busy as a defense against the negative effects of aging. They prefer to continue to work and wonder how and what kinds of corporations practice compulsory retirement.

## Compulsory retirement in corporations

The likelihood of an employee being forced to retire at a specific age varies with the kind and size of the company. The National Industrial Conference Board's survey of 974 companies, 700 of which were in manufacturing, showed that compulsory retirement appears to be the general practice among public utilities, banks, and insurance companies. Among manufacturing companies, about one-fourth differentiate between hourly and salaried employees—salaried employees have less opportunity to work after sixty-five than hourly workers.

In manufacturing companies, compulsory retirement at sixty-five is related to the size of the company: about one-fourth with less than 500 employees insist on retirement at sixty-five. About one-half having 500 to 5,000 employees and almost three-fourths of the companies with more than 5,000 employees insist on retirement at a mandatory age. In the wholesale and retail trade companies, only one-half reported compulsory retirement at sixty-five.

Approximately 65 percent of the 974 companies reported having some type of preretirement counseling program to help their employees prepare for retirement. One-half of those who do limit the counseling sessions to an explanation of the company pension system, Social Security, and other postretirement company benefits and services. Other companies add counseling in regard to health problems and the use of leisure time. About one-fourth regularly distribute retirement-planning literature to employees who are nearing retirement. Twenty percent of those companies that offer general counseling also invite the wives to counseling sessions. A few companies, 21 or about 2 percent in this survey, help employees to prepare for retirement by allowing them to taper off work through a program of extra time off during the years near the retirement year.[6]

## The retiree who applies for a job in a company new to him

### GETTING A JOB

The man who is psychologically dependent on his job for his personal happiness should, when he knows the time of his imminent retirement, have a satisfactory substitute in mind to take the place of the former job. It may be a purposeful project, some hobby, a program of study, or a travel itinerary. Many, however, prefer to think in terms of getting another job. Some, of course, actually need the money.

Strangely, some intelligent retirees who have had years of experience as successful executives, salesmen, personnel managers, department heads, engineers, and in other responsible positions will apply for a position as though they were novices in business. They will, for example, talk about themselves and their need for a job. They will even remind the interviewer that he would be getting a bargain by hiring a man with the kind of experience the applicant represents. They mention influential people whom they know. Some will overstate or understate the salary they got and fail to describe accurately the functions performed in the positions previously held.

If you decide to apply for work with an employer, you will find your task easier by developing answers to the following questions:

1. Just what would you bring to a new employer in the form of services he might need?

2. What advanced or proven techniques in production, marketing, research, accounting, finance, or other aspect of business do you know so well that you would be able to provide a new employer with a service that he needs?

3. If you have been an active member of a research or other group working on confidential projects in your former place of employment, can you get clearance from your former employer? (Managements of integrity do not want to antagonize a competitor by hiring a man who might be accused of peddling confidential information.)

4. Assuming that you could get clearance from your former em-

ployer, just what evidence can you present, or at least legitimately claim, in regard to systems or procedures you helped to develop and make effective?

5. Just what can you do to increase sales, improve profits, reduce costs, improve research techniques, handle responsibilities of specific operations, or contribute to other aspects of another company's efforts?

The emphases in your answers should be on what you have done and why you believe in the values of doing it again for a company that is new to you. If you have honest respect for what you have done and can do, you will have interesting interviews with employers who, in some instances, will be glad to discuss their problems with you.

As I write this, I can name seven acquaintances who retired from university teaching at approximately the same time I did and later made more money than when they were teaching. They are also very happy. What type of work are they doing? In each case, their work is closely related to or a part of the same work they did years ago, but they had developed an answer to question 1 above. I do not know whether they asked themselves that question, but their work history indicates they put into practice answers to that kind of question. Some of the seven had one exceptional ability—they had the ability to sell their special service by defining it very clearly and tying it into the needs of prospective employers.

### YOUR RÉSUMÉ

Retirees who wish to work for a new employer are likely to need a résumé. Most conventional résumés have headings such as "Educational Background" and "Work History" above the typed data. This kind of form has its values, but if the applicant's past employment record involved managerial responsibilities, it is better to add to the résumé a special kind of organization chart with a letter of transmittal. (See pages 68 and 69.)

As a retiree who has had tested experience in dealing with business problems, you should apply for an opportunity to solve specific kinds of problems with other employers. You are not likely to get employment if you apply for a vacancy. Instead, it is up to you to apply for a privilege to solve certain business problems, the kinds you know that you can solve or, at least, tackle intelligently.

An applicant may decide to conduct his own direct mail campaign or he may wish to register with "Executive Search Consultant" firms. These firms can be classified into two major groups in regard to their charges. Those who *do not charge the applicant* develop their own files of desirable men whom they refer to employers, who pay the fee. Some of these consultants do not care to consider anyone who, on his own initiative, *comes to them.*

Those firms who *do charge the applicant* may or may not explain their charges very clearly before accepting the applicant. Some are purposely vague about their explanations. These "vague" outfits are more likely to charge fees that are much larger than the unsuspecting applicant may anticipate. Hence, you should find out exactly what the fee will be and what services are assured before you sign any contract. The Yellow Pages of the telephone directories of the larger cities list many good and some surprisingly expensive firms, but each should be thoroughly investigated regardless of their claimed services or the fact that prestige publications accept their advertising.

If a nearby city has a Forty-Plus Club, you should consider it as a likely means of providing job-getting aid. (See page 168.)

For a list of employment agencies, you may wish to write to *The New York Times*, 229 W. 43rd St., New York, N.Y. 10036, for a free copy of their annual guide to employment agencies that advertise in the *Times*. People who want a temporary job should ask for "So You Want a Temporary Job."

Manpower, Incorporated, has offices in numerous cities and is especially interested in placing the mature worker. The president, Elmer L. Winter, has a chapter on the subject in his book, *Women at Work* (New York: Simon & Schuster, 1967, chap. 14).

For writing a résumé, you can write for a copy of a helpful booklet, *Guide to Preparing a Résumé,* available to those of the New York City area from Professional Placement Center, Division of Employment, New York State Employment Service, 444 Madison

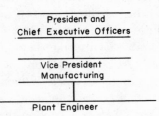

President and
Chief Executive Officers

Vice President
Manufacturing

Plant Engineer

A managerial position. Responsible
for capital and expense budgets,
utility mgt., plant construction,
maintenance, facilities planning.
Worked closely with corporate staff
in originating plans, financial programs,
and governmental agencies.
Responsible for 25 engrg. staff
members and 200 other employees.

General Foreman - Maintenance

Responsible for maintenance,
modification and installation of
plant facilities and production
equipment. Hired and trained
supervisory personnel. Developed
and implemented cost improvement
programs: work measurements, work
sampling, methods analysis, wage
incentives.

Assistant to Plant Engineer

Provided technical and advisory
services to management in the
design and development of
specifications for a variety of
projects, including financial
considerations as a primary
responsibility.

Project Engineer

Investigated engineering
aspects of major projects.
Recommended solutions with
evaluating justifications,
specifications, and schedules.
Responsible for utilizing
computers for the control
of plant engineering functions,
resulting in a computer-
processed maintenance
system, that produced
desired cost reductions.

68

Avenue, New York, N.Y. 10022. Those in other parts of the nation should write to the Public Relations Office, Division of Employment, State Office Building Campus, Albany, N.Y. 12201.

If you wish to know more about executive-counseling services whose advertising is peppered with offers of "career analysis" and "job advancement," you may refer to "Job Counselors under Fire," *Business Week*, Sept. 21, 1968, p. 92.

### LETTER OF TRANSMITTAL

Vice-president, Manufacturing
Address

Dear Sir:

The enclosed outline of my qualifications may interest you, particularly if you are in need of an engineer who has had training and varied experience in developing, justifying, implementing, and managing a program that would reduce maintenance costs by means of a computerized-process system.

Recently I retired from my position as plant engineer in a company that manufactures electrical equipment. Annual volume of sales is $100 million. This required me to perform managerial functions in labor relations, work measurement, budgetary controls, and computer applications.

My abilities to attain cost-reduction goals have been demonstrated through computer applications to production problems of varied kinds. I would like to continue to do the same type of work in a company that is new to me. This, to me, is the one best method of reducing maintenance and production costs.

The enclosed organization chart and accompanying résumé indicate my seasoning over the years as I moved through several position levels in the plant's organizational structure.

Very truly yours,

Signed Name

### INTERVIEWS

Normally, you would be likely to know some of the main facts about a company that would respond to your mailing, but your own ingenuity in getting pertinent additional information should be helpful to you. One purpose of the facts should be to provide subject matter for your use in stimulating the prospective employer to discuss some of his problems with you. If not, you can say to the interviewer: "Would it be helpful to both of us if you were to tell me about the nature of your needs that might apply to me? If you care to do so, I should then be able to discuss more helpfully whether I might fit into your company's operations." His answer should lead to an objective discussion of the company's problems.

Bear in mind that an employer wants to talk with you long enough and often enough to develop his image of you. He wants to know, for example, how rigid you are in your thinking as to what you want to do and how you want to do it.

The image an employer has of an applicant is very important in enabling him to judge the probable abilities of the applicant. Let us consider the image idea in hiring as exemplified in interviewing retired officers of the Army, Navy, and Marine Corps. Most commissioned officers retire in their early fifties. Many are very able men who want to continue to work and so they very logically seek jobs in industry.

Many employers will shy away from hiring retired officers, not only because they are rated as too old to train for important future responsibilities, but also because their ways of life tend to develop an authoritative manner which is quite appropriate in the services but is not appropriate in private industry. An officer while in the services does not have to learn how to present his requests or state his ideas in a friendly manner. A firm direct command is easier to give and more effective. In civilian life, tact and permissiveness are far more essential to effective communication than in the armed services. The retired officer who applies for a job in industry should have some civilian friends observe his manner in communicating, for his brusqueness and tones of finality, then have them advise him *tactfully* before he goes to his first interview.

If in the course of an interview you think your services should be considered further by the prospective employer and you like the psychological climate of the company as you experience it, you may wish to agree on topics to be discussed further in another meeting. Each meeting should lead to a stage where you become more aware of the factors that would be involved in a definite working relationship.

## AVOID THE DEFENSIVE STANCE

Do not visualize yourself as the ordinary hat-in-hand type of young applicant. Think and talk as a colleague who feels at home with the management men whom you meet. You need not ask for an "opportunity" in the manner you probably used when you applied for jobs years ago. You are now a mature person. You should direct your conversation toward the prospective employer's problems in your field of interest, not toward your need or desire for a job.

Do not talk about how little you are willing to accept. Defer any discussion of salary. If you are asked to name a figure, try to pass the responsibility back to the asker. Let him, if possible, name the figure. In some instances, the figure will be higher than you had in mind. If it is too low, state why you think that the job under consideration should have a higher rate.

After a series of important interviews in a company has been completed, write a thank-you note to those who spent an appreciable amount of time with you. Write the note even though you were turned down.

Most of your interviews will be pleasant conversations with people whom you respect. Presumably you functioned as a colleague of management men in the company from which you retired. You should continue to feel the same way when you visit another company. Unfortunately, the "retirement shock" that hits some retirees in their first stages after retirement causes them to lose their normal self-confidence. They develop an apologetic manner, especially when they view retirement as a letdown in their self-worth. They tend to feel an aimlessness in life. This feeling is accentuated by the probability that getting a satisfactory problem-solving opportunity may and does, in some instances, require a year or even more.

Do not assume that nobody ever hires anyone over sixty-five. The University of California's Hastings College of Law in San Francisco has been consistently hiring overage professors who have been uprooted by compulsory retirement rules at other schools for more than twenty-five years. This galaxy of overage professors has been dubbed "The Sixty-Five Club." Currently, the faculty of twenty ranges in age from sixty-five to eighty-five. The school, now third largest law school in the country, is regarded by some authorities as an outstanding law faculty.[7]

Admittedly, few retirees want to become law professors, but it is usually possible for the determined overage applicant to find something to do that enables him to feel that he is still very useful. The specialist or technically trained man who knows the companies which are doing research or development work in his field of interest is likely to find that employers are glad to know of his availability and to interview him.

Harold R. Hall's study of retired executives indicated that of those who had been retired less than two years, 30 percent were actively and productively engaged in work. Of those who had been retired more than two years, 45 percent were in the active and productive classification. In general, the data showed that many executives in their early retirement had done inadequate programming for later productive activities but in the course of two years a higher percentage found their way into such activity. These figures offer some hope for the executive who retires without a job in mind but tries to obtain one later.[8]

**INSTRUCTIONS TO YOUR WIFE AND
OTHER MEMBERS OF THE HOUSEHOLD**

When you plan your program to get a job, you can prevent some of the feelings of uselessness that are likely to develop if you will give your wife and other members of the household instructions regarding their conduct while you are job hunting. Most wives and other members of the family are sympathetic and interested when a man spends many days in trying to get relocated. When he comes home at the end of the day, they greet him with the same old question: "Well, did you get a job today?" After a few of these quizzings, the question cuts deeper and deeper into your feelings of self-worth. Your morale falls lower and lower, and your disposition gets worse.

So, do not let this happen to you. Tell the members of the household that you have mapped a campaign of several months and that you will inform everyone about your progress whenever you have something important to report to them. In the meantime, they can be most helpful to you if they do not ask you any prying questions. Ask them to conduct themselves in the same cheerful manner that they usually display to you.

## Continuing employment in your present company

### PART-TIME EMPLOYMENT AS
### CONSULTANT TO THE COMPANY

Very few older men are needed in their company as a consultant. Only those who are geniuses in a highly specialized field can contribute enough to justify asking for a consulting arrangement. Most men who ask for it do not get it and are usually deeply offended. Those who do get that kind of arrangement seldom enjoy it more than a few months.

Company officers who are members of the board of directors and those who have heavy financial investments in the company can "demand" the privilege of maintaining a satisfactory working relationship after they are sixty-five. Men in this category can supply helpful counsel in some cases but even they are likely to discover that they are part of the company's nonessential overhead.

Occasionally, a member of the engineering or research department has some specialized knowledge that should be available for a year or two after he retires, but this is exceptional rather than typical for retirees. In certain technical fields such as mineral-ore dressing, hydrometallurgy, and geology, retirees may continue to work productively for several years on a consulting basis. The shortage of competent men in fields so specialized as these explains the special arrangements.

There are, of course, the few exceptional men such as the very able retirees who are young for their age. Most of these do not, as a general rule, want to continue in their old companies—they usually have new projects of their own which they want to try.

The new project that many of these very able retirees follow is to offer a consulting service to companies other than or in addition to the former employer. This kind of part-time consulting service usually succeeds so well that the retiree finds himself working on a full-time basis and more busy than in his regular preretirement job. Consulting businesses or arrangements of this nature have been very successful in those instances with which I happen to be acquainted.

### PARTIAL RETIREMENT OF AN EXECUTIVE

Some executives who will hold their title until they are 64 years and 364 days of age resent mandatory retirement because they like to imagine that they are carrying all the responsibilities of the title until the very last day. Perhaps they are being allowed to think they are carrying on their responsibilities as always, but top management may have had a trainee "warming up in the bull pen" for several years. He may have been handling some of the responsibilities, but the younger man has not wanted the older one to be especially aware of it. If you are in the near-retirement category, you may have become aware not only of a chosen successor's presence but, more importantly, of the fact that you are no longer getting the stimulus of day-to-day contacts with responsible men of your own company, as well as with the competition that a corporate executive needs.

You will note certain changes in reactions to you as a result of your mixed old-new status. Old friends and customers try to be as friendly as formerly, but you sense that their relationship has changed or is changing. You are motivated by the old picture of yourself, but the picture you are gradually forced to see is somewhat less glowing than the one you liked in the past.

The other employees are not antagonistic to you as a person, but they recognize that your appointed successor should have freedom in building a new team, one whose members identify with him, not with you. Your day as the unquestioned leader is passing. The successor wants to bring in his new men, men who will acquire the training, new points of view, and techniques that will fill gaps in the old organization. The successor deserves a chance to conduct his programs as he wishes, and you will gradually admit it to yourself. And the sooner you actively and openly prepare the way for your successor, the better.

## Why most modern companies should retire employees at a definite age

The financial men of modern corporations can cite figures which show that, costwise, it is necessary to have relatively few employees who have passed the mandatory retirement age. I do not know those data, but I have seen ample psychological evidence of men, usually owner-managers or major stockholders, who remained too long in managerial control of their companies. The effects of their delay in retirement point up the harmful effects of similar delays on the part of other members of an organization, though perhaps to a lesser degree.

The man who owns or controls a company is in a position that enables him to plan the rate of his own retirement. Usually, he imagines that he wants to remain only long enough to be sure that his successors are properly trained and competent to carry on. Unfortunately for their businesses, many remain too long.

The typical owner intends to let go, but he cannot quite accept the idea that anyone else could ever take his place. An example occurred in one of the New England states. The president, who was also the main stockholder, of a small bank decided at the age of sixty-five that a younger man should be brought in to be trained to take over the presidency. Accordingly, he selected a nearby bank officer who had a successful record and gave him the title of "Executive Vice-president," but the older man continued to remain in order to "train him," as he explained to others. Twenty years later, the executive vice-president had retired at age sixty-five, but the old man was still president at the age of eighty-five!

Obviously, an owner-manager who hangs on too long fails to develop a competent successor. A correlative of this weakness in his organization is that his company will probably have a weak staff—as long as the old man decides every important question, the younger men cannot develop and they know it. The effect on the ambitious men of good potentials is to cause them to obtain jobs elsewhere.

The owner of a company who likes to think that he has partially retired but, in reality, is still the controlling influence is apt to have a bad habit of taking his leisure trips away from work when he feels so inclined. Maybe he ought to be on the job at those times in order to make the decisions about the many matters he keeps under his control. Gradually, the business suffers because of too many delays in decision making.

Some smart owners of businesses foresee all these and other hazards—they retire, completely, near the time of life when most executives of large companies retire. Others find reasons to delay the date.

If you happen to be the owner-manager of your company and you delay the naming of your successor, or you name the successor but withhold the proper authority that usually goes with the managerial title, you are producing noticeable conflicts in loyalty on the part of the able younger men who identify with you, are loyal to you, and want to be helpful to you even though you are past the usual retirement age. In spite of their personal loyalty, some younger men think of you as a block to their advancement.

Bear in mind, too, that through the years of your managerial responsibility you helped to build a team of younger men of talent to support your programs. Some of these men are ready to succeed you. They are impatient to take over. You should therefore view their impatience as a sign of your ability to select good men and to build a strong organization.

If you remain, you will sense the conflict on the part of subordinates. As a result, you will become defensive. You will become overly conscious of some of their deficiencies or shortcomings. You will note faults and weaknesses which did not seem important years ago, but you now perceive them as more evidence of the need for your "hanging on" another six months, a year, or two years!

You, like most men who have held responsible positions in business, will find it easy to justify in your own mind why it is "absolutely necessary for you to remain another year or two." Of course you are one of the few who see it that way, but your colleagues are too kind to tell you.

If you feel that you must stay, you should get out of the main management stream and into staff activities such as developing new products or arranging new mergers. Besides, it is always possible to make indirect contributions to your company by doing an original project for the industry as suggested in Chapter 5.

### First reactions to full retirement

The usual emotional reactions of a man from the higher occupational levels who moves out completely are not as simple as people at the retirement party assume. Not at all. His emotions are a mixture of outward geniality, release from pressures, inner bitterness, and a kind of determined hope. These are my findings after observing and working with many able men of business who retired under mandatory policies. The general pattern of their reactions can be described as follows:

1. Ostensibly, they left their company with good feelings on the part of the board, top management, and the retiree.

2. *Intellectually*, the retiree accepted his retirement in outward good spirit, not because he really wanted to retire, but because it was necessary, chiefly because the corporation would benefit from following a policy of bringing in new and younger men.

3. *Emotionally*, he was convinced that he still had a lot to offer the corporation, far more than the younger men realized. He felt pushed aside, rejected, resentful, and embittered, mildly or decidedly, at times.

4. Sometimes he relieved his throttled feelings by blaming someone or something for his departure. At other times he felt better

when he congratulated himself on the release from the pressures of the old job.

5. As a result of his ambivalence, the coexistence of the conflicting forces and feelings that beset him, he *determined* to enjoy his retirement "even if it killed him," as one phrased it.

6. His next step, if the feeling of resentment against his retirement was strong, was to get away: pack the car and head for some recreational or other place where he hoped to reorient his feelings and enjoy life by eventually devoting himself full-time to his favorite sport or some other activity. In some cases he moved to a retirement area, where he was apt to play golf with "ferocity," not in a relaxed manner. In other cases, he returned to his home, where he tried to find a satisfying hobby or other absorbing interest.

7. Later interviews usually indicate that the favorite sport or other interest of most of these men rarely becomes as satisfying as the old job, even though the retiree tells you about how he was harassed by the pressures he experienced in his former active, tempestuous days, and how glad he is to be enjoying retirement. Actually, his tone of voice and wistful manner imply that he misses the thrills of achievement and the feeling of being useful in doing work that he rates as worthy of his ability.

As one would expect, this pattern was not at all evident among the men whose careers were in the creative fields—the fine arts, writing, inventing—nor in research, nor in the professions of law and medicine. Most of these men never retire mentally. Even though they may talk about a retirement, they are pursuing their lifetime interests almost as much as ever. Nor have I found the above pattern of resentment to retirement appreciably often among men of the lower occupational strata.

The men who do exhibit the described pattern represent the higher occupational levels of modern industry, particularly among executives, their work associates, and specialists who work closely with management men, and among other trained employees. However, we cannot assume that this pattern of frustration and the attempts to make satisfying readjustments is inherent in the job the individual has held. Rather, the pattern is characteristic of those men who devoted themselves wholeheartedly to a kind of work which they can no longer pursue in their retirement from the corporate life of today. The wholehearted devotion they gave to their work without developing equally satisfying other interests was a necessary part of their work life. Small wonder that they find adjustment to retirement very difficult. They deserve more admiration than they usually receive.

*Abruptness* in causing devotion to a career to cease is a common factor in the difficulties of able men of business who are suddenly forced to adjust to their retirement. Their problem is similar to that of the artist who suffers a sudden illness or physical handicap. When we see the problem of unexpected need for adjustment on the part of the pianist whose arthritis or deafness handicap him or the painter who cannot see colors clearly, we sympathize with him for his inability to continue his art. But we fail to recognize the equally frustrating emotionality that befalls the businessman who is forced to quit his "art" more suddenly than the physically handicapped artist.

The answer does not, I fear, lie in the oft-recommended procedure of having corporations give prospective retirees gradual retirement. At least not in the gradual retirement procedures practiced today. Currently, companies that encourage gradual retirement do not require or counsel the prospective retirees on how to adjust to retirement. As a result, most of those in a gradual retirement program merely "loaf" for two months instead of one month during their last preretirement vacations. They learn little or nothing about the ways in which they might utilize extra time by means of really self-fulfilling activities.

Gradual retirement programs are not geared to train the individual how to adjust to a twelve-months-of-the-year schedule of idleness.

Let us review the factors involved in dealing constructively with severe emotional effects of retirement on these high-grade men in whom we are especially interested:

1. The individual, in his work life, has concentrated consistently for a number of years on his work. He learned to enjoy his work life.

2. He neglected to develop other interests that were almost or as fully satisfying as his work.

3. Retirement at a specific time brings an abrupt end to the enjoyment of his pleasant way of life.

4. He is not prepared to utilize constructively and satisfyingly the leisure time available to him.

5. He needs preparation and stimulation in finding and pursuing purposeful projects that utilize his best potentials, projects that will enable him to associate meaningfully with the people and the problems he knows or at least respects.

The purposeful project as one approach to solving the adjustment problems of high-grade men who retire is in an early stage of development in our culture, but I believe on the basis of my own experience that it would be helpful to many retirees. The next chapters will emphasize this type of approach as well as suggest other retirement activities.

## REFERENCES

1. Nancy C. Morse and R. S. Weiss, "The Function and Meaning of Work and Job," *American Soc. Rev.*, 1955, 20, p. 191–198. At the time of writing, this was the latest available representative survey on this subject that included men of all occupational levels.

2. Committee of Retired Army, Navy, and Air Force Officers, *Retirement from the Armed Forces*, Harrisburg, Pa.: Stackpole Books, 1957, p. 49.

3. Harold R. Hall, *Some Observations on Executive Retirement*, Boston: Graduate School of Business Administration, Division of Research, Harvard University, 1953, p. 123.

4. See Harry M. Rosen, "Who Are the Elderly?" *Proceedings of Senior Center Directors Short Course*, Oklahoma Center for Continuing Education, Norman, Oklahoma, May, 1967, p. 3. These figures vary with definitions. When consumer units with head age over 65 are considered rather than individuals, 23 percent are self-employed or employed by others. See Dorothy S. Projector and Gertrude S. Weiss, *Survey of Financial Characteristics of Consumers*, Board of Governors of the Federal Reserve System, August, 1966, p. 151. The third study data are taken from a Veterans Administration study for year 1965, reported in *Aging*, June, 1968, p. 7.

5. See Charles M. Crowe, *Getting Ready for Tomorrow*, Nashville, Tenn.: Abingdon Press, 1959, p. 66.
6. Harland Fox and Miriam C. Kerpen, "Corporate Retirement Policy and Practices," *Studies in Personnel Policy*, no. 190, The National Industrial Conference Board, Copyright 1964.
7. See David E. Snodgrass, "The Sixty-five Club," *The Journal of the Michigan State Medical Society*, May, 1960.
8. Harold R. Hall, *op. cit.*, p. 90.

# PART TWO

# Purposeful Projects and Other Retirement Activities

## CHAPTER FIVE

# Project: "I'll Find Possible Answers to a Need of the Industry I Know Best"

*"How dull it is to pause, to make an end,*
*To rust unburnished, not to shine in use,*
*As tho' to breathe were life!"*
—ALFRED, LORD TENNYSON, *Ulysses*

PSYCHOLOGICALLY, the prospective retiree who is embittered by the thought of retirement can be understood when we think in terms of the couplet by William Congreve:

Heaven has no rage like love to hatred turned,
Nor hell a fury like a woman scorned.

The woman who offers her love naturally becomes infuriated when it is scorned. A prospective retiree reacts in the same emotional way when he wants to continue to work for a company he likes but management declines his offer. He himself is not clearly aware of the reasons for his emotions when he thinks of retirement, but he does know that he would like to continue to give his warm personal attachment to the organization and to the people with whom he has worked, the company to which he has given years of devotion at some self-sacrifice. He has given his company and his work a kind of identification somewhat similar to that a woman gives the man she loves.

What he is trying to say from his subconscious pleadings is "Look at me, not merely in terms of what I have done for you in the past but in terms of what I would like to do in the future, in spite of the fact that I am scheduled to retire. As a prospective retiree, I feel lost, useless, unwanted. Please, somehow let me continue to be a friend."

## *Recognize the possiblity of ambivalence when you plan your retirement activities*

The emotionally pleading employee who undergoes mandatory retirement continues to nurture the hope that management will somehow make an exception of his case. When he finally realizes that management must follow its retirement policies with some consistency, that his pleadings are of no avail, and that he will be retired on the scheduled date, he is apt to project with some vehemence his feelings against management. He is not conscious of the ambivalence that is taking place, even though ambivalence, the coexistence of opposite and conflicting feelings about a person or object, has frequently been recognized by him in his past human relations.

An example: many a husband has had the experience of irritating his wife, as when he spilled coffee on her new dress and she shrieked: "You oaf—get away from me. I don't want to have anything more to do with you!" Of course he knew that she didn't really mean it. Her *basic* feelings toward him would continue as in the past. He realized that her anger at the time was *incidental* and not at all important enough for him to change his basic relationship toward her. He continued to act and feel toward her as he had before the incident occurred.

Unfortunately, when a man plans his retirement activities while still reacting emotionally against the thought of his retirement, he tends to fail to differentiate between his basic long-term feelings toward his old company and his incidental irritation about the event of retirement. This failure on his part in planning his retirement activities is likely to cause him, when his offer to continue is rejected, to say to himself: "I don't want to have anything more to do with my old company." He should realize that in his state of ambivalence his negative feelings are temporary, incidental, and not really characteristic of his relationship with the company and, usually, not at all characteristic of his attitude toward the industry in which his company operates. He seldom does at the time. Usually, he wants to get away from his colleagues and the place where he has worked, even though he realizes that he knows so much about that kind of business that he could give information of value to many companies of the industry.

## WHY PLAY GOLF WITH "UNDISCERNING FEROCITY"?

If he makes an adjustment by going to a country club or resort in order to try to forget all about his past work and the company for whom he worked, he can release his pent-up energy, as many frustrated retirees do, by playing golf with "undiscerning ferocity," a term used by David Riesman. Riesman thought of this kind of adjustment for the retiree as an "ersatz preservative" and not as one that results in an inner transformation that encourages self-renewal.[1]

Most able retirees from business have a feeling of frustration in greater or lesser degree. Many do not express the feeling openly, but it is there for years, at least in mild form. In this book we assume that you as a retiree are susceptible to some of these feelings but that you would like to prevent such negative feelings or to redirect them into positive channels. One approach is to achieve a sense of usefulness, *not* by working for the old company as an employee, but in a new relationship with the same kinds of people and problems that you dealt with on the old job. You can do a project that would be helpful to your industry as well as indirectly to your company. In this way you will contribute what you know to the industry you know best. If you do, you will be able to enjoy golf or any other recreational activity for its usual benefits, not merely as an outlet for your pent-up resentment.

This does not, by any means, suggest that you should write a summary of what you learned in your old company and try to peddle it to other companies of the industry. Far from it. Instead, you should use your background to conduct a study of one problem of the industry and make the study with the cooperation of members of the industry—the findings to go to every company.

### A possible answer

Let me describe where this is now practiced to some extent in American life. It is practiced by those retirees from the academic world who continue to study a problem of professional interest to them and to their scientific colleagues. They work on a project of their own, usually an important scientific question. The faculty member who retires knows the men in his field and keeps in friendly contact with a chosen few. He discusses his project with them, not for the purpose of advising the scientists what to do about their work, but for adding to his information on his own project. He knows that he would not be welcome if he visited his colleagues frequently or if he tried to influence the work and thinking of the men where he worked before retirement. He realizes that he is no longer an employee of the institution, but he is still a friend. When he has completed the study or significant parts of it, he presents a report to his colleagues in an open meeting, in a published report, or by personal interviews with interested individuals.

Note, however, that in this entire relationship, whether it takes place with the faculty members of an institution where the retiree was employed or at another institution, the relationship is not organized or planned by a dean, a chancellor, or a faculty—it is informal and takes place at the initiative of the retiree. It never begins at all nor stops at any specific time; its end as well as its beginning depends upon the wishes of the retiree. And the retiree sets his own pace.

As a retiree you now realize more fully that one factor which made your career friendships meaningful before you retired was a mutuality of interests—you and your colleagues dealt with problems common to both of you.

One of the pleasant side aspects of pursuing a project is that a retiree from the academic world can often establish friendly informal relationships at institutions of another area, an area to which he may wish to retire. He is welcomed or ignored in the degree to which he seeks to do creative work that applies to fields of interest to the active workers of the institutions of the area. When I first retired, I noted that my former colleagues were friendly in a polite but a hurried way. They did not want to continue the conversation as they had formerly—they had work to do. But when I talked about subjects of interest to them, they were less hurried.

This means that if you can hope to enjoy friendships with work colleagues after you retire, you will have to develop a project that involves genuine interest on the part of some other people of your industry as well as yourself.

Of course, pursuing a project will not bring you many chatty new friends—it will, however, enable you to enjoy the kinds of friendships you enjoyed when you were working. And it can aid your rehabilitation in many ways.

Gerontologists have found that the rehabilitation of older people depends largely on their developing purposes in life and achieving a forward orientation through the pursuit of those purposes.[2]

### DEVELOP A PROJECT OF YOUR OWN THAT APPLIES TO THE INDUSTRY YOU KNOW BEST

To reiterate for the purpose of emphasis, in the project idea you give the benefit of what you know and can learn about a problem to the industry. The problem and your contacts in finding answers have broad relationships. Whatever you do of this nature should be of interest and value to many companies, not just to one company or the company where you worked. If you worked in a company of the chemical industry, for example, the project would apply to all or many companies of the chemical industry.

Every industry has some challenging problems which no one is solving. Let me offer an example from my own field of work. As a teacher of industrial psychology I often wondered how other teachers of the subject were conducting their instruction. I looked for ideas better than those I was using. I found a few by asking a lot of questions, reading, and some observations of classroom teaching, but I was unable to obtain a comprehensive description of the methods used, the advantages and disadvantages of various procedures, or even the extent of usage of specific methods. Accordingly, when I retired I pursued my own original project for two years, doing what should have been done more productively many years before. The report was published and distributed to the members of the professional organization to which the findings applied. Seven years later, I still receive requests from teachers for a copy of the report. Copies are no longer available—all have been distributed —but another teacher should redo the study and publish a better report, one that meets the needs of these times.

As a retiree from an industry, you undoubtedly know some executives personally. Discuss with a few chosen ones your desire to continue to be of service to the industry. Mention to each several possible projects that might benefit the industry, projects you might like to do. You can explain to the executive that you enjoyed your years of service with a company of the industry, that you are retiring, that you are not looking for any job, but that you would, in an informal way, like to be of service to the industry as a whole. Explain a tentatively chosen project to him and ask for his comments and criticisms. Modify the plan and purpose of your project and explain it to other executives. With relatively little time and effort, you can develop a program for a project which has a purpose that you can respect and pursue enthusiastically.

*Do not assume that you must deal with a wholly new problem.* Some old problems which have been studied for years have not been completely solved. Consider working on a problem that challenged you when you were working, one that would direct your retirement thinking in much the same way that your old job was a focal point of your daily mental effort in the past. Later, you would probably discover new slants on the old problem, aspects that would stimulate your thinking in new directions and be of interest to others as well as to you. As a result, you and your associates would realize that you are still growing mentally and not going into the stage of mental dullness and deterioration that characterizes too many retirees.

The objective of gaining mental stimulation is just as important as finding possible answers to an industry problem, in some ways more important. Perhaps you can appreciate the benefits to you of working on an industry project if you will think of the answers that you will get when you ask some of the older men who are still working: "What are some of the things you intend to do when you retire?" One kind of answer will be of the project variety: "Oh, I am going to add a wing to the house, build a sailboat, improve my golf score, learn to read lips, take a trip abroad, etc." Answers of this kind are good normal personal projects, probably suitable for you as well as for almost every retiree. Their one serious missing aspect is that for you they do not utilize the tremendous background of information you learned on the job, knowledge of the industry's practices, or the many pleasant social relationships you enjoyed. Most serious of all, personal projects will not enable you to feel that you are still a worthy member in the mainstream of usefulness in the world. A project of personal benefit only will not enable you to feel that you are still a worthy member of the world of affairs when you are retired. If you have an unsatisfied desire for the continuation of that kind of feeling, you may want to consider the pursuit of an industry project.

## POSSIBLE INDUSTRY PROJECTS TO CONSIDER

You will be able to think of several possible projects if you will recall some of the occasions when you said to yourself: "I believe that a company of this industry could make more money, reduce their costs, increase their sales, or improve their profits in regard to the problem of . . ." Here are some old problems, all previously studied but still challenging as projects which are in need of attention by interested retirees:

1. A *traffic man* has estimated mentally how much his company

loses each year by shipping its products to customers from distant rather than nearby warehouses, but he does not take time to give management a report on his ideas. It would be easy for him after he retires to interview traffic managers of other companies and to work with them in developing facts and suggestions that would improve the services of all the traffic departments of the industry.

2. A *marketing man* with a varied background in sales has wasted thousands of hours sitting in customers' reception rooms. He believes that costs and effectiveness of personal selling could be improved. He decides that on his retirement he will develop methods that will reduce costs such as the waiting time. After he has retired he programs a project to find better methods. He is sure that other salesmen and sales executives will be glad to discuss with him the problem and to describe their methods.

3. A *credit man* of an industrial firm wonders why managements do not utilize their credit services more often to increase sales, by helping customers through special financing methods that would reduce losses and at the same time increase sales. When he makes it a retirement project, he finds that he is welcomed by other credit men, company treasurers, and marketing executives.

4. The *customer-complaints* man of an equipment manufacturing company retires. Through the years he has discovered that many electricians who install the equipment really do not know how to install it properly. He decides to study the same kinds of problems of other companies by conferring with executives and electricians. As a result, he is welcomed by the many men whose problems he understands. He makes contributions to both manufacturers and customers, and he enjoys his retirement even more than the old job with the one company where he had a pleasant career.

5. An *accountant* says: "Why don't more people in the company utilize what we could do for them?" This question has probably been applied most often to marketing. "Why don't the people in marketing ask for the accounting department's records of sales of specific products by areas?" For many marketers, distribution costs exceed production costs. Effective cost accounting procedures help assure the most efficient distribution expenditures.[3]

6. A man from research and development says: "What *developments*, particularly recent inventions and new product designs used in other industries, are likely to affect sales or methods of our industry, the industry in which I worked?"

7. A *production* man in a large manufacturing plant has selected for purchase millions of dollars worth of production equipment. He has tested the equipment and developed techniques for reducing a wide variety of manufacturing costs. When he retires, hundreds of manufacturing executives would be glad to buy an industry report on the significant findings gained in his own plants and from other plants that he could visit in his retirement. He might need a coauthor to help do the writing of the report, but that could easily be arranged.

8. "What are the *personnel needs of companies* of the industry regarding trained personnel, particularly in regard to men trained in the sciences and the ability to use program-evaluation review techniques and new types of equipment?"

9. *Retirement counseling* offers one possibility of your doing a project for employees of your industry. Most managements recognize that any plan for stimulating preretirement thinking by the prospective retirees should include a counselor who has experienced the problems of retirement. Management men would agree that attainment of the age of fifty-five is when a first stage of personal "stocktaking" takes place. This, ideally, is the age when most men are becoming receptive to programs of retirement planning, but relatively few employees do very much about it.

10. If, after your retirement, you do not care to conduct discussion-group meetings of prospective retirees, you may be able to arrange through the personnel department of the company where you worked to get the names and addresses of employees who will retire within a year or two. Write each one of these a friendly letter telling him that you would be glad to correspond with any prospective retiree concerning his retirement, describe your experiences in seeking work, the climate and cost of living where you live, etc. Depending upon where you live and how much you like to write, you may find yourself busy.

*Trend studies* offer opportunities for projects by retirees of every industry. If you will think of bothersome problems in relation to trends, and recall some of your readings in the trade journals of your field, you will probably come up with a challenging problem or two that excite you as suitable topics for follow-up or as a definite project for you in your retirement. Discussions with several knowledgeable colleagues should lead to a better definition of a problem and suggest appropriate procedures for getting answers. After that, you may want to correspond with or interview members of the industry's trade-association headquarters.

*Trade-association staff members* should be considered when you choose a problem—they have certain functions to perform and jobs to protect. Hence, avoid any implications that might cause association staff members to become fearful of your trying to encroach on areas which they wish to protect for themselves. If this possibility is obvious, develop the program in a way that will enhance or at least not threaten the image or functions of the trade-association staff members. If you approach them in the right manner, they will very probably help you in many ways.

### THE FINANCING

Where will the money for expenses come from? The answer will vary with the purpose you have in mind. The purpose is likely to be one of these three:

1. *What the project will do for you as a retiree.* Your main desire may be to do something that will utilize the background of your experience, give you a sense of personal fulfillment, and offer genuine pleasure while doing it. The money for this kind of purpose usually comes from the retiree—he thinks of the expenditure in much the same way that he thinks of spending money for travel or a vacation.

2. *To put you into favorable relationships with men who may offer you a job.* If your financial situation requires you to improve your retirement income in the course of the next year or two, you may dislike the thought of taking the usual routine, low-salaried job you might be able to get. If you realize that the image you pre-

sent to a prospective employer is that of a retiree who must accept what he is offered, your job prospects are likely to be rather limited. Why not, therefore, try to portray yourself as an exceptional retiree? The ideal way to build a favorable image is to do something so worthwhile for your industry that a top executive will ask you to do a special project or take a position with his company. If you build a reputation for yourself as an alert, competent performer, somebody is likely to forget your age and offer you an opportunity that puts you above the level of the usual retiree.

3. *To use available special funds.* Some men who want to do a project know of sources of money that can be tapped for the purpose: governmental bureaus, industry associations, foundations, or a wealthy individual who wants to make a contribution to the industry in which he made his money. Generally, the man who wants to do a worthwhile project that benefits others as well as himself is likely to find a source of income that will enable him to perform the service he has in mind.

### THE REAL ENJOYMENT IN DOING A PROJECT

Each of us has his individual emotional needs at different times in life. Right now, as a retiree, you probably have a need to feel that you are useful by doing something for someone else, to be making a constructive contribution in this world of ours, and to give yourself some meaningful excitement instead of empty hours of idleness. Retirement activity should, at times, be as exciting as mountain climbing as described by one explorer who had experienced its pleasures: "The concentration required on a difficult climb is demanding and therefore relaxing. All the everyday problems of your life must be forgotten. There is no tendency to daydream. You have to think of what you are doing at every moment and of nothing else."

As Dr. Ralph W. Sockman well stated:

> If we are to grow old gracefully, we need more than the ability to throw ourselves into the present and to capitalize the memories of the past. We need something to look forward to, something to live for.

Dr. Karl Jung, the eminent psychotherapist, reported that most of the patients who came to him were persons who had made their pile and were bored with it. They had no purpose or zest in life. Recently a retired man in Baltimore gave me his card—*No Phone. No Address. No Business. No Ulcers. No Money.* He was trying to make a joke of his retiring, but I am not sure that he was making a joy of it.[4]

If you undertake a purposeful project you will discover that you gain certain benefits which only you as a retiree can appreciate. You will feel that you are not throwing overboard all that you learned in the past, but that you are a worthy, though an unofficial, member of an active group; that you are exchanging ideas with people whom you respect; and that there is added purpose in your life, a kind of purpose which you are uniquely qualified to give.

You gain prophylactic benefits. As you know, aging people who are busy performing interesting activities have less tendency to relive the past by the usual boresome talkativeness. Busy people with important purposes in mind do not need to glorify their past when the present is exciting.

As a prospective or actual retiree, you need recognition for the person you are now in your present years of retirement, not for the person you were years ago. If you are unable to attain a satisfying kind of self-evaluation as a retiree you either have to be a very mature individual, psychologically speaking, or you are likely to fall into the defensive kinds of adjustment such as bragging about past achievements, trying to dominate the people around you, belittling yourself, or even becoming despondent, isolated, and unhappy. Much, of course, depends upon the degree of involvement that you feel in regard to the current problems and ideas which are important to you.

The need for people to feel useful has been demonstrated many times. When a person feels that he is tremendously necessary, he is more likely to be in good mental health. This was dramatically illustrated by the findings of a Russian physician, Feodor Mochansky. He found that the rate of mental breakdowns on the part of the people was less during the stressful period of the seventeen months of the siege of Leningrad than in peacetime. Doctor Mochansky attributed the low rate of psychiatric disorders to the fact that every man, woman, and capable child was needed in his country's defense. Each realized that he was definitely needed.

## GUIDELINES IN DOING A PROJECT

1. Try to have a project or similar activity that enables you to work with acquaintances and colleagues, men whom you respect. You have become accustomed to working with others as a member of a team. Most retirees need the privilege of exchanging ideas with colleagues, even though the team may be very loosely structured.

2. Set time schedules for each workday; they should be flexible, but at least definite enough to enable you to feel that your day is orderly. You should feel that your project is too important to let you get lax and lackadaisical in your work habits. You were under time pressures years ago, and you will probably be happier now if you have datelines to stimulate you.

You will appreciate the benefits of time schedules when you observe the oft-met type of retiree who senses unknown dangers in his uncertain future and who then becomes meticulous about timing small activities as a substitute for important losses from his old job. He performs minor chores at regular hours, walks to certain places at specific times, and meets the same cronies each day. The *regularity*, not the importance of the activities, gives him the feelings of protection and importance that he needs. Obviously, these useless efforts could and should give way to efforts that are more meaningful and rewarding, such as those which can become part of a purposeful project.

3. Let the project keep you mentally active by its incentive to read business or professional journals, preferably more than you read before you retired. Your project should give purpose to your reading of current events magazines and newspapers. Reading will become more enlightening as you run across ideas that give you another slant on some aspect of the project on which you are working. Investment reports, industry conventions, and correspondence with friends are likely to have added bright spots for you when you are mentally alert and looking for ideas or answers to specific questions.

4. When you are looking for answers to a specific problem, you

won't be likely to talk about your past or your own ego-centered interests only. You won't even talk about your age unless someone asks you. In that case, you will give whatever answer you wish, but add: "That's incidental—let's go on with the main topic."

5. If you are interviewing an active member of a company in order to get information relative to your project, you should plan for a brief interview. To keep the conversation from becoming a lengthy social chat, it is well to conduct most interviews while you are standing. Do not sit down unless really necessary because you want to have the interviewee think of you as an active, productive member of the industry, not as a retiree. If you must sit down, sit on the edge of the chair. The more businesslike your manner and the sooner you leave, the greater the likelihood that you will be welcome the next time.

6. When you call on a member of your industry for information, have a specific topic in mind. Prepare your questions in advance. Talk about those, not about incidentals such as your retirement or current newsworthy happenings.

Bear in mind that you can always become interesting to a busy man by asking intelligent questions about his work or his other vital interests. You lose that interest as soon as you talk about the subjects that interest you only.

7. When you have gotten the kinds of information and developed the ideas that might be helpful to active members of your industry, present your report to those who will welcome the opportunity to hear and discuss your findings. Do this first in interviews with individuals who contributed their ideas to your study. After you have obtained their reactions, you may want to present your findings to the members of the industry at a group meeting or annual convention.

### Find some exemplars for your retirement

When you were growing up as a boy you found some exemplars, personalities, whom you admired. They inspired you. Now that you are a retiree, you need a different kind of exemplar, one who has adjusted effectively to his aging. You may not be able to find many nearby retirees who are active in a manner that would inspire you but descriptive examples are available in our literature. Here are several that may fit your emotional needs at this time.

1. Written by a college administrator who was about to retire:

> An administrator has all too little time and all too little residuum of energy left him for reflection. . . . However, it takes but a modicum of reflection to realize that even saying "I don't have to" must after a time pall as an occupation. When I don't *have* to come back from a vacation, will I want so much to prolong it? I fear not. Enjoyment will still be in the pursuit, rather than in the achievement. So, it follows unless human nature changes, which it won't, that the retired man must have—must find, if he doesn't have it—a pursuit.
>
> I think that perhaps the happiest man I have ever known intimately throughout his retirement was the late Dean Charles B. Benjamin of Purdue. An engineer, he not only planned for retirement, but during retirement, as the years passed, he was always foreseeing days when his then avocation might be too much for his physical powers. He knew so much about the animals, the birds, the trees, the flowers, the geology as we tramped over California mountains, that, like nature, he spoke a various language. But all this time he was learning to paint, so that when he could no longer tramp the mountains he could sketch them. Later he exhibited in Pasadena and in Washington. After a while, he got himself a small but respectable telescope and from his front yard fraternized not merely with the mountain peaks but with the heavens. And finally, after deafness and near blindness shut him off from much that he loved, his mind to him was still a kingdom in which he roamed master almost as long as he breathed.[5]

2. Written by Malcolm S. Forbes, editor-in-chief of *Forbes:*

> At the Newcomen Society of North America dinner honoring FORBES Magazine on the occasion of its 50th anniversary, among the dais guests was 92-year-old J. C. Penney, founder and for more than 40 years chairman of the board of that phenomenally successful retail giant. You and I at our present age should be as alert, lively, keen.
>
> I couldn't resist telling him how well I remembered one of FORBES' editors coming to my father over two decades ago to sug-

gest that we push up a scheduled article on Mr. Penney: "He's pretty old now, and if we don't do the article very soon he'll probably be dead." Mr. Penney's eyes twinkled when I told him the story and added that I was of a mind to write this editorial.

"You needn't hurry to get it done," he said with a chuckle.

Wonderful, isn't he? [6]

3. Norman Cousins, president and editor of the *Saturday Review*, has described several elderly famous men whose vigor has been frequently mentioned:

> I have a vivid recollection of Albert Schweitzer at the age of eighty-two crawling under one of the crude hospital bungalows at Lambaréné on a day when the sun was a frying pan under your helmet and the humidity a boiler room strapped to your chest. He was on all fours, carrying heavy carpentry tools, in order to repair a break in the flooring. You witnessed this phenomenon with mixed admiration and despair. Despair because you were half his age. Also, I might add, incapable of helping. Later, you asked *le grand Docteur* whether he was not exerting himself unduly. After all, there were workers at the hospital who could do the crawling. And *le grand Docteur* would fix a baleful eye on you from under his poodle mop and tell you that no one should dare to think of depriving him of hard labor. He was eighty-two; that was how he got there.
>
> Pablo Casals is probably the last man in Western civilization who could be accused of ferocious tendencies; but if you want the privilege of a punch in the nose, just suggest to Don Pablo that he give up conducting at Marlboro next summer because it is exhausting work for a gentleman over ninety. When Don Pablo dies, it probably won't be because he has run out of gas but because he has run out of strings.
>
> Some people are baffled that Picasso at eighty-six should be able to maintain a rigorous schedule as practicing artist and as father of a young family. There need be no mystery. Confidence creates capacity.
>
> The will to live requires neither conscious decision nor definition. It creates its own compatible chemistry and draws its own lines to longevity. And the will to live has a natural tendency to become consonant with the universal design; in this sense, the life-force is omnipresent.[7]

4. Dr. Irving S. Wright, clinical professor of medicine at Cornell University Medical College and president of the American College of

Physicians, believes that retirement based on age is obsolete. His views on retirement derive from interviews during the past fifteen years with hundreds of individuals personally or administratively involved in various aspects of the retirement problem.

There is no gain in longevity, even with good health, if the extra years are without meaning to the individual. The benefits of medical progress are but empty gestures if the beneficiaries must be dependent on pensions, social welfare, or the support of others, while still capable of self-supporting effort.

Those workers who looked forward to retirement often become disillusioned and depressed, observed Dr. Wright. They lose their appetites, are listless, develop a host of body aches, pains, ailments, and other complaints, and become highly neurotic. "The good life has become a poor life."

There are other more constructive approaches to the problem. Dr. Wright suggested:

One of the most interesting and successful experiments was initiated by the proprietor of an engineering works at Darlaston, England. Moved by the pleas of retired employees that they be permitted to go on working, he set up a shop for them in an unused building. In addition to lathes, presses, grinders, drills, and other tools, the building is equipped with easy chairs, game tables, a dartboard and a radio. The men do not have to clock in, there is no foreman or supervisor, they can work or play as they wish. But they are paid the going rate for all machine parts and other items produced.

The experiment started with 15 retired workers. Of their own volition, they come to work regularly at 8:30 each morning and put in a full day's work. Absenteeism is low, production high. With their pensions, many of the elderly workers now have more money than they did before retirement. Several have learned a new trade. A 75-year-old bricklayer became a riveter, for example; at the end of ten days he was producing as much as the average skilled worker.

Instead of operating at a loss, as expected, the program actually has returned a profit, which was invested in more equipment to accommodate more retired workers. Creative ideas have come out of the shop and been adopted in the main plan. A 76-year-old retired worker, for example, came up with a new idea for a broaching tool and jig that increased production from 200 to 2400 units per day. His ingenuity earned him a substantial bonus.[8]

# REFERENCES

1. See David Riesman, *Individualism Reconsidered*, Glencoe, Ill.: The Free Press, 1954, p. 487.
2. See Raymond G. Kuhlen, "Changing Personal Adjustment During the Adult Years," in John E. Anderson (ed.), *Psychological Aspects of Aging*, Washington, D.C.: American Psychological Association, 1956.
3. An excellent treatise on this topic is available in Letricia Gayle Rayburn, "Accounting: Aid to Effective Distribution," *National Public Accountant*, official publication of National Society of Public Accountants, 1717 Pennsylvania Avenue, N.W., Washington, D.C.
4. *Proceedings of the Fourth Annual Governor's Conference on Aging*, sponsored by the New York State Office for the Aging, 11 N. Pearl St., Albany, N.Y., May 7, 1965.
5. Shirley W. Smith, "Preparing for Retirement," *Michigan Alumnus Quarterly Review*, vol. XLIX, no. 20, p. 240.
6. Malcolm S. Forbes, *Forbes* magazine, Feb. 1, 1968, p. 12.
7. Norman Cousins, "Art, Adrenalin, and the Enjoyment of Living, *Saturday Review*, Apr. 20, 1968, pp. 21–22.
8. From *Geriatric Focus*, vol. 6, no. 11, a publication of Knoll Pharmaceutical Company, Orange, N.J.

## CHAPTER SIX

# Project: "I'd Like to Be Helpful to Young Men in Business"

*"Youth, large, lusty, loving—Youth,*
*full of grace, force, fascination,*

*Do you know that Old Age may come*
*after you with equal grace, force,*
*fascination?"*

—WALT WHITMAN
"Youth, Day, Old Age and Night"—1881

"I'D LIKE to do something for young men in business" is a statement you are likely to hear occasionally from retirees who worked their way upward from beginning jobs to successful careers. They think of some of their own long, lean years of hard work and what those years taught them of possible value to young men.

Another influence that arouses the desire to develop young men stems from a man's inner pride in his past contributions to the discovery and development of good men for important jobs. A common statement by older employees and retirees when they talk about a man who has been promoted to a responsible position is "When he came into the company, he worked for me. He was awfully green but I taught him a lot and he learned fast—fact is, he's way ahead of me now but I helped him a bit, too." Perhaps the old paternal instinct is influential also. As one successful executive told

103

me: "Every man who has advanced to a responsible position will, if he is worth his salt as a leader, take an interest in and keep in touch with several bright young men after he retires."

The retiree who identifies with both his industry and the younger generation wants to see able young men come into business and have successful, happy careers. He knows that business as well as every other honorable field of work must grow and fulfill its socio-economic responsibilities by selecting, training, and inspiring men who have good potentials for growth. If the interested retiree wishes, he can make his contributions in these directions by either of two procedures: (1) He can keep in touch with and contribute his friendly influence to the few young men of the industry or his family whom he knows and admires (he can do this in many informal ways), or (2) he can utilize his background of knowledge and judgment through the more organized procedure of a planned project, to which he gives almost as much considered attention as he gave to his work. In this chapter we assume that he will pursue the former possibility.

### What an older man tries to pass on may be obsolete

When an older man tries to advise a younger person about the way he should deal with a problem, the older man usually states how he would have solved the same problem if he had encountered it when he was that age. Thus he fails to recognize how the thinking of young people and the influences on their thinking have changed. To the typical retiree, telling a young person what to do means doing it as he himself did it, and that does not always fit. Let's face it, fellow old-timers, you and I dealt with a lot of our problems with young men in the same way we were reared as children—by means of authority, quite often well-meant and usually effective but dictatorial and enforced by means of an implied threat of punishment. Some of the younger parents of today are getting smarter. See "Don't Let Anyone Know You're Mom." Children who have had this new kind of parental influence will become tactful parents and supervisors in their adulthood.

## "DON'T LET ANYONE KNOW YOU'RE MOM"

### by Erma Bombeck

My children are in that stage of life where they can tolerate my presence if I lurk in the shadows, am mute and in no way indicate that we are related.

They have been in this stage since they were able to say, "Wait in the car."

The first time I discovered my presence was a humiliating experience was when I served on playground duty. I thought I had cleaned up rather well, was reasonably dignified and didn't pick my nose. However, that evening I was approached by my son who said, "You had to do it, didn't you?"

"Do what? I asked.

"You had to call me by name."

"What am I supposed to call you?"

"Other mothers just say, 'Hey kid'."

I had rather hoped they had outgrown this phase last week when I transported a carload of kids to the local skating rink. As 10 children piled out of the wagon, I turned up my coat collar and slid across the seat to go in. My son gasped, "You're not going inside, are you?"

"Gee, I don't know," I said evenly, "I toyed with the idea of sitting out here in the car and inhaling carbon monoxide until I lost consciousness. However, the prospect of watching 400 kids skate round in a circle to deafening rock 'n roll music made me lose my head!"

He kicked the tire and began to mutter, "You've ruined everything. If I skate with a girl, you'll smile dumb at me."

"I promise I won't smile dumb."

"If I fall down, you'll raise your eyebrows like when I goof up."

"I will not raise my eyebrows."

"If I skate by you, you'll say hello."

"I will not say hello. I will simply sit on a chair in a state of self-hypnosis and meet you here in the car at the end of two hours." It was agreed.

Nearly an hour went by before he skated up to my chair. "Hi, Mom," he yelled. "Did you see me make that turn?"

I looked at him blankly, "Hi, kid, did you lose your mother?"

"Quit kidding around, Mom. How about a quarter for a snack?"

"I saw your mother a minute ago. She was wearing a sack cloth over her head."

"Aw Mom," he grumbled and skated away.

"Isn't that your son?" asked the woman next to me.

"Sure," I said, grinning, "but a mother has to have a few good innings just to stay in the ball game."

SOURCE: Reproduced with permission by NEWSDAY, Inc.

Many parents of today realize that they should improve their methods. Recently, when I was in a New York City skyscraper, I passed the office of a fifty-year old corporate executive who knew me. He asked me to sit down to have a chat about his fifteen-year-old son who is in high school. The father said that the boy is a good student, has always obeyed him in the past, and had never rebelled against parental instructions. Surprisingly, during the previous evening the boy had suddenly rebelled. After dinner, the boy started to study and the father turned to doing several routine family chores. One chore was to write a note to one of the boy's teachers, explaining to the teacher why his son had to be absent from school on a certain half-day. The reason was that the parents had made a dental appointment for the boy on the date of absenteeism. The father, however, did not know the teacher's name, and so the following conversation took place:

Dad     "Son, I want to write that note to your teacher to explain your absence when you had to go to the dentist. What's your teacher's name, so that I can address it to her by name?"

Son     "I won't tell you.'"

Dad     "Son, apparently you didn't hear me, or I didn't hear you correctly." The father explained the question again bust in a rising, threatening tone.

Son     "Dad, I heard what you said, but I am not going to tell you her name!"

Dad     "All right, son, I'm going to let you have it." The father removed his belt and walloped the boy. (Incidentally, the father has a physique of the professional football type.)

Dad     (Exhausted) "Now, son, what is the name of that teacher?"

Son     "Dad, you can beat me all you wish. But I am not going to tell you!"

Of course, the father who told me the incident asked: "What should I have done? How could I have handled the situation in a smarter, better way?" My answer to him was "You handled it in the same way in which you and I were reared. We accepted that kind of discipline, but a better approach might have attained the right ends more easily and far more effectively—by being ingenious without shifting from the one extreme of the old, firm discipline to the opposite extreme of unguided permissiveness.

You would have been more effective if, at the time of your second request for the teacher's name and the son's refusal, you had stopped to think and asked yourself: 'Why is he defying me? What does his unusual behavior really mean?' You probably would have concluded very quickly that he was trying to become a man by defying parental authority. You should have gone to the boy, given him a handshake, and said: 'Son, I see you're trying to prove to me and to yourself that you are becoming a man, and your defiance was your way to show it. Do you think that the method you used was really a grown-up way of proving it? Don't answer me now; I'll get the teacher's name by telephone tomorrow. Later, after you've thought about it, you may decide that you can prove your growth toward manhood in more intelligent ways. You tell me when you're ready?' "

## We retirees have to learn how young people think about older people

To many young people, we older men are walking backward into the future. The accent on youth has elevated the younger into the limelight. Young people do not believe that the older a person becomes the greater his wisdom! They know that most people carry many of their early prejudices and stupidities along with them into their old age. Certainly, the younger generation will not be impressed when we claim that we know something because we learned it years ago.

In Biblical times, Job could say that "Wisdom is with the aged, and understanding in length of days," but the younger generation of today would not accept it, because the wisdom of old men in Job's time did not require a basic foundation of the kind of scientific information that the young people are learning today.

In the primitive agrarian cultures, the elders had the funds of knowledge which in our culture are stored in libraries and textbooks and quickly taught in the classrooms to the young. This is a major reason for the shift away from the high social status of the elderly that was found in some old cultures. If you and I as retirees can hope to receive the respect of the young, we shall have to earn it by proving our values to our society in ways appropriate to the developments of this age.

No use pleading for return to more respect for the aging. Nor asking that everybody should ascribe more recognition to the aging. Some writers argue that since parents sacrifice for their children when the children are young, the children when adults should sacrifice for the parents when they are old. Government has changed the old feeling of financial responsibility for the care of the aged by assessing the young for the cost of taking care of them.

When our Social Security system was changed to increase payroll deductions in order to increase benefits to the recipients, a research analyst for a tax foundation pointed out that since people who were retired or about to retire could receive more in benefits than they contributed in payments, the tax really amounts to a transfer of funds from the younger generation to the older generation.

Is it any wonder that some young people think of "senior citizens" as burdensome? Those who feel this way about the aging are not aware of any challenges to active living that the retirees are offering the young.

Formerly, the role of the older people was to give direction and leadership to the younger members of the family. Now influences outside the family give the members of the family increasingly greater amounts of direction. These influences are the schools, the mass media of communication, and the other cultural changes. Bear in mind, too, that the automobile transports people away from the home environment to distant areas where new customs and standards of conduct are learned.

## The intergenerational difficulties in communicating

DeWitt C. Reddick, Director of the School of Communications, University of Texas, gave a talk at an annual conference on aging, in which he discussed some of the barriers to communication in a changing world:

A concept that is fixed and central to most young folk today may throw roadblocks before clear communication between generations. It may best be described as *one-worldness*. The youth of today represent the first generation that has grown up exposed to the ceaseless outpourings of the mass media. Through the glaring eye of television they have seen starving babies in India, . . . mobs on college campuses; they have been entertained by violence and bloodshed and mystery and comedy set against backgrounds of cities and small towns at home and abroad. To them the world is one place, one big mixed up confused place in which people have not yet learned to live together and to solve their problems. Other generations tend to think in terms of countries, of refuge from world problems, of the patient eternal upward struggle of mankind that must continue for centuries. But to today's children there seems no escape from the turmoil of problems that must be solved in their lifetime for the world, not for just a segment. This world one-ness colors all their planning, their dreams, their conversations, and they find conversations of older folk hard to understand. And older folk are disconcerted to discover that youth no longer looks to them for advice or leadership. The estrangement between generations widens. . . .

An additional barrier is that which results from distortions which may result from a misunderstanding of the mass media or a misuse of the media.

Perhaps I can clarify this point in the following manner:

The most intensive listening-viewing age for television, surveys indicate, is the five-six year old bracket. Children of these ages tend to spend about four hours daily viewing television. What do they see? The surveys indicate that parents give little direction in program selection for the children. Almost the reverse is true—often the parents choose an adult program; thus the children settle down to witness a western shoot-out or the agonizing of divorced couples or a foreign agent being neatly killed by the man from UNCLE. Imagine, then, these five and six year olds going the following year into their first school class—what kind of concepts of the world must live within their minds? We in education have come to recognize that we must take into account the world which the individual student brings from his environment into the classroom.

These children of the new world have been exposed already to the world of the adults, to the world of all peoples, of all countries. Their education must be adjusted accordingly. And the difference continues into high school and into college. Older folk, speaking from the memories of their own school and college experiences, may find difficulty in communicating.[1]

We have to realize that by the time the average American youth graduates from high school today he has seen 500 movies and viewed 15,000 hours of television, according to a community relations director of the Motion Picture Association of America. When, however, we study these young people, it is found that most of them want to improve mentally and morally. Many have developed an idealism of their own. Most will eventually become good husbands, wives, and citizens.

The more we demonstrate to them that life's experiences have taught us the benefits of holding to certain basic values, the more pleased they will become regarding the prospects for their own future. They admire the older man or woman who constantly adds inner strength and meaningful living to his life as he grows older.

## YOUNG PEOPLE VISUALIZE THEMSELVES IN THEIR EVENTUAL OLD AGE WHEN THEY SEE US

The one pleasant fact that we should recognize when we think of the various ways in which younger people perceive us is that to them we portray what they, too, may expect to become.

When you accept retirement supinely, your acceptance registers mightily with your children and other young people. Young people want to see you happy and comfortable but even more, they want to see you conduct yourself in a manner which increases their respect for you and the way you deal with your adjustments in retirement. They, too, expect to retire some day. They do not want to see you give up too easily.

This means that we should determine to redirect our self-centeredness, stop the boring talk about our ailments, forget about what we did in the past, and think and talk about the future and the roles we can play as long as we can possibly keep active.

Research studies indicate that retirees who are active and productive tend to have greater self-esteem, a more positive concept of the future, and a better identification with children or child-surrogates. They are likely to have better morale than those who are nonactive and nonproductive.[2]

We seniors can admit without feelings of inferiority on our part as mature men that most high school students know more and better physics, chemistry, and mathematics than we old-timers do, even though we may have kept ourselves up to date or even contributed to advances in our own special field. We do not expect young people or adults to look up to us for what we learned in the sciences outside our field, but there is one important area in which many of us can offer the young people ideas they are still trying to learn in their interpersonal relations—the art of getting along with people. Young people do not learn that from books. They have to learn the lessons involved in the same ways we had to learn them—by experience, by observation, by exchanging viewpoints, and by getting suggestions from men of seasoned insight.

## Choose the kind of young people with whom you would like to communicate

Most young people have good potentials, even though many are trying hard to find themselves, and some are failing miserably. A small percentage will become drug addicts, criminals, or other deviants, but that has been true throughout human history. And it will continue indefinitely. That simply means that if you want to make a contribution to several members of the younger generation, you will have to decide which kind of young people you wish to reach. Well, why not decide to understand a few of the ambitious young people who are working in companies of the industry in which you had your career? You probably know more about that category of young men than any other one classification.

To supplement what you learned from experience, it would be advisable to do some library reading and confer with personnel men. If you do, you will run across published reports on "discontented young men" who have entered business. The surveys over the years reveal the same old problems: promotions are too slow, the pay is too low, the boss isn't very smart, the management ought to adopt different methods, and so on.

The problems are much the same as they were when we were young fellows in business, but some very helpful researches have been published in the field of counseling individuals who have problems in adjustment.

Another reason for doing library work to prepare yourself for constructive relations with young men is that well-educated young men will not be impressed by your statements about what your own years of experience taught you, unless you also can occasionally cite data from at least a few systematic studies reported in journals and books written by researchers. The trained young men of today are accustomed to the authority of research—they will accept research findings as more important than your unsubstantiated opinions.

You might begin your reading with the systematic studies of the growth problems of college students by reading Graham B. Blaine, Jr., and Charles C. McArthur, *Emotional Problems of the Student* (New York: Appleton-Century-Crofts, 1961), a collection of articles, understandable by the layman, describing the psychiatric problems of Harvard University students and the manner in which they are dealt with by a University Health Service. One of their main findings about the confused adolescent is that he is trying to develop for himself an appropriate believable "map" of his world so that, as he develops, he will have a place where he belongs and can function successfully. This kind of problem of bright young men generates a brooding interest in abstractions which the young individual only partially understands but likes to imagine that he does understand: communism, evolution, right, wrong, God, duty, and a host of others. "By sorting them out, he sorts himself out."[3]

Similarly, the main questions of students counseled at the UCLA's Student Counseling Center are: "What shall I do and be as a person now?" and "What shall I be later in life?" The Center provides a place where students can discuss their questions and make their decisions without worrying about approval or displeasure of parents or faculty members. "Staff members say students show a tremendous need for contact with an adult other than a parent or a faculty member."[4]

## What you can do to help young men define their place in business

You, as a retiree, can make significant contributions to the development of several young men in business if you decide to prepare yourself to do so. Many young employees, though out of college and working, are only a few short steps beyond the confused college adolescents mentioned above. As ambitious young men they are trying to answer for themselves their questions: "What shall I do and be as a person now?" and "What shall I be later in life?" They need someone with whom they can talk without worrying about the approval or displeasure of a parent or a busy supervisor.

Obviously, you cannot be helpful by simply going to a young employee and implying: "Young man, talk over your problems with me and I'll give you the answers." Most of your preliminary preparation for effectiveness is in making the mental shiftings mentioned above. After that you might test your skills by chatting with several young employees whom you know and like. Measure your ability to counsel young men by the extent that you have acquired the knack of asking questions that enable the confused employee to answer his own questions.

If you are successful in establishing rapport to the extent that he wants to ask you questions about his work situation, you may be able to counsel him *indirectly* without his thinking of you as a counselor. Later, in the course of additional interviews, he may begin to think of you as a friend to whom he turns for counsel occasionally. Bear in mind that your objective is not that of becoming a counselor but a trusted friend with whom certain young men discuss their problems.

The kinds of questions young men ask will vary, but your interviews are likely to be productive if you keep in mind one basic principle: *each man has two pictures of himself in his own mind: the kind of man he thinks he is and the kind he would like to be.* The more you can stimulate him to talk about himself and his hopes for the future, the more he will enjoy your conversation and the more you will learn about how he thinks of himself and what his thoughts are concerning his future in the company where he works.

## Problems you are likely to find

Do you want to guess what you are likely to discover as the most common problem of young men in regard to their advancement? My answer on the basis of several decades of interviewing young men of modern corporations is: *They are waiting for somebody to tell them what they should do in order to advance in their work.* There are many other classifications that you will find, but this category will be the one you are likely to meet most often. The thinking of these men is that of the "waiters"; they are waiting until management needs the employee's services in a better job.

### "THE WAITERS"

*Characteristics* of a man in this category are that he *hopes* his potentials will be discovered. He has developed an attitude of letting the company decide his future: "I'll let the company decide the ways I am needed, my pay, and my advancement. In the meantime, I'll do a good job." The desire to do a good job is a requirement for advancement, but it must be supplemented with intense intellectual curiosity about the company's business objectives, competitive advantages, innovation in suggesting new methods, or some venturing into unknown technical pathways. When the young man does this kind of thinking, he "finds himself" as a functioning, productive personality in the world of work. His need for establishing his identity is being answered. He becomes a full-fledged adult and he knows it. Unless he does this largely by his own initiative and ingenuity, he becomes just another "waiter." The "waiters" do little or no pioneering in ideas or pacesetting. They merely keep up with what happens near them, and so they get few merit increases in pay.

*Management men* recognize the presence of these men. Executives suspect that many could be stimulated by thrusting new challenges before them. But some executives do not take the time or give thought to the arousal of the potentials that have gone into quiescence. The reason for their neglect of these men is twofold: (1) every organization needs some quiet, middle-of-the-road doers who cause no trouble, and (2) it is much easier to offer challenges to men who have proven their enthusiasm in tackling the company's needs. Why give time and thought to arousing dormant spirits when several go-go fellows are all set to tackle big problems before they are asked to solve them? The go-aheads do not usually wait until management picks them up and thrusts opportunity upon them— they are always looking for a loose ball before it is handed to them. To the executive, it is vastly more hopeful for the future when he must hold in check the men who have too much initiative than to try to arouse initiative where it has not appeared.

Some managements have recognized that employees wish management would develop a program or system for analyzing every employee, reviewing his strong and weak characteristics once or twice a year, and then telling each man just what he should do and how to advance himself. Indeed, this is one of the most frequent requests I have heard from many employees of the companies with whom I have worked.

This request usually comes from the academically oriented young men who left college recently and are now expecting to advance at regular intervals as they did in school. It is natural for them to expect to be given this kind of feedback—they are products of a "lockstep" educational system of eight years in the elementary schools, four years in high school, and four years in college, with semiannual examinations and reports on their standing. Industry, by contrast, is a big confusing arena where all kinds of diffused, nonspecific influences are controlling events that the individual cannot always identify or even foresee. The lockstep-minded want someone to provide a model, preferably one that can be computerized to provide easy answers for them.

At first thought, one may wonder why more managements have [5] not adopted a system of rating all employees. Some are using such systems, but the systems do not provide the kind of thinking that has made American business successful in the past. That American business has moved forward through the years is not because some all-knowing authority studied each man, told him what to do, and then coordinated his personal desires with those of perhaps thousands of others of the same company. Instead of a lockstep system, business has allowed each man in the organization to apply his ingenuity and initiative to make his contributions in the most appropriate manner.

In addition to the lockstep influence of academic training, the management-trained graduate has been taught to think in terms of the big overall corporate and national economy perspectives. In his courses, he analyzed and "solved" problems on a high theoretical level. Now that he is working in an actual corporation, he is dealing only with simple gritty problems that could be done by a person with an eighth-grade education. He feels let down. He becomes more conscious of shortcomings in the management above and the employees around him than in seeing the whole picture of which he is a part or in learning from the employees with whom he is working.

*Your role as a friendly retiree* is to be of help to a man of this category, if you and the man can communicate with each other.

First of all, do not give him the usual advice or pep talk that he lacks initiative nor that his education must be unlearned. Also, recognize that the man does not want sympathy—he needs a colleague who can offer useful suggestions and a friend who likes him and believes in him in spite of the evidence that others have thus far ignored his potentials. This means that the more you can get him to talk about himself and express his feelings, the clearer your picture becomes of how he sees himself.

*Your questions* may be pointed toward the ways the individual defines himself: as aggressive and as sure-to-succeed or as one who is wasting time in feeling sorry for himself? How much time is he giving to thinking about his superior's problems and the company's needs? To what extent is he making suggestions that apply to his job rather than to top-management's functions? Is he reaching out for more responsibilities? When he and his ideas misfire, does he take aim at another target and try again and again or does he give up after a few failures to get management excited about his suggestions? When he gets slapped down by his boss does he sulk or still treat the boss in a manner which shows that he is enthusiastically working with him and for him?

You and he can discuss some of the work problems of the company and those of the employee's superior, problems in the area of the younger man's range of experience and job specifications. Let him develop an action plan that he wants to use in dealing with his own situation.

*An action program* for an employee must be developed by himself. An appropriate action program should help him establish the kind of identity he is seeking to become. You become helpful when you ask an incisive question or offer a suggestion that will stimulate him to think through his situation and develop his own feasible action program. In this way, he "sorts himself out."

The action program can be simple or comprehensive and complex. With the higher-grade men such as the technically trained and the business specialists, the action program usually consists of writing up a proposal for a procedure that might help the superior get certain work done in his department with less effort, at lower cost, or with greater goodwill from the employees.

If the action program is complex and involves other persons, as it often does, you and the employee may want to meet several times to polish the proposal and, after it is presented, discuss the reactions of management to it.

### THE RANDOM-EFFORT, TRIAL-AND-ERROR EXPERIMENTERS

Every large company has one or more of these young men, for a time. They usually have a history of some aptitude in one of the fine arts, a few years in selling insurance, some feeble efforts in public relations or newspaper reporting, graduate work in one or two of the sciences, a foreign-service job perhaps, plus some other uncoordinated efforts. When you get them to describe their educational and occupational records, you are reminded of the youth who worked in a bird store during the day, studied architecture in evening school, and had an ambition to become a sea captain! If this kind of individual graduates from high school or college, you will find him taking evening courses that are not focused toward any recognizable vocational objective. When he obtains a job that might lead to a worthwhile objective, he reads a wide variety of journals, but none is related to an objective he claims to have in mind.

Surprisingly, many of these vocational wanderers have high intelligence. They can learn almost any subject they choose and study the subject diligently for a brief period. Some are individualistic in their thinking and their attire. Some are also quite tactless, consciously and purposely so. They like to shock people by their disdain for the social conventions. Some take pride in being creative, but very few produce any worthwhile works of art or original plans of any useful value.

These men are very responsive to invitations to lunch for almost any stated purpose. If you can induce one of them to talk freely about his childhood and how adults reacted to him, you are likely to find that as a child he felt unable to meet the expectations of his father or an older brother, or someone else who helped to rear him. When he failed to please as a child, he turned to other tasks or activities. He used the trial-and-error technique in attempts to gain adult goodwill. We all did that to some extent as children, but most of us, in the process, discovered that we could also gain the desired goodwill or our self-respect by pursuing consistently a certain few objectives. Some of those who fail to develop a consistent pattern of self-training continue in their adulthood to flounder in their randomized technique, and so they leave any promising field of effort before competence and self-worth are attained.

*Your role as a retiree is* not to lecture the individual on the importance of pursuing a consistent program until he attains success. Instead, you can probably be of more help by pointing out his opportunities for gaining self-worth where he is now working. Your emphasis on what he is doing well and on facets of the job he has not as yet explored, plus your friendly support, may not solve his problem for him, but you are at least suggesting a program that is likely to help him do what he would like to do, namely, to work consistently toward a kind of self-respect that he could not attain in the past.

## "NOBODY IN MANAGEMENT NOTICES ME."

One of the big problems of many young men during their first few years in the business world is the fact that no management man gives them as much attention as they want. This is to be expected when we realize that as children they were the center of a lot of admiration from parents. In school they got less attention, but their work was evaluated every day and they were often praised for efforts, good or poor. In high school and college their work was evaluated frequently. When, therefore, they come into a somewhat impersonal business world, the adjustment pains to being "another employee" may be severe. Those who do not make a satisfactory adjustment with the first employer are likely to seek employment elsewhere for what they describe as "a better opportunity." Actually, most do not know of any better opportunities with the second, third, and fourth employers than they did with the first one. What many should say when they leave the employer is "I have not as yet found a satisfactory 'father image' in this company."

This search on the part of a young man is, on the whole, desirable, but he should have some insight as to what his search signifies about himself. Instead of looking for a father image, he should become acquainted with the supervisors above or around him and look for a good coach. An important factor in a man's advancement is to work for an executive whom he likes as a coach, though not necessarily as a person. This has been revealed in research studies as well as stated in conversations with successful men.

General Electric Company, for example, made a statistical study of 3,000 G.E. managers' records. Depth interviews were conducted with a sample of 300 of them to find out what made them successful managers.

These managers were asked in effect: "How did you get where you are? What were the things that held you back? What do you consider were the strongest factors in your development to your present position?" and so forth. The answers when analyzed for significant factors showed that 90 percent of these managers consistently stated, "I got my best development when I was working for so-and-so and so-and-so." [6]

The men who advanced in the company had learned how to work with and to learn from certain superiors. No doubt some of these superiors had difficult personalities and were hard to please, but the younger men had matured to the level where they ignored the negative aspects of the situation and concentrated on the positive. As a man who has had years of experience in industry, you know that almost every young man who has ever advanced to a job of real importance has been reprimanded, really bawled out a number of times, but he had the inner maturity that enabled him to see the benefits from his superior's constructive attention. Any man who advances in the business world has been seasoned—he has learned to adjust to difficult personalities and to work happily with supervisors regardless of their peculiarities and cussedness.

*Your role as a retiree* friend is to help the young man realize that an executive cannot take extra interest in any *one* young man. That would alienate the other employees. No sensible executive will treat one employee as a "crown prince." Instead of the young employee assuming that a management man will treat him as an "only child," he should realize that it is up to him to learn from everyone in the organization, fellow workers as well as supervisors. In time, he will discover that he learns decidedly more from one individual than from the others. This one may provide the kind of work relationship mentioned in the General Electric study.

*Check the technical-reading habits of young men.* The young man who is aggressive in his desire to learn a business can find many helpful people and sources of information. Journals and books abound. Men of other companies who perform operations related to those of the young employee can be met at industry-association meetings. Stimulating relationships with peers are essential to growth. Much can be learned without violating confidences or dealing with matters of a competitive nature. Indeed, two questions can be asked the ambitious young man: "From whom are you getting the kind of coaching that will make you a more competent man this year than you were a year ago?" and "What business publications, applicable to your field, do you read?"

## "HOW CAN I DEVELOP A FAVORABLE IMAGE WITH MANAGEMENT?"

When you meet this kind of question from a young employee, your first answer is likely to be: "Do a good job by doing what management wants done and more." Sometimes a young man will answer: "I have been doing good work, I believe, but management men do not turn to me for help when new and bigger problems are to be handled—they give the assignment to somebody else." The answers that would explain such a situation vary so widely that no one explanation can apply to every person. In some instances the real reasons are so integral a part of the young man's mental makeup or personality that the problem is too big for you to tackle it. Some men who graduate from college and appear to be smart just simply do not have savvy. They somehow never do catch on to the world of their work, regardless of the amount of coaching they are given. Bear in mind that it is much easier to inspire capable men than to give "savvy" to men who lack it. Perhaps they should seek a career elsewhere?

Sometimes you can be of some assistance by discussing a potentially capable man's skills in communicating with others. Many inabilities to communicate effectively are caused by simple factors in speaking: voice is too low for many people to hear it clearly, words are muddled, speaking is in monotones without inflections or emphases, or English usage is poor. The individual may be decidedly introverted and has not learned adequate social skills. His manner may be too reserved to engender warmth or to present evidence of leadership abilities. Some men, too, talk too much. They talk a good line but do not follow through on assignments, or when they do, they fail to keep management men informed on the degree of progress and reasons for delays.

*Your role as a retiree* is to ask questions about his arts of communication. He may believe that these arts are so simple that they can be ignored. Actually, these arts are essential to the development of a favorable rate of advancement. Besides, it is better to talk about weaknesses in communication than to discuss personality character- istics. It is unpleasant for a person to hear that he should change his personality, but he is not usually embarrassed when his ineffective habits in communicating are discussed.

### "MY POTENTIALS ARE MUCH HIGHER THAN MY WORK REQUIRES."

This claim is often correct—some men do remain too long in jobs much lower than their potentials call for. Let us consider those reasons which are caused by management rather than the individual.

Management may rightly place a capable man in a low-ability job for a time because that experience provides a background of knowledge that is necessary to the performance of a related higher- level job. Problems arise when the employee is kept there much longer than necessary. Perhaps the more difficult job is not available on the first day the young man decides he has learned all he can on his current assignment.

Many an executive finds it easy to keep a good man indefinitely on the same job when no competent replacement is available. Too often, however, a good man is kept on the job so long that his potentials deteriorate.

*Your role as a retiree* is to ask the employee whether he has discussed the situation with his superior to find out the employee's limitations or shortcomings. You can often help a young man realize that a supervisor will not criticize a thin-skinned, defensive em- ployee. It is partly up to the employee to prove that "he can take it" in the right spirit before he should expect a supervisor to "lay it on the line." After this factor has been faced by the employee, you can ask him questions about his work attitudes and conduct on the job.

You might ask the employee whether he has demonstrated that he has an interest in his current job or in a higher level of responsibility in some other field. Does he ask incisive questions about this or any other kind of work? What technical journals does he read to build up a background of specific value? Does he make suggestions about his willingness to do tasks that would indicate his unused potentials? If men of higher ability are around him in the company, does he talk with them about some aspect of their work? Do his after-work activities cause management to realize that he has a lively interest in applying his potentials to another job level? Does he attend technical or professional meetings that signify a definite area of interest?

Is he conducting himself when on the company premises in the manner of an up-and-coming young man or like an hourly worker —does he leave the plant or office the minute that his workday has ended? Does he avoid overtime unless it involves extra pay? Is his level of aspiration insofar as management knows on the level of the typical factory worker? Perhaps so far as management knows the younger man's growth curve has leveled out.

### The retiree's compensations

You, as a retiree, may ask: "Assuming that I try to do these things for some of the younger men of the industry or the community, what do I get out of it?"

The answer is that you will get all the pleasures of some fine friendships plus certain benefits that only you as a retiree can appreciate: you will feel that you are still giving of yourself in common with others, that you are a worthy, though an unofficial, member of the business community, that you are exchanging ideas with people whom you admire, and that there is added purpose in your life, a kind of purpose which you are uniquely qualified to give. You will be active in the mainstream of modern work life as you know it. The psychic income you gain as a retiree will be far more satisfying than money income would be.

If you have had years of experience in working with and supervising others, you have developed valuable abilities to perceive, to interpret, and to evaluate the mental experiences that your young colleagues in business are undergoing. Their psychological needs are never-ending. You will never run out of opportunities. The way is open for you to develop new and heartwarming relationships for yourself as well as for others.

## REFERENCES

1. DeWitt C. Reddick, *Proceedings of Governor's Committee on Aging*, Texas Agricultural Extension Service, Austin, 1967.
2. See Walter G. Klopfer, "The Inter-personal Theory of Adjustment," chap. 3, in Robert Kastenbaum (ed.), *Contributions to the Psychobiology of Aging*, New York: Springer Publishing Company, Inc., 1965, p. 41. Page 43 lists the original sources of related findings.
3. See Graham B. Blaine, Jr., and Charles C. McArthur, *op. cit.*, p. 94.
4. "What Students Want," *Modern Maturity*, April–May, 1968, p. 27.
5. See Harry W. Hepner, *Psychology Applied to Life and Work*, Englewood Cliffs, N.J.: Prentice-Hall, Inc., 4th ed., 1966, chap. 17.
6. Reported by Moorhead Wright, Consultant in Decentralized Manager Education, General Electric Company, "Stop Looking for Loose Geniuses and Start Growing Your Own," *First Advertising Personnel Workshop*, Association of National Advertisers, Jan. 26, 1956.

## CHAPTER SEVEN

# Project: "Where to Live?"

(The setting: Retirement party for teacher of
philosophy.)

FIRST QUESTION     *"Now that you are retiring,*
                        *where do you want to live?"*

FIRST ANSWER     *"The same place where I've*
                        *tried to live in the past."*

SECOND QUESTION     *"And that is?"*

SECOND ANSWER     *"Wherever I can come close*
                        *to living life at its very best."*

OF ALL THE retirement projects that can be mentioned for
retirees, the one to which you probably have given most thought is
"Where to live?" Many foresighted men begin to investigate possible
areas several years before the date of mandatory retirement. Vacations are planned to visit certain areas. Books and magazine articles
are likely to be chosen because they offer needed information.

The reasons often cited for wanting to move to a new area can be
classified into two major groups: logical and psychological.

## Logical reasons

*The old house is no longer suitable.* Most retiring couples have a
house that was purchased when children were growing up. Now
that the children have married and moved away the old house is

125

unnecessarily large. It probably has a garden and lawn that require attention. In northern areas, snow must be removed during the winter. Hiring workers for cleaning and gardening is likely to be difficult. Besides, the neighborhood real-estate values may be deteriorating, and the sooner the place is sold, the greater the likelihood of getting the expected price.

The old house becomes a problem when you wish to travel. Who will give it protective care while you are gone? If you move into a retirement center, you can lock the door and forget about the house by simple arrangements with neighbors.

*Old friends have moved away or died.* The longer a person lives, the more he realizes that to have satisfying friendships in the later years new friends must be found and new friendships must be cultivated. This is more difficult in a community that has a heterogeneous age population than in an area where the percentages of older people are much higher, as in the retirement centers.

*Health.* When an individual has a health problem that might be cured or eased by living in a different area, he naturally wants to move, especially when the problem causes severe pain or inconvenience. In a few cases, this reason is "another good rationalization for moving"; not a reason recommended by the family physician, but it offers acceptable rationalizations.

*Climate.* People who live in cold or smoggy areas have a natural tendency to think that if another area has more sunshine or less smog, the area is better for retirement.

Harold R. Hall's study of executives who retired indicated that one-fourth move to distant points, and about half of the group select "good-climate" spots for purposes of health, pleasure, or for both reasons.[1]

Climate as a reason should be supplemented by answers to "How do we want to enjoy life in retirement and which places make our desired kinds of enjoyment easy to attain?" If you, as some prospective retirees do, choose a climate just to enjoy loafing, try loafing in one specific area for two or three weeks to test whether you want to continue to loaf during all the years of your retirement—you might be doing it a quarter of a century, you know!

## Psychological reasons

When you investigate possible geographical areas for retirement living, you should ask yourself: "What symbolic meanings am I trying to find in a new area? Subconsciously, am I looking for a place where I can get back the feelings of status, importance, and social relationships of the job I left, or am I looking for a more pleasant climate where I can associate with others of my age who are good company and are enjoying life in new ways that I, too, may enjoy?"

Any environment where a retiree has lived and worked for years is likely to have some features disliked by the retiree who is hoping to find a new Garden of Eden. He may feel that the climate is too severe, the people too uninteresting, the local stores too limited in suitable merchandise, the prices too high, and so on ad infinitum. These generalized statements are likely to be rationalizations for the individual retiree's feelings about his own limitations when he was working: his inability to get as much social recognition as he had desired, failure to make as much money as he wanted, imagined rejection by professional or business associates, or some other symbolical shortcoming which he now attributes to the community where he lived, not to himself. A new environment may appear to provide the answer to his needs. And in some cases it very definitely does.

If you feel resentful toward younger people because you imagine that they have displaced you in your job or in the social position you had occupied, you may be happier in Florida or some other area where there are concentrations of retirees. Climate may be less important for you than the opportunity to regain a satisfying social life.

When you read the advertising and talk with the salesmen of the successful real-estate developers of retirement centers, you will find that their emphases are on the pleasant social life: country-club living, beautiful golf courses, big swimming pools, dancing, card playing, etc. And when you visit the center, you will find that most of the retirees who live there may not be using the country-club facilities, but they are very friendly, sociable, and glad to meet and talk with another retiree. They, too, are pleased to meet a person who needs friendliness—that, not the country-club facilities, is very probably why they took up residence there.

The retiree who felt rejected in his old work environment is likely to be especially anxious to move to a new area. He imagines that there he will not have to feel as "uncomfortable" as he did with old associates who did not appreciate him. When you investigate places to live in retirement, bear in mind that your deepest impulsions may be to find a place that fits your "dreamiest" moments about the ideal home: warmth, physical comfort, security, and full acceptance as a member of the group by associates. You may be trying to find answers to your dream expectations, not just answers to your logical needs. If, in a new environment, you do not perceive the place as answering your dream needs, you are likely to return to your old environment.

### Does your present area offer what you are really seeking?

One of the most illuminating experiences of a retiree who wants to investigate ideal places to live is to begin investigating his own community and area *first*.

You might begin by counting the number of friends in your present area. How many are so important that you doubt whether you can ever find equally delightful substitutes?

How well do you really know the opportunities for enjoyment of your present area? Even though you may have lived for many years where you have been working, you probably never really took a good look at the area. Example: how many of the colleges, schools, factories, community organizations, churches, orphanages, governmental offices, and places of historical significance have you visited? As a start, you might begin your little survey by visiting all the nursing homes and retirement centers of your area.

## Facilities and places to consider

Homes designed for retirees are increasing in number and varieties, ranging from old hotels and apartment buildings to well-designed retirement centers that have the houses on one level, located near entertainment and shopping centers. Of course a retiree who contemplates moving into any retirement building or center should investigate carefully and extensively before he invests.

*Retirement housing* has been classified into categories such as the following:

1. Real-estate developments
2. Supervised and planned communities
   a. Dispersed-dwelling communities
   b. Trailer villages
   c. Retirement hotels
3. Full-care homes

*Real-estate developments* are operated on a profit basis. They do not provide for serving food or medical and nursing care to residents but they are likely to provide facilities for socialization.

*Dispersed-dwelling communities* are usually operated on a profit basis. Some provide medical and nursing care, others do not. Some provide planned activity programs. The sponsorship, facilities, and costs of living in these communities vary widely, and each must be considered on its own merits.

*Trailer parks* or villages are usually operated for profit. Trailers are owned by the occupants. Though mobile, many occupants remain in a village for years.

*Retirement hotels* provide retired persons with living accommodations similar to those available in a hotel, but on a contract basis.

*Full-care homes* are not usually described as operated for profit. Actually, some are. Sponsorship, accommodations, financial arrangements, eligibility requirements, and policies vary widely. Church and fraternal organizations are the most likely sponsors. Anyone who is considering such a home should be very careful to investi-

gate the institution's definition of "lifetime care" even though a
lifetime right of residence may be granted. The "right," however,
may be subject to an adverse decision by a governing board, particularly when the member becomes difficult to manage or care for.

Managements may require substantial down payments, plus
monthly rental charges with additional charges for utilities or use of
recreation facilities. Consideration should be given to the usual
services: number of meals per day and quality of the food, as well
as peripheral facilities for shopping, recreation, and transportation.

Obviously, a prospective retiree who wishes to consider membership in any retirement house or full-care home should investigate a
wide variety of factors. Some want fees so large as to confiscate all
the resident's wealth. Be sure to verify any assumption on your part
that homes which are sponsored by a religious organization will give
you better value for your dollars than a private-enterprise builder or
sponsor.

Life-care homes for the aged run by churches or fraternal organizations may have account books which show no profits, but some
are constantly buying and building larger facilities from their
profits.[2] Some are peopled with snobs. Generally, a good rule is to
avoid "founder's fees" unless you have had an attorney read the
contract and you are sure of what you are getting. You should
consider how many rooms you will occupy. If one room, must it be
shared with another resident? How can you get away from a room-
mate whose company wears you down? How can you get away
from other residents whose company you do not enjoy?

*In a retirement center,* every individual gives up some of his in-
dividuality. He is another member of a defined group. As long as a
person remains a member of the general population, he is less easily
categorized. In a retirement home or center, your identity relates
almost entirely to the defined group of which you are a member.

On the other hand, we should also realize that a strong factor that
pulls people into a retirement community is the desire to break out
of their loneliness. "Rev. Bidle, when administrator of First Community Village, Columbus, Ohio, stated that loneliness forces more

people to come to the Village than any other single factor. Healing for loneliness is one of the Village's most important stocks in trade." [3] When a retiree moves to a community where other retirees live, he and they have things in common in much the same manner as each man had in his former social or work life.

Some retirees look upon a retirement center or home, with its group provisions of well-balanced meals and medical care, as one aspect of regaining desired social life as well as emotional security. Most retirees, however, want to maintain their independence as long as possible. A home for the aging is avoided until its facilities become necessary or, at least, highly desirable for the care and protection of the individual.

### CONGREGATE LIVING

Congregate residences provide living accommodations which may be cottages with flower gardens and patios or apartments in a multi-story building. They serve three meals a day, provide maid service, and furnish certain linens. Most require payment of a substantial entrance or founder's fee that may be a few hundred or many thousands of dollars. This fee covers life occupancy of the specified accommodation. In addition, a monthly fee for meals and other services is charged. The monthly fee varies, depending upon the cost of living, the services given, and the health or hospital services.

An important question is *"How soon* do you want to adopt that way of life for all your remaining years?"

Before you sign any contract, you should have your attorney read and explain the contract to you. You should also make a careful investigation as to whether you would fit into the group socially. You can get some idea of the likelihood of finding congenial associates by meeting and talking with the residents. When I visited a well-known retirement community, I asked a resident "What kinds of people live here—how would you describe them?" He said: "I can answer most easily by citing a recent incident on the golf course. I was sitting on a bench waiting for some players to move ahead when a stranger came up and sat beside me. He said: 'This is a beautiful day.' I agreed. And then he said: 'Yes sir, this is so beautiful there's only one thing that could spoil it, and that would be if you turned out to be a Democrat!' "

Do you have to guess that the men in this retirement community consist mostly of individuals who worked their way up from ordinary circumstances to high-income positions of the business and professional world, that they are opposed to welfarism, and that they hold to belief in the values of personal character developed by hard work and seasoned integrity?

## How well do people who live in different facilities like them?

Most aging persons in retirement centers and in homes of the aged are very happy there. They seem to be happy in a fairly wide variety of housing, as indicated in a report by researchers of the School of Public Health, University of California at Los Angeles:

> A five-year study of some of the psychological effects of retirement housing was based on a census of retirement housing in California, totaling 299 licensed and 330 nonlicensed facilities. Six cities, representing different modes of housing for the aged and a wide range of socio-economic levels, were investigated.
> 1. A retirement hotel in Los Angeles which provided rooms and meals at a total cost of $103–$145 per month;
> 2. A low-cost suburban retirement village in central California, offering apartments at a rental of $75–$101 per month;
> 3. A new high-rise apartment building in the downtown section of a city in Southern California, where rentals ranged from $66 to $111 per month;
> 4. A middle-income retirement village in a desert area in Southern California, with houses in the $13,990–$27,290 price range;
> 5. An upper middle-income retirement village in Northern California, selling cooperative apartments for $21,000–$32,000.
> 6. A life-care facility in a college town near Los Angeles, licensed by the State and offering rooms, apartments, and cottages at an initial investment of $5,000–$25,000, plus maintenance of $175–$700 per month.
> Queried about contacts with young people other than children,

about 38 percent of the subjects said they had friends less than 40 years old. Only one third expressed yearnings for greater contact with youth. About 60 percent denied that having young people around would be "more fun."

Findings in the study seemed to sustain the contention that retirement communities provide old people with added opportunity to develop friends and acquaintances.

A common fear among older persons living alone is that there will be no one to help if they become sick or disabled. Retirement housing allays such fears, the study showed.

In the relatively prosperous, college town, life-care facility about 90 percent of the subjects attended lectures or concerts, 80 percent went to the theater or movies, over 50 percent engaged in volunteer work or church activities. In the middle-income village, over 70 percent went in for gardening, more than half occupied themselves with arts and crafts. The mean number of activities at these two sites was nearly twice as high as at the low-income hotel and the rental village.

The great majority of the subjects in this study appeared to be well satisfied with their situation and with life in general. When asked directly how they liked the site, more than two thirds replied "a lot"; more than 90 percent liked it at least "quite a bit." The highest degree of satisfaction was found in the life-care facility, which was liked at least "quite a bit" by all respondents. The lowest was in the low-income retirement hotel; but even here only 17 percent of the respondents liked it "only a little" or "not at all."

Morale was generally high at all sites, the report stated. It was highest in the upper-income groups, but only slightly lower in the others.[4]

Generally, the psychological climates in all of the retirement centers which I have visited were good. However, I have not visited enough of these places to be qualified to generalize. A feature that seemed evident in most of them was that the activities of the residents are mostly of the "retirement *from*" and little of the "retirement *to*" variety. The activities were almost entirely of the time-filling kind, few in the direction of using time in meaningful or creative ways.

A look at a weekly calendar of a typical retirement community usually provided such choices as social dancing, potluck suppers, shuffleboard tournaments on the fifteen outdoor courts, weekly movies, bridge, canasta and pinochle, folk-dance classes, art and craft classes, language classes for beginners, and beach parties.

When Professors Sidney L. and Alice D. Pressey, Ohio State University, retired, they kept count of the number of business and social contacts when they lived in their own home, in three apartment complexes (one primarily for older people), and in two retirement communities. After two years of retirement, he became a visiting professor half-time in a Southwestern university for a year. The number of social contacts there in a week was ninety. This was about twice as many as for the apartment residence. When they went to a fine church-founded retirement community of some 250 residents, where they had an apartment, ate at least one meal a day in the dining room, and participated in the community life, the social contacts were about sixty-six in a sample week. The nature of the social contacts varied from routine business and casual conversations to those with faculty colleagues and highly meaningful professional varieties. As they stated about the contacts in the church-founded community: "Most important was the nature of them and certain qualities of life in the retirement community—a feeling of belonging but more as inmate than participant, little feeling of worth or purpose. In such a place and group, such lacks may seem largely inevitable." [5]

The Presseys recommended that managements of retirement homes could do more to give the community life less of the "inmate" atmosphere and more of the "participation" kind.

Of course individual differences in reactions to retirement homes vary greatly. One woman member of a home said: "Older people here feel at home and comfortable. They enjoy the company of others who are the same age. Their friendships are warm and genuine. When they leave for days or weeks to visit relatives or friends who live at a distance, they are all happy to get back in spite of all the regimented ways of life: eating at set hours and being served the same foods in the same way."

In contrast, another woman who lived in a home that practically duplicated the one described so favorably said about her place: "The greatest disadvantage is the curse of propinquity. Old persons who see nothing but other old people, three times daily at meals, day after day, and year after year, do not have the best effect upon each other." She then described her weariness from listening to hypochondriacs who dramatize their ills, their gripes and special requests, and the maliciousness of the grapevine that passes around slanderous rumors.

When Harold R. Hall made his study of executives and their retirements, he found marked differences in the behavior of retirees in a very well-known Florida community in comparison with retirees of the North. In the Florida community, there was a sameness in the activities that was not evident among Northern retirees whom he had surveyed. In Florida, much time was given to outdoor activities of a sports or recreational character such as shuffleboard, lawn bowling, fishing, and golf. The pace was slower. Interestingly, Hall found not a single case of distinct unhappiness, but neither were there cases of what might be termed outstanding happiness among those interviewed in Florida. He also found some evidence which indicated that long-time residents had been happier during their first years of retirement than they were later.

One possible explanation for the finding of "sameness" among the Florida retirees was that constant sunshine has both advantages and disadvantages. For building bodily health it is excellent, but continual living in warm, constant temperatures tends to bring some enervation and a degree of lassitude. These findings certainly do not condemn the Florida area as a place of retirement for executives, but as Hall stated:

> Unquestionably, such communities have filled and will continue to fill satisfactorily the needs of many executives for their retirement purposes. Important for the prospective retiree, however, appears to be the need for careful scrutiny of any such location in advance of retirement. He and his wife should see whether their needs and desires will be served in sufficient measure to make a specific retirement community the answer to the important question, "Where shall we live?" [6]

Some observers of retirement communities have reported that the men adjust more easily to the social life than the women. The reason seems to be that the women are giving up established social lives whereas the men, for the first time in their lives, can give more time to the establishment of their social life in an area where many congenial associates are available. In contradiction, an intelligent woman who lives in a large retirement community believes that men do not adjust more easily: "Men are in the minority as to numbers, and I would say they cling together—rather in self-defense in retirement communities."

## Basic questions in deciding where you want to live

When you contemplate a move, to what extent would it affect your participation in the mainstream activities with which you still identify? Or, have you cut yourself off entirely from the industry in which you had your career? "I'll go where the action is for me" was your guideline when you were younger and ambitious. It should still be a guideline for you as a retiree; that is, if you think of retirement, not as a period of quiescence, but as a new stage in a different program of activities.

When you are thinking of moving to another area, ask yourself: "Would this move mean that I am now leaving one stage of participation in the mainstream of life as I know it and moving into another stage? Or am I moving into boredom?" The where-to-live question cannot be answered satisfactorily without consideration of the "how-to-live" questions, which the retiree should first decide. How does he intend to live so that life has worthwhile values, meaning, and depth for him? These decisions should take precedence over the "where" question. The *where is secondary*, not primary. A basic principle of worthy living in retirement as well as in the active work life is: *The motive of life is to function.* Where, in your retirement, can you function most usefully, happily, and appropriately in this stage of your life? The *way of life* you wish to enjoy is basic to your answer of *where?* This was well stated and exemplified at a conference of the Indiana Commission on The Aging

and the Aged. One of the speakers was the director of The First
Community Village, Columbus, Ohio. Some of his comments offer
important fundamentals to be considered by anyone who is seeking
a place to live in his retirement:

> Those who work in the field of geriatrics very long are bound to
> come across case after case of individuals who are residing in the
> most exquisite surroundings and yet who are slowly dying of bore-
> dom and meaninglessness.
>
> So, we cannot merely create a place to live but we must create
> *a way of life* . . .
>
> Let me describe in two concrete illustrations what I mean.
>
> About six months ago, I had interviewed a lady in her mid-70's and
> she decided to move into our retirement center, First Community
> Village. The day she was to come in, her sister called and said, "You
> had better not take her. She can't even walk from her apartment to
> her mail box."
>
> Her doctor's report, however, indicated that she was capable of
> walking *if* she wanted to do so, and that is a mighty big "if." So, we
> went ahead with our processing and received this lady into the vil-
> lage. Within three weeks the mood and the environment of the Vil-
> lage, the other people whom she met, the stimulation of programs
> and ideas—all of these had combined to bring about a remarkable
> change. It was on a Saturday afternoon three weeks after entering
> First Community Village that I saw her with four of her friends get-
> ting into a taxi. She told me she had organized a trip to a matinee
> downtown with a group of the "girls" she had met at the Village.
>
> Since that time she has become head of one of the Village Commit-
> tees, the Garden Committee—to be exact. And the other night when
> a group of the Villagers went to a local racetrack, she was in the
> front row!
>
> Or, here in another person, is a man who had been living in an
> apartment house for two years. In all that time he had met only one
> couple. He spent most of his time reading and looking out the win-
> dow. His doctor convinced him that he should move into First Com-
> munity Village. After a good deal of discussion and thought, he did
> move in. In four weeks' time, this man who had been so lonesome
> had become associate editor of the Village newspaper, he was one of
> the tour guides for visitors who came to see the Village, and he had
> talked three times before different groups. He was thoroughly
> amazed at himself. He said, "Never before have I been able to get up
> in public without stammering and becoming frightened to death."

For the two years before coming to the Village he had had to take a sleeping pill each night, but that was no longer necessary.

We could go on and on, but the point of all this is—neither one of these people needed a place to live. They both had that. They were looking for a *way of life*.

The speaker mentioned certain needs of typical retirees and then described how the particular village that he directs is meeting the needs:

Is it possible to build to meet all these needs? Yes, to some degree. This is possible and indeed several sponsors have done this. First Community Village, for example, has built congregate housing of the hotel type, a high rise building and also garden type apartments, located in the same acreage, and moreover, has located there separated cottage type apartments. Thus, for the 500 people moving into First Community Village, 20% will live in their own cottages, handling their own cooking and having a high degree of independence; 60% will live in garden type apartments, eating together for maintaining maximum freedom from care; 20% will be under closer assisted type living.

It is rather interesting that of all the housing projects now in the United States which have been written up in the most recent and comprehensive book in this field, "Buildings for the Elderly"—there are only 8 projects listed which have attempted to build both congregate and proximate housing under one project. . . .

In the remainder of this conference, I assume you will gather many statistics and details of immense value. So let me reiterate again— when you put all these together and sum them all up, make sure they answer not just a place to live, but more important, a WAY OF LIFE.[7]

No matter where you live, when you retire you may think that you should live somewhere else. You can find a better climate very easily, but you will probably discover after a year or two that a good retirement is not in any place but is to be found in your mental life in relation to activities and associates. And no matter where you go, there will be some problems, as well as many pleasures. This means that you should investigate the possibilities thoroughly before you make your choice. I found one couple who spent the entire first year of retirement in answering the question. Immediately after his retirement from a business position of the New England area, they stored their furniture. The two went on an exploratory trip down the Eastern Seaboard, through all of Florida, along the Gulf Coast, through the Rocky Mountain and Pacific Coast areas up to Vancouver. They spent one year on their project. At the end of the year, they reviewed what they had learned and chose a retirement community in Arizona. The reasons stated were "its fine friendly people, the activities we could enjoy with them, the climate, the nearby scenery, the designs of the houses, the good police protection, and the businesslike management of the community." When I interviewed him two years later, he and his wife were happy about the way they had made their choice and the choice they made. The important point to keep in mind is not the specific place they chose but the factors in their choice and their systematic way of going about it. Other retirees will, no doubt, go through a similar procedure and come to a quite different decision, one that fits their needs and their preferences.

## Sources of information

Helen Heusinkveld and Noverre Musson, *1001 Best Places to Live When You Retire* (Chicago: The Dartnell Corporation). Ask for latest edition.

*A National Directory on Housing for Older People,* National Council on the Aging, 315 Park Avenue South, New York, N.Y. 10010. This publication is revised every few years, but the contents are not inclusive, because listings depend upon the return of a mailed questionnaire.

Write to your state capitol, letter addressed to State Commission on Aging and Aged. Ask for their Directory of Services for the Aging: the listings of philanthropic homes for the aged and licensed nursing homes. Ask for copies of any *Newsletter* prepared for distribution to persons concerned with the problems of aging.

Anyone who is vitally concerned about the selection of a nursing home for a relative or friend should read Bertram B. Moss, *Caring for the Aged* (Garden City, N.Y.: Doubleday & Company, Inc., 1966). Also, send for a copy of the pamphlet: "What to Look for in a

Nursing Home," American Medical Association, 535 N. Dearborn St., Chicago, Ill., 60610. You can also get helpful information on selecting a nursing home by writing to the American Nursing Home Association, Suite 1008, 1101 Seventeenth St., N.W., Washington, D.C. 20036. Ask for their booklet, *Thinking About a Nursing Home*.

## REFERENCES

1. Harold R. Hall, *Some Observations on Executive Retirement*, Graduate School of Business Administration, Division of Research, Harvard University, 1953, p. 239.
2. See Leland Frederick Cooley and Lee Morrison Cooley, *The Retirement Trap*, Garden City, N.Y.: Doubleday & Company, Inc., 1965. Chapters 12 and 13, as well as the remainder of this book, offer very helpful information to retirees who want to become aware of their problems.
3. Helen Heusinkveld and Neverre Musson, *1001 Best Places to Live*, Chicago: The Dartnell Corporation, 1964, p. 7.
4. Reprinted from *Geriatric Focus*, vol. 5, no. 16, a publication of the Knoll Pharmaceutical Company, Orange, N.J. Reported at a meeting of the American Psychological Association, New York, 1966, by Susan R. Sherman, Wiley P. Magnum, Jr., Suzanne Dodds, and Daniel W. Wilner, the authors of the report.
5. Sidney L. Pressey and Alice D. Pressey, "Two Insiders' Searchings for Best Life in Old Age," *The Gerontologist*, vol. 6, no. 1, March, 1966.
6. Harold R. Hall, *op.cit.*, pp. 254–263.
7. James Bidle, "Retirement Village Housing for Older Persons," *Proceedings of the Sixth Annual Conference, Housing and the Well Older Person*, Indiana State Commission on the Aging and the Aged, Indianapolis, 1963.

CHAPTER EIGHT

# Retirement Activities
# that May Appeal to You

*"Age is only a number, a cipher for the records.*
*A man can't retire his experience. He must use it."*
—BERNARD BARUCH

MANY A VOCATIONALLY successful man has said: "I have no hobbies or special recreational interests. Does that mean I am doomed to boredom in my retirement?" On second thought, some add "But I do want to keep mentally active, to know what is going on in the world, and to get as interested in something as I was in my work."

These men may get some hopeful thoughts from a significant study made by Dr. Otto Pollak for the Pension Research Council, Wharton School of Finance and Commerce, University of Pennsylvania. He and his associates selected from a large number of retirees those whose retirement was believed to be very successful. Forty-seven of those selected were studied systematically. One of his main findings was that successful retirement is not so much associated with the pursuit of new interests as it is with the cultivation or the renewal of old interests. Unfulfilled wishes that furnished motivation and led to satisfaction in retirement were utilized after they had been created, either by or as a result of a man's work or by childhood experiences: "Success in retirement is first of all attention to unfinished business in terms of an individual's own experiences." [1] If he enjoys a specific retirement activity, particularly a voluntary service, it is likely to be motivated by the continuation of much earlier emotionalized experiences. (See page 173 for an example.)

A second important finding was that in another class of successful retirees, the retiree had a successful retirement because he defined himself in terms of a larger whole which could be a civic movement, a charitable enterprise, a local community, or the universe. Chiefly, the individual had a sustaining philosophy of life that provided a frame of reference in which his waning capacities, failing health, and the cessation of former activities, however meaningful, seemed to lose their threat.

These latter findings of Pollak agree with those of leading thinkers in religion, philosophy, and related fields who have been pointing out for centuries that the satisfactions from the here and now, as exemplified by the business or professional man's ability to function in his full powers, should be complemented by another kind of growth of the mental life, the development of a sustaining personal philosophy. Eventually, the individual must develop his orientation, his interpretation of the scheme of things, one that subordinates his waning powers to something larger and more enduring than the individual himself. Chapters 11 to 14 of this book deal with the quest for developing a personal philosophy. This chapter and the next two deal with the meaningful continuation of interests in work, service, and recreational activities.

### Recognizing your unfulfilled wishes

A natural question on your part might well be "How does a retiree recognize his unfulfilled wishes that were created by work or childhood experiences, in order that he can satisfy them in ways that will improve the likelihood of a successful retirement?" Theoretically, the answer might be "Have several mature psychologists study you," but this is an obviously unnecessary and impractical answer. *You* will have to make the study of yourself. You will have to do it by the simple method of reading about, observing, and in a few chosen instances, experimenting with available outlets for your mental energies. Chapters 5 and 6 have treated some of the work-related interests that appeal to some retirees. But there are more work-related interests that can be followed by simply "keeping abreast of the times." The importance of these follow-through mental activities is so great that physicians often mention them in their advice on health to the aging.

When Dr. G. M. Young, M.D., Gary, Indiana, spoke before the Annual Governor's Conference on Aging, on "The Counseling of the Older Person—Medicine," in which he summarized how the older person can continue to enjoy good health, he listed as first a continued interest in the world you live in:

> I would list the following objectives for the oldster:
>
> *First,* keep interested in the world you live in, specifically in the fields of your own life's occupation during your active years of employment. That is, if your work was in the fields of engineering or mechanics, then by all means keep abreast of developments in these fields. If on the other hand, your work was in law, accounting, medicine, or in the building trades, then by all means keep an active interest in these fields. Do this as the first thing to keep alert.
>
> *Second,* keep abreast of the times in current events, in politics, and in world history and changes.
>
> *Third,* develop a sense of independence in your life and do not let yourself become dependent upon other members of the family or society for your care and support.
>
> *Fourth,* develop new interests and hobbies. Take an interest in community affairs, the church, fraternal organizations and clubs. Take an active interest in worthy community projects and create a desire to help others who need help. Do all the things you had looked forward to doing when retirement came. Keep young and stay young by keeping busy and above all do not become moody and introspective.
>
> *Finally,* maintain good health. Have periodic physical examinations. These should be carried out regularly. Counsel with the doctor regularly and do not put off seeking medical advice on ailments that may seem trivial. Help at these times may prevent some more serious condition in the future and "an ounce of prevention is worth a pound of cure." [2]

The important suggestion for you as you read about, investigate, and experiment with various suitable retirement activities is that *you* note when the thought of pursuing a specific activity grips you. When an interest "seizes" you, you have discovered an unsatisfied interest that probably developed in work or childhood—its source or origin is not important—the fact that it stimulates you to pursue its possibilities is important.

If you find that you do a lot of sleeping that is not induced by fatigue from work, bear in mind that the extra sleeping and intermittent dozing on the part of older people is one way to overcome boredom. The older person who has a zest for living is interested in what goes on in the world and tends to follow the same sleep pattern he has had for years. If you adjust your thinking and attitudes to keep mentally alert during your retirement years, you can add a lot of extra living by simply keeping awake, being mentally active, and thereby enjoying more hours per day. Here are some work-related services that stimulate some retirees to keep mentally active.

### Service Corps of Retired Executives (SCORE)

This program was established by the Small Business Administration, Washington, D.C., to use retired executives as consultants to small business. The work is done by volunteer members, retirees, who have had experience in fields that can be of value to small businesses. The work of the retirees may have been in retailing, production, office management, accounting, banking, sales, advertising, wholesaling, or any one of many other fields. The volunteers stand ready to share their experience and know-how with any small businessman who needs help. Any business firm that employs twenty-five or fewer people can obtain their services by simply writing or telephoning to the nearest Small Business Administration office.

SCORE developed from the pioneering work begun in 1950 by Maurice du Pont Lee, Wilmington, Delaware. (His father was a cousin of General Robert E. Lee and his mother was a member of the du Pont family.) His service was known as Consulting and Advisory Services.

To his surprise Mr. Lee found that managers of small businesses are often willing to help a competitor. One of his first examples of this willingness, as described to a writer by Mr. Lee, occurred in Wilmington:

> A young woman who owns a small beauty shop was in difficulties, unable to meet a debt. She appealed to the old-timers for advice. They knew less about operating a beauty shop than they did about building igloos, but they decided to find out in the simplest way. They went to the successful competitors of their client, stated the problem, and in turn asked advice.
>
> Did the competitors turn a cold shoulder, smile at the possibility of a rival's failure? No, they turned their own businesses inside out to show what made them successful. They disclosed their early mistakes and advised how to prevent them, suggested ways to gain customers, in the hope of helping their rival help herself.
>
> "There's enough business for everybody," was their attitude. "The town is growing."
>
> "If," said Mr. Lee, "we had been trying to make money for ourselves, or if we had been 'passing the hat,' we wouldn't have been welcomed. But as soon as we made clear that our mission was to aid another who was trying, and whose main difficulty was her inexperience, every door was opened."
>
> He believes thousands of doors will be opened everywhere on behalf of the "little fellow" who needs and is deserving of help, once the right knock is given on them—but there must be that knock, and the unselfishly interested retired man is ideally placed to give it. . . .
>
> There is nothing mysterious or difficult about how they started in Wilmington. First, Lee satisfied himself of the soundness of the idea. Next with a few friends advising, he drew up a list of the retired and about-to-be-retired men who seemed most capable, if they would, of being helpful to the city's small businesses. Twenty or so of them met one afternoon in the board room of one of the banks, at the president's invitation. Fifty attended the second meeting.
>
> The bank donated the room. It furnished secretarial service. Moreover, it invited other banks to send officers to the meetings, and most of them did. After the initial confusion arising from everybody having a plan, the present Consulting and Advisory Services, Inc., was born.

Beginning in 1964 and later, Congress appropriated funds seeking volunteers to do work similar to what Maurice du Pont Lee had started. In the course of SCORE's first three years of operation, 4,000 volunteer workers cooperated. It was estimated that in one twelve-month period they helped to prevent bankruptcy in 21,000 small businesses of 200 communities in the United States. A current descriptive circular of SCORE offers the following excerpts:

SCORE services

• Who qualifies for SCORE assistance? Actually, any small businessman—in most cases with 25 or fewer people—can apply. Your shop doesn't have to be "in trouble" to qualify. Whether you have a specific worry—or whether you simply feel the operation is a bit stale and needs a new "slant"—you qualify.

• Suppose you haven't made a thorough review of your production line in 10 years; SCORE will be glad to help. If you're wondering whether you can afford to put some of your bookkeeper's load over on computers, ask SCORE. If you don't know how to measure the sales you're getting from your advertising, SCORE will send an expert.

• You don't have to have an SBA loan to qualify. Whether you are already receiving SBA assistance in one form or another, makes no difference. Many times SCORE volunteers have been helpful to businessmen that didn't even know about SCORE and came to SBA seeking management advice, but not seeking loans.

• In fact, you don't even have to be in business yet. The man who is seriously thinking about going into business can use SCORE experts to help him plan soundly.

• Too, SCORE is happy to help you stay ahead. Hundreds of thriving businesses are using SCORE counselors to improve and grow.

• SCORE, you see, is heart and soul of the purpose behind SBA itself. The volunteer members, like the agency, are dedicated to helping small business stay strong, progressive, and abreast of new technology.

What does SCORE cost?

• The counselor's time is free. SBA asks only that the businessman who uses SCORE reimburse the expert for his out-of-pocket travel and other expenses. Otherwise, the expert serves without fee.

SCORE successes

• Yes, hundreds of businessmen are showing new profits—because they called in SCORE, then followed the expert's advice:

• A Houston clothing retailer, who runs two shops, has doubled sales in six months, because he and his son followed the advice of a SCORE volunteer. He expects to increase sales by another 50 percent in the next six months.

• Writes a chair manufacturer in Oregon: "I have been amazed to see the way a SCORE volunteer can bring a difficult problem into clear focus. The SCORE program taps one of the greatest resources of this great nation."

• A St. Louis baker is saving $200 a week—thanks to a SCORE inspection and analysis of his operations.

• The president of a New York firm told SBA: "It has been three months since the analysis of my business was completed. . . . I have changed my method of operation and have extended my line. I have added an additional salesman. I'm beginning to realize a profit."

• In Utah, the volunteer who helped a car-wash operator cut his overhead was a man who had been president of his own firm and the controller also of a national firm.

## Volunteers for International Technical Assistance (VITA)

Nicknamed the "Postal Peace Corps," VITA has its headquarters on the campus of Union College, Schenectady, New York. Everyday practical problems of rural-village life in foreign countries are referred to VITA for solution. Typical problems are: Can you design a simple pump to pump river water up onto hillside rice paddies? How can we harvest jute growing 6 feet under water? We have very little scrub wood or other fuel to burn—can you tell us how to build a stove that cooks by solar power? Questions such as these are referred to qualified American scientists and specialists, some 6,000 in number, who are available for VITA services. The files of VITA and a related group in California contain answers to more than 12,000 questions. Consultants receive no pay for their information.[3]

## The International Executive Service
## Corps (IESC)

IESC, with headquarers at 545 Madison Avenue, New York, is popularly known as the "Executive Peace Corps." Another term is the "Retired Management Missionaries." It was founded as a nonprofit project by a group of private businessmen, headed by David Rockefeller, President of the Chase Manhattan Bank. IESC receives financial support both from private business sources in the United States—individuals, corporations and foundations—and from the United States government, through grants from the Agency for International Development. It has two major objectives: to contribute to a strong base of vigorous private enterprise in developing nations and to provide opportunities for retired and semiretired businessmen to continue to use their know-how and experience. The Corps also enables some younger executives to broaden their management abilities by serving in foreign countries. The requests for assistance come from overseas companies. Companies assisted have ranged in size from 12 to 5,000 employees. The volunteer serves without salary, but IESC pays all travel expenses for the man and his wife, plus a tax-exempt per diem allowance scaled to the project country to cover all reasonable living expenses. The average age of volunteers is in the late fifties, the majority of whom are retired executives. The companies which are assisted pay part of the cost. IESC deals directly with the individual businesses and not through the governments of the United States or the host country. Fees are charged, but they are scaled to what the foreign company can pay— the purpose of the fee is to screen out worthless requests and to stimulate the client to use the advice for which he pays.

*An IESC project begins when* a locally-owned company in a developing country asks for assistance—usually through the resident IESC representative in that country. Then a series of basic steps follow: the company is carefully screened. Is it a private business or a government-controlled enterprise? Does the firm have a growth potential and a management that can benefit from IESC help? Will its survival and success be of benefit to the local economy? Is no other professional help obtainable, either because of its cost or because it is not available locally? Finally, is its management serious enough about wanting assistance to be willing to contribute to the cost of the program?

*The types of projects handled* are as varied as business itself. IESC executives have helped a bakery in Thailand and reorganized a dress manufacturing plant in Brazil; worked with a dairy in Iran and a provincial bank in the Philippines; and served the fields of appliances, aviation, broadcasting, building materials, construction, engineering, foundries, leather and shoes, hotels, millwork, machinery, motion pictures, plastics, fruit and vegetable canning, textiles, travel, and a host of others. All types of skills have been furnished: general management, production, marketing, finance, personnel, and others.

## Cleveland Senior Council

This Senior Council was founded in 1956 by a group of community leaders who saw the need and the opportunity for continued valuable service by retired people, and the possibility of supplying their counsel to a wide range of civic, welfare, charitable, and educational groups and to small businesses and individuals. In the first ten years of service thousands of people with problems have come to the Cleveland Senior Council and its members for advice and ideas based on the sympathetic understanding of others who have struggled with the same kinds of problems.

The Cleveland Senior Council is organized to:

• Supply helpful counsel on community projects which will enhance the civic life of the city and make the city more attractive to its citizens.

• Provide a central group of retired executives and professional people to which companies and institutions may refer their retirees for membership and community activity.

• Provide the means of educating companies in the necessity of preretirement preparation for their personnel.

• Provide counseling service from its reservoir of experienced talent for individuals and organizations.

• Find interesting opportunities for its members to keep themselves active and to utilize their abilities.

• Encourage individual and volunteer activities of members on community problems.

• Promote fellowship among its members through closer association in such activities and through monthly luncheon meetings.

Approximately 160 members make up the Cleveland Senior Council. Both men and women are invited to membership. New members are proposed and recommended by present members. Previous executive or professional experience and the time and willingness to participate in counseling activities are the only requirements. Members come from a broad variety of previous background and activity.

No charge is made for the counseling services and therefore the Council can be as selective as the members—they help where they think they can be most effective.

The group has preferred to remain independent, and its members maintain its modest office in the Hanna Building. They are in effect paying dues of $25 a year or more for the privilege of giving their services to the clients who come for advice. In addition, the Council has some twenty-five industrial and commercial members, including some of Cleveland's leading companies. They contribute to the Council's support and refer their retiring executives for membership.

The Cleveland Senior Council has found that it is very difficult to attempt to advise people outside of the Cleveland area. When members of the Council can sit down around the table as a project committee and talk out a problem, helpful ideas are likely to develop. Advising by mail has not been practical because problems are more or less personal. However, a number of similar groups have been started in other areas, and some of them have operated profitably.

## Volunteer talent pools

This type of community service has been developed most effectively by the Volunteer Talent Pool for Winnetka, Glencoe, Northfield, and Kenilworth, Illinois.

It came into being as a by-product of the Winnetka Senior Center. The Center is a community effort to provide a congenial meeting place, together with recreational, educational, and hobby activities for its members, retired men and women of the area. In 1960 it was recognized that the Center had a pool of talent and know-how waiting to be called upon for volunteer service to the communities in which they lived.

A first step in implementing the idea was to make contact with the superintendents of schools of Winnetka and Glencoe. The Winnetka schools invited informed adults to talk to classes at the junior high school level on subjects the pupils were studying.

Later, a financial breakthrough came when the National College of Education of Evanston and the Winnetka Schools, under a grant from the Wieboldt Foundation, undertook a research project directed toward the underachieving child. A professional social worker was named coordinator of this project. She sought adults who would provide good adult images—people with interest and enthusiasm for specific subject matter—those who could bring a warm interest in children, an unusual skill or knowledge, and an ability and willingness to share their wisdom with young people. Such individuals were located and referred to the school project coordinator. The school coordinators assigned the adults to the child or group of children with whom they were to work.

A close check was kept on how each relationship was working out in actual practice. It was the sensitive handling of these human relationships which contributed greatly to the success of the project.

In June of 1963 the research project conducted under the Wieboldt Foundation grant was completed, but the Winnetka School Board decided to support and continue the program.

Participation by volunteers in the school system expanded. The

Volunteer Service was no longer limited to work with "under-achievers." Volunteers, regardless of age, were requested to aid in the enrichment of school programs.

Steadily the range of services provided by the volunteers broadened. People of all ages were needed, and responded with enthusiasm when asked to give of their time and talents. One of the personal values for the older adult was the opportunity to associate with younger volunteers and with people still in the mainstream of business and professional life.

Then came requests from parochial schools, the schools for retarded children, the Hadley School for the Blind, the brig at Great Lakes Naval Training Station, and the public recreation departments and the like.

All wanted to expand their services and asked for carefully selected, competent, responsible volunteers. Public welfare agencies and the public children's service agencies also asked for qualified, prescreened volunteers. Official village departments were ready to use volunteers to supplement the work of their paid staff.

To build liaison and morale among the volunteers, they are periodically invited to a social get-together where they hear from inspirational speakers concerning the significant contributions volunteers are making to the nation.

All of the services required in the administration of the Talent Pool are voluntary, and many of the essential project materials used by the volunteers in the schools are contributed. The current Project for Academic Motivation (PAM) began in a single elementary school with the services of four retired businessmen, each working with one child or a small group for forty minutes each week. This has expanded to nine communities with more than 500 men and women of various ages serving as volunteers.

Further details of the Winnetka idea and PAM program may be obtained from Mrs. Janet Freund, Winnetka Public Schools, 1155 Oak St., Winnetka, Ill. 60093. See also Aging magazine, July, 1968, p. 6.

Anyone interested in forming a similar service for a community should purchase a copy of a comprehensive *Operating Manual for a Volunteer Talent Pool* (price $2.25) by writing to the Volunteer Talent Pool, 620 Lincoln Avenue, Winnetka, Ill. 60093.

## Reading and educational programs

If you have been so fortunate as to have established the habit of reading during your early life, you are likely to find adjustment to retirement easier. Books to you can become old friends who will never leave you. Or, if you developed keen interests in certain subjects years ago, you can make many hours and days very rewarding now that you have more time available than in your earlier years. The habit of reading the daily newspapers and the business journals of your field is probably so firmly established that it will enable you to feel that you are still an active member of the changing, pulsating world about you. Reading about current affairs helps you keep yourself mentally alert.

### STUDY PROGRAMS

Home-study programs offer opportunities to take any one of a wide variety of courses, even piano tuning and upholstering. The student can progress at the rate he prefers.[4]

The American Association of Retired Persons has offered pilot programs in Washington, D.C., and Long Beach, California. In a recent year, the Institute of Lifetime Learning opened with a curriculum offering sixty-six subjects, with most of the classes filled, and with more than 500 students over the age of fifty-five. The oldest admitted age was ninety-two. These institutes serve as prototypes for local continuing education programs.

Physicians have recommended the Institute and other study programs to men and women who are seriously challenged by boredom —suffering from loss of contact with people and events. Retirees who are interested in study programs usually investigate the schools and courses available in their area.

**THE INSTITUTE FOR RETIRED**
**PROFESSIONALS**

The IRP, developed at the New School for Social Research in New York City, offers an outstanding continued learning program. It was organized in 1962 as a center for those who have retired from the professions and executive positions in industry, government, and public institutions. It is designed for those educated people who wish to continue their education and to engage as a group in intellectual and cultural pursuits. The Golden Age clubs (or the Sixty-Plus clubs) meet the social and recreational needs of the average retiree, but not those whose special skills and talents are in danger of eroding from disuse. Their minds crave the intellectual excitement of new educational vistas.

The IRP's major goal is to provide "an opportunity for continued educational and intellectual growth." In addition to taking courses at the New School as regular students, its members conduct forty courses of their own in all the disciplines on a volunteer basis. This constitutes almost a university within the university. Since no one is paid, this program is the largest do-it-yourself project of its kind. Every opportunity is taken to develop social relations so important for older persons. Such projects are often in the nature of neighborhood socials, luncheons, film programs, and travel.

Eligible for membership are men and women who have retired from at least twenty years of active professional life in such fields as medicine, dentistry, the law, the various sciences, engineering, and teaching, as well as the creative and performing arts and executive levels in business and industry. Ranging from fifty-five to eighty-five years of age, they are integrated into New School classes attended by other students and taught by instructors usually a good deal younger than themselves.

The results of a survey questionnaire distributed among IRP members indicated that more than four-fifths of the membership spends three or more whole days a week at the New School; a quarter of them spend four days, and a fifth spend five days.

New opportunities for education in the arts and in learning foreign languages were most often mentioned.

About half the surveyed members claimed they were reading more than before joining IRP, and exercising a more selective choice of literature.

Others mentioned the stimulating intellectual exercises of preparing papers for the various study and discussion groups. There seems little doubt that IRP is one answer to some of the problems of New York's retired professionals who, as a specific group, had too long been neglected in the planning and execution of programs for older persons.

The IRP Council and officers are very conscious of the need for similar programs at universities in our urban centers. It stands ready to help retired professionals anywhere to develop a project in their own communities.

Other educational programs have been developed in many other cities. The University of Kentucky, as an example, offers special scholarships to persons over sixty-five. High school diplomas and fees are not required. For more information about this nationwide program, write to the Council on Aging, University of Kentucky, Lexington, Ky. 40506.[5]

## A CHALLENGING QUESTION OR THEME
## WILL ENLIVEN YOUR READING

If you held a responsible position when you were still working, you had problems that concerned your work. You wanted to keep yourself informed about what others were doing who had related problems. As a result, you read some journals and books that applied to your field. You can continue to enjoy reading about the same subjects in retirement. To many able retirees this is their most enjoyable intellectual activity.

Some men, however, lose this kind of reading interest when they retire. If this has happened to you, you may not want to try to force yourself to read again about the same old problems that you would prefer to forget. If, as a result, you now find in your retirement that your reading has become randomized and less interesting, you might rearouse your interest by choosing a new problem or theme. A good example of the influence of a purpose in reading can be recognized if you try to read an airline timetable without special need for the information. When, however, you have a definite place in mind to which you wish to go, your interest becomes accentuated. Similarly, the student who wants to pass a course gains far more knowledge from his reading than the casual reader who reads the same text but only wants to add to his general information. As a retiree, you can enliven your serious reading by first choosing a challenging question or theme that arouses a continued interest. Without it, your reading is not likely to be very stimulating to you.

The typical retiree from business has had many experiences which are likely to give him feelings of involvement that offer themes for his reading. Problems within his work experience that have not been solved and may supply a theme are those dealing with management training, supervisory skills, labor-union practices, trends in certain fields, and a host of others. Currently, as well as in decades past, one of the universal questions that has bothered businessmen has been widely discussed: "Is all business evil?" The critics have claimed that the nature of our business society is not creative, not designed for social benefit but to benefit a fortunate few. This question can be a challenging theme in the reading by retirees who identify with business life and organizations.

Abram T. Collier, President of New England Mutual Life Insurance Company, has described the nature of our business society as a creative society:

> I put forward this simple proposition: that our society is a creative society; that its prime objective, as well as its great genius, is its creativeness; and that, as creative accomplishment is the actual day-to-day goal of modern business, it is also the keystone of our business philosophy.
>
> I am thinking of creativeness in its widest and deepest sense. Thus, business does not exist merely to produce more goods and services, or better goods and services for more people, though that is no small part of its task. Business also, particularly in these days, affords the principal or the only means whereby individual men may gain the

satisfaction of accomplishing something more than merely sustaining their own lives. Pleasure, power, and fame appear to be but by-products of the efforts we make to be useful members of society and to leave it with something more than it had when we arrived. Perhaps we leave only the grain of sand that Robert Frost said he wished to leave on the beach of history, but at least, if we do that, we can feel that we have fulfilled our role in living.

What I am suggesting is that the great goals of happiness, freedom, security—even goodness and truth—are values which should be viewed as subordinate to, and resulting from, a new and positive creative ideal. Our people in business and elsewhere seem to be driven by an urge to build, by a longing to explore and reach out, by a desire to realize, through men and for men, such things and experiences as humanity has never known before. In this light, our vaunted freedoms of thought and action, our sought-for freedoms from worry and want, and even our ethical standards of behavior (products as they are of other places and times) are not ends in themselves, rather, they emerge as important values just because they support and make possible a creative society of men.

This is the modern heresy: that it is not enough to be good, to lead a blameless life, we must also be creative.[6]

Do you agree with Mr. Collier? Do you think that young people agree with this point of view? Would you be prepared to discuss this with young people?

Of course there are many other kinds of socioeconomic problems that can add zest to a retiree's reading: juvenile delinquency, the stability of marriages, migration to the suburbs, adequacy of educational facilities, housing, government versus private enterprise, public transportation, costs of hospitalization, and the numerous factors in social evolution.

As an example of a continuing theme, anyone, young or old, who wishes to center his reading around the question as to what part poverty plays in social and political revolutions can keep busy during all his remaining years. Do the poor, those on a borderline of starvation, lead purposeful lives directed toward revolution? Many students in this field believe that the very poor nurse no grievances and dream no dreams when they are engaged in a desperate struggle for food and shelter. If you have any top-of-the-head beliefs on these or other subjects, why not do some systematic reading to confirm or to modify your easy assumptions?

Do civilizations die as the result of conquest by enemies from without or by degeneration from within? What do the historians think? If you will study the decline and fall of civilizations, you will find that some began their descent into oblivion when they became soft as the result of too much leisure and too little necessity to keep themselves strong. They had too few problems to stimulate their continued development. Certainly, the people of the United States have gained much leisure as a result of technological advancements. Few people in our nation fear hunger. We do not have to labor in order to eat. However, we do have some serious social problems: lawlessness, underprivileged citizens, and drug addiction.

Perhaps you can challenge yourself to study the histories of civilizations and be able to decide for yourself whether our contemporary social problems are really giving us spurs or hindrances in our advancement.

If current social changes do not arouse any dormant interests to influence your reading, how about following the stock market? Before retirement, you thought of your occasional investments in securities as a form of recreation, but your attitude after retirement is likely to change to one of crucial earnestness. Success or failure in making investments after retirement may have important bearings on your standard of living. As a result, you will study your investing far more seriously and systematically than you could when you were working full-time. By the time of retirement you have learned that all the advice you get from friends, bankers, brokers, and investment counselors requires far more careful analysis and evaluation than you applied previous to retirement.

Finally, if reading by having a continuing theme or problem in mind does not appeal to you, you can at least keep yourself informed about your former place of employment by asking the public relations department to include you on the mailing list for all important releases, the company house organs, and employee publications at plant locations where you worked.

# REFERENCES

1. Otto Pollak, *Positive Experience in Retirement* (monograph), Homewood, Ill.: Richard D. Irwin, Inc., 1957.
2. See *Proceedings of the Governor's Sesquicentennial Conference on Aging*, Indiana Commission on the Aging and Aged, 1966, p. 20.
3. See Hallowell Bowser, "New Uses for Old Bicycles," *Saturday Review*, Sept. 21, 1968, p. 26.
4. A *Directory of Accredited Private Home Study Schools* may be obtained from the National Home Study Council, 1601 18th St., N.W., Washington, D.C. 20009.
5. A four-part "Time for Learning" series of articles, published in *Harvest Years*, June–September, 1968, presents a comprehensive report in this field. The series was inspired by material presented at a University of Michigan Conference on Aging.
6. Abram T. Collier, "Business Leadership and a Creative Society," *Harvard Business Review*, January–February, 1968, p. 155.

## CHAPTER NINE

# Information and Services
# Available to Retirees

*"Age, I make light of it,*
*Fear not the sight of it.*
*Time's but our playmate, whose toys are divine"*
—THOMAS WENTWORTH HIGGINSON

WHEN I WROTE to the Commission on Aging of the State of Colorado, Denver, for information helpful to retirees, I received a reply from Robert B. Robinson, Director, Older Americans Division, which included this paragraph:

> I firmly believe that the people who suffer most after retirement are not necessarily those with inadequate incomes but rather retirees who do not know what to do with their new-found leisure; for example, the person who has worked in industry all of his life and has not participated in the community has no way of knowing how he can utilize the talents that he does have. I hope that some moves toward correcting this will develop under the leadership of knowledgeable people.

You should, for your own benefit, have a desire to know about the various facilities that are available to retirees. These are so numerous and proliferating so rapidly that you could keep yourself mentally active in the first stage of retirement just by learning what and where they are, to whom they apply, and whether certain ones might

161

add to your enjoyment of retirement. Indeed, every community should have one or more retirees who have specialized in learning about the facilities and services that are available to retirees.

Governmental facilities operated for retirees vary from one community and one period of time to the next. If you try to keep a yearly list of them, you will find that they come and go rather rapidly. Federal and state laws change, appropriations are added or dropped, the rulings of courts change interpretations of laws, and bureaucrats vary in their decisions as to the requirements for participation in the use of aids.

Private projects to serve retirees who seek employment, counseling, or recreational services are developed, flourish, and die—the initiating personality of the project moves on to other interests, or he may decide to retire completely and let the younger retirees take over. Thus, a needed and effective service that may have been organized and operated by a retiree for the benefit of other retirees disappears. These and other influences make it necessary for the knowledgeable man in the field of retirement services to constantly revise and update his information. Still, every retiree should try to get acquainted with the services or facilities that happen to be applicable to him in his time and place.

## Where to begin

An easy and rewarding approach is to subscribe to magazines which are edited for retirees:

> *Harvest Years*, monthly. 104 E. 40th St., New York, N.Y. 10016.
> *Dynamic Maturity*, a bimonthly preparation-for-retirement magazine. 408 E. Grand Ave., Ojai, Calif. 93023.
> *Modern Maturity*, a bimonthly magazine, free to members of AARP. 408 E. Grand Ave., Ojai, Calif. 93023.

The latter two are published by the American Association of Retired Persons. Membership in AARP entitles the member to the use of the AARP drug service, insurance plan, and the travel service, as well as to other services of value to certain retirees. Dues are nominal.

*National Council on the Aging*, 315 Park Avenue South, New York, N.Y. 10010. NCOA is a nonprofit, nongovernmental agency concerned with the opportunities and needs of older people. NCOA believes the extent to which older people can continue to contribute to family and public life, remain independent and self-directing, and receive such services as they may need, will depend not only on themselves but also on attitudes and leadership in the communities in which they live. Through its library, consultant staff, and its publications, NCOA provides information and consultation to organizations and leaders in the field of aging. Write for a publications list. Its library of books on retirement is one of the most complete in this country.

## Federal government sources

Administration on Aging, Department of Health, Education, and Welfare, HEW, 330 Independence Ave., S.W., Washington, D.C. 20201. Ask for "Publications Available to the Public." This list is divided into two sections: publications that can be purchased from the Government Printing Office and those obtainable without charge as long as the supply lasts.

*AGING* of HEW is a monthly newsmagazine that provides information about programs, activities, and publications in the field of aging. The subscription price is $1 a year, payable in advance to the Superintendent of Documents, U.S. Government Printing Office, Washington, D.C. 20402. The most useful content in this magazine for readers of this book—those who are healthy, have adequate income, and wish to remain mentally active—is the section on "Publications." Most of the other articles deal with the problems and services for those retirees who are on a welfare basis or near it.

The Administration on Aging dispenses money to the various states, usually to a state agency that grants funds to local communities for programs that provide job training, recreation, health benefits, and social opportunities to retired people. These programs, as one would expect, seem to come and go without apparent reason to the retiree who is trying to find out what services are available to him. Of course the durations of programs vary somewhat with the changing conditions of a locality and the funds allocated to them.

## Social Security Administration, HEW

Your local Social Security office can advise you in many ways, including the availability of pamphlets about payments to retirees, survivors, and for disability. Some of the most helpful pamphlets require payment of a small fee and are available from the Superintendent of Documents. Examples are:

*Planning for the Later Years* is an example of a pamphlet that is written to help employees plan for their later years well in advance of their retirement. A series of seminars conducted by the Social Security Administration for the purpose of making retirement-planning information available to its employees led to the development of this pamphlet. Except for one chapter on the U.S. Civil Service Retirement System, the rest of the pamphlet has information on finances, health, housing, etc., useful to anyone.

*You—the Law—and Retirement* by Virginia Lehmann, of the Office of Aging, Welfare Administration, is another helpful pamphlet, designed for persons getting ready to retire and for those who are already retired. It informs older people how to know enough law to avoid certain mistakes: why, how, and when to see a lawyer.

## State commissions on aging

You should write to the commission on aging at your state capitol and ask to have your name and address listed for mailings that go to retirees, particularly those mailings which explain benefits and services available to citizens. The great majority of our states have such a commission. Several publish well-edited newsletters as well as occasional research reports and records of proceedings of annual conferences on aging.

## National Council of Senior Citizens, Inc.

Located at 1627 K St., N.W., Washington, D.C. 20006. The purposes of this organization can be recognized from the promises printed on the cover of one of their pamphlets which makes an appeal for memberships:

*Now You Can Help Win A Better Life for ALL Elderly People!*
* *Bigger Social Security*
* *Improvements in Medicare*
* *Better Housing for Seniors*
* *Consumer Protection*
* *New opportunities for full-time or part-time work in community service*
* *Homestead Tax exemptions*

————*Through membership in the National Council of Senior Citizens you can help support the campaign to bring dignity and respect to ALL older Americans in retirement.*

## The theme of most governmental printed matter in this field

When you get acquainted with the publications mentioned directly above, particularly those of governmental sources, you will realize that the readers for whom most of the articles are prepared differ markedly from those for whom this book has been written.

This book has been written for the prospective and recent retirees who are of an independent, self-reliant character. That, however, is not the kind of emphasis that appears in most governmental and many other publications in this field. As one expert stated: "Our society acculturates dependency, and much of the talk about being independent is just so much window dressing. Many gerontologists, I submit, are busily fostering dependence while loudly proclaiming that they are maintaining independence."

The above statement was made by a director, Office of Aging, Welfare Administration, U.S. Department of Health, Education, and Welfare, who elaborated further by stating:

> We are sure that older people want to be kept in the mainstream of life and equally sure that we should be creating activity centers geared to a specific age group. We are sure that older people want to be independent, yet we have conferences, on how to provide services and do things for them. We profess that we should never talk down to the aged and then proceed to design programs that would be patronizing to a 13-year-old. We advocate an income approach to meeting needs and spend much time developing programs of reduced fares, food stamps, and other devices that erode the income principle.

To the above statement, he added: "Even more important than the welfare programs discussed is the development of the basic ingredient—the *sine qua non*—of successful aging—a philosophy of life." [1]

If you will examine the publications put out by state and federal bureaus that deal with the aging population, you will find that a few are directing their efforts toward providing older people of average and above-average means with alternatives of choices but a high proportion of the writers and speakers equate the aging with the poor, the deprived, and the neglected in our population. Low income, inadequate housing, and poor health are emphasized. Caseworkers assume that they should look after these people. That, of course, is not what most healthy recent retirees are looking for. To aid the retirees whose problems differ from those served by governmental and welfare organizations, many corporate managements turn to privately prepared publications. Also, individual retirees develop special services on their own initiative.

## Preretirement counseling booklets and services, privately published

Several organizations publish preretirement counseling booklets for distribution to employees nearing retirement. As an example, Retirement Advisors, Inc., 4 West 57th St., New York, N.Y. 10019 publishes four booklets a year in a cycle of twenty extending over a five-year period, designed for people still at work but approaching retirement. Their purpose is to help these people anticipate some of the problems and opportunities that retirement will bring and induce them to plan for a good transition into retirement. The titles of the twenty booklets are listed below. Every five years each booklet is revised, updated and reissued in a completely new edition in the cycle's sequence.

*Financial Problems*—Making Ends Meet
*Problems of Physical Health*—Keeping Well
*The Question of Housing*—Deciding Where to Live
*The New World of Opportunity*—Keeping Busy
*Savings and Investments*—Making Your Dollars Work For You
*Food, Diet, and Weight*—Eating to be Healthy
*Community Resources*—Getting Help When You Want It
*Travels, Trips, and Tours*—Going Places
*The Eyes, The Ears, and The Feet*—Getting Around
*Family Matters*—Getting Along Together
*The Benefits of Social Security*—What's Coming To You
*Rackets and Swindles*—On Guard Against Frauds
*Money Matters*—Handling Your Taxes
*Personal Records*
*Exercise and Rest*—Keeping Fit
*Protecting Your Rights*—Legal Affairs
*Making Retirement Happy*—They Did It
*Recreation*—Enjoying the Leisure of Retirement
*Mental Health*—Having Peace of Mind
*Medicare*—Insuring Your Health Costs

RAI publications are part of a program that consists of booklets, published at quarterly intervals and distributed by employers to their senior employees, and a *Monthly Newsletter* distributed by employers to their retired employees. RAI serves no individuals as such. All of their publications go out in bulk to the employers, who distribute them to the individuals covered by the service that the employer is providing to his people.

*The Pierre-the-Pelican Retirement Series,* The Garden District Educational Services, 1528 Jackson Ave., New Orleans, La. 70130, a section of the publications division of the Louisiana Association for

Mental Health, prepared by Lloyd W. Rowland, director of education and research, provides a well-planned service of twelve letters for corporations who wish to have the letters mailed monthly to employees during their last year of employment.

Harvest Years Publishing Co., 104 East 40th St., New York, offers a special program for employees of corporations. The corporate retirement program gives employees:

1. A fifty-two-page monthly publication, *Harvest Years* magazine, devoted to their retirement needs, plans, and projects

2. A "Planning-for-tomorrow" kit—booklets and other materials regarding problems faced by the retiree

3. A reader information service

4. For the employer, a four-page bimonthly newsletter to keep the management personnel informed about the latest developments in the retirement field

Other services are their film "Financial Planning" and the special report "Death: The Way of Life," a study that presents death as a natural part of life.

In addition to the above-mentioned services, several hundred firms are utilizing the help of the American Association of Retired Persons in their work with retired and older employees. Information on this program and how it assists firms is available by writing to the Director of Retirement Planning, AARP, Andrus Building, 215 Long Beach Blvd., Long Beach, Calif. 90802.

*Forty-plus clubs* are locally organized clubs that set their own field of service according to their own rules. They are not nationally organized but Forty-plus groups can be found in cities such as New York, Philadelphia, Los Angeles, and Washington, D.C. They serve only persons over forty whose incomes fall above a specified level. The groups have no paid employees, are operated by members only on a voluntary basis. The initiation fee for active members varies but is likely to be about $15, plus $5 a month as dues. Each active member agrees to work for the club at least two hours a week. If he obtains a job, he pays no commissions or fees. The percentage of members who get jobs varies from group to group but runs as high as 80 percent under some conditions.

## New directions for yourself

One of the effects of reading the publications about retirees and retirement is their stimulating influences in the direction of "That is not what I want—I'll strike out on my own or join up with others who are like-minded." This is what happened with Maurice du Pont Lee and many others. When Dr. Julius Hendel, senior vice-president for marketing at Cargill, Inc., a grain merchandiser of Minneapolis, retired, he brooded over the "apparent relationship between retirement's placidity and mental and physical atrophy." So he formed Experience, Inc., a consulting organization that has more than fifty consultants, two-thirds of whom are retired.

In Norwalk, Connecticut, the Senior Personnel Placement Bureau was developed and is staffed entirely by volunteers whose average age is about sixty-five. The minimum qualification age for placement assistance is sixty.

In Denver, Colorado, a retiree, Lennig Sweet, initiated the development of a preretirement training course and induced the Adult Education Council of Metropolitan Denver to sponsor it. More than 500 people have participated in this demonstration project that gave leadership training to volunteers who conducted small-group discussions on the problems of prospective retirees: legal, health, financial, residential, recreational, and others. The project was funded by a title III grant of the Older Americans Act, Colorado Department of Public Welfare. For further information, write to the Council, 1314 Acoma St., Denver, Colo.

The need for comprehensive information about facilities available to retirees is evident in most communities. If you will call at the office of a community organization to inquire about the situations where your talents could be utilized, you are likely to be disappointed about the information you are given. It will probably apply only to the organization on which you call. I have yet to find the community organization which has staff members who can give an interested retiree an intelligent description of the community's needs for retirees' services, needs that apply to the entire community, not

just to the one organization where he happens to call. (Senior
citizens' centers in a few cities can provide some of this information,
but they are not likely to know the needs of local churches, schools,
fraternal orders, or some of the hospitals and nursing homes.)

But let us not blame the good people where one happens to call.
They are visited by many retirees who call once to offer their services
but fail to follow through when they are asked to do something.
Most staff members of the community agencies have plenty of work
to do and will welcome anyone who can help them do a better job.
This means that there are opportunities for one or more retirees in
each population center to carry out continuing, purposeful projects
of learning all about the needs of each community: of the individual
agencies, churches, schools, and clubs, all identifiable needs for
which the services of retirees could be utilized. This is a need only
partially answered in almost every community. So why not develop
your own project by collecting the information needed, keeping it
up to date, and making it available to other retirees?

## To make your collected information available to others

If you want to tackle this idea, you can start with any community
service agency or person you happen to know or read about in the
daily newspaper. It may be a church that is starting an athletic program for the boys of a slum neighborhood, an admired political
party that is trying to elect a mayor, a college that is planning to
raise its endowment fund, or any agency or organization that serves
people of the community.

If you should attempt to make such a survey, do not become dis-
couraged when the agency head or staff member whom you interview happens to give you little encouragement or obviously considers you to be "an old man" who must be humored and gotten
rid of as tactfully and quickly as possible. Make notes of whatever
useful information you receive, and go on to the next agency on
your list. Later, you can come back to the agency where you got a
brush-off and perhaps suggest how you might be helpful to the
agency.

After you have made several interviews, you are apt to say to yourself that you need another retiree or two with whom you can discuss your gleanings of information. You realize that you need a colleague or two who can help develop a standard outline that will enable you to organize the information into a systematic form. Find the kinds of retirees you need. Get them interested in working with you. Then you can have a committee, if desired.

Later, when you believe that you have made a systematic survey of the community's needs for the volunteer services of other retirees, you will have to arrange the obtained information into a form that you and others can use in describing to a new retiree the community's needs, the kinds of abilities and the skills needed by volunteers. Does your information enable a retiree to make an intelligent choice? Do you present the information in a form that he can apply to himself?

## Factors involved in the retiree's choice

Put yourself into the "shoes" of a new retiree to answer his questions. If you as a retiree would like to contribute your informative services to other retirees who want to contribute their volunteer services where they may be needed, you should consider factors such as the following:

1. *Does the need call for knowledge or skills which were learned in the individual's work life?* Example: A man who had been an accountant or finance man in business might welcome a chance to look after the financial records and make reports involved in the business operations of a service agency.

2. *What kind of people would the volunteer associate with on the job?* Would a retiree who has a lifetime record of drive and initiative in business care to spend his working hours in the company of the workers of a typical social agency, employees of a governmental bureau, certain religious groups, or others whom we recognize as worthy citizens but are not the kinds of individuals that a typical entrepreneur has worked with in the past?

3. *What kinds of people would the volunteer be helping by his*

*service?* Volunteer services are frequently needed in a hospital, but would the individual enjoy being with and helping the sick or patients who have suffered accidents? How about working with the patients in a mental hospital or the feebleminded of an institution for the mentally retarded?

4. *Would the ordinary factors of available transportation and sanitary facilities be satisfactory?* The transportation problem might be easily solved or very difficult, depending on the volunteer's situation. The sanitary facilities would have to be evaluated by visiting the place of work, and those are a pertinent factor in some cases.

5. *Would the work contributed cause the volunteer to feel that he was performing a service worthy of his abilities?* Many retirees who start to contribute their time and effort to a community service agency drop out very quickly. They will not, in many instances, voice any specific complaints, but the reason is a feeling that they are just doing routine, meaningless tasks: no skill or judgment required, no pay, no status, no responsibility, no leadership, and no feeling of growth as a person. No wonder they quit—someone failed to give the task any significance that was worthy of respect by the volunteer worker.

### Emotionalized childhood experiences motivate many a volunteer

If you will become acquainted with the life histories of those retirees who enjoy doing volunteer services, you are likely to find that performing the service satisfies a deep-seated urge that developed in the childhood of the specific retiree. Most of us have had certain childhood experiences which caused us to identify with certain individuals who represent us and our emotional needs. Perhaps I can illustrate this by using myself as an example by telling you that my father died when I was four years of age, and it was necessary for me to be reared by the kindness of a relative, a Pennsylvania Dutch blacksmith, and his wife. They accepted responsibility for me. He was a strict disciplinarian who believed in hard work and the usual virtues that are basic to the development of character. He meant well and I gained much from his influence, but I felt unwanted and soon determined to depend on myself as much as possible. I earned the money to pay for all my own clothes from the age of eleven onward. At fourteen I was taken out of school to learn the blacksmith trade. I continued to study at night, taught a country school, and then worked my way through college. As a result of these experiences I developed an urge to help students who want to learn. It is probable that when I finally retire, I shall look for a school that has lots of students who are willing to give up their own ease and comfort in order to learn. To me, that is an important requirement for my giving a volunteer service in my own retirement. (My motivation confirms Pollak's findings mentioned on page 141.)

If you will apply the same kind of analysis of your own background, you will probably find a different urge to satisfy but one that you developed in your childhood. If you can identify the urge and choose a feasible way to satisfy it, you should be able to enjoy volunteering your services in retirement. Your rewards would not be in the attainment of any status, money, or power but in a kind of giving of yourself that would be especially beneficial to others as well as satisfying to you.

## REFERENCE

1. Donald P. Kent, *Aging: Fact and Fancy*, OA no. 224, U.S. Department of Health, Education, and Welfare, Welfare Administration, Office of Aging, 1965.

## CHAPTER TEN

# Volunteer Services
# and Hobbies

*"Doing nothing is the most tiresome job in
the world, because you cannot quit and rest."*
—ANONYMOUS

SOME NEW RETIREES, when they are asked to help out by contributing their services to a church or other organization, have an
emotional upset. They feel irritated and disgusted by the thought:
"Now that I am retired, have I become worth so little that I'm good
only for that?" (Of course this kind of reaction will not occur if the
retiree has been doing church work for years—he will be glad to be
asked to do more of what he knows he likes to do.)

## Rewards from giving your services
## in retirement

The new retiree from a responsible position of business or the
professions usually needs some time to realize that he must consider
factors other than money, status, or professional achievement when
he thinks of overcoming his boredom and feelings of uselessness by
volunteering his services. Without realizing it, he develops new
measures of the kinds of rewards he seeks. These are likely to be of

the kinds mentioned in these three statements made by successful volunteers:

1. *"I became an interested and interesting person again."* When a man is working at a regular job, his day has purpose. He has experiences which not only hold his interest but help to make him an interesting person. The daily experiences give him different slants on numerous aspects of life. He develops ideas from contacts with other persons who have ideas. And when he comes home at the end of the day, he usually has some observations to report to and discuss with his wife. As a result, he is an interesting conversationalist at home.

Can a retiree from business or professional life be happy if he has almost no social contacts in his retirement?

The retiree who prefers to be a social isolate who is happy in his own little world may not feel lonesome, but he misses the satisfactions which come from involvement in shared activities that promote human survival and individual strength.

Of course not all social isolates develop the kinds of peculiarities of certain aged recluses, but one interesting study in this field was made in England. We occasionally read about aged recluses who deliberately choose to live in indescribable squalor. Most people assume that they are psychotic. However, a four-year study of such recluses has been reported in the *British Medical Journal* by the research-project physicians and their assistants.

The study was made of twelve men and sixty women ranging in ages from sixty to ninety-two. No evidence of psychosis was found in about one-half of the persons studied. Each patient's personality history was studied by interviews with relatives, neighbors, and friends. "The pattern that emerged was that of a domineering, quarrelsome, independent individual."

> In many instances the windows were heavily curtained or papered to shut out the outside world. Chronic alcoholism was found on the part of 3 patients and another 20 were known to be heavy drinkers. Alcoholism was suspected but not confirmed in 5 other cases.
>
> A number of the patients were induced to accept home help services. Although most of them refused to permit anything to be thrown

away or even moved, 6 had their rooms transformed into "reasonable" cleanliness and others showed some degree of improvement.

Most were obviously very lonely, they lived alone, and had poor or non-existent social links with their community. They were of the independent or domineering type but they had developed a rejection of and hostile attitude toward the outside world. Even though they usually refused help they appreciated visits.[1]

This type of extreme self-neglect often is an expression of "hostility to and rejection of the outside community." All of which suggests that we ought to practice the art of making new friends and maintaining old friendships before as well as after we retire.

One of the benefits of giving time and effort to a church, luncheon club, industry group, professional organization, or political party is in the social contacts. Of the friends we have at age sixty, only about 20 percent are likely to be available at age seventy. The other 80 percent have moved away, died, or changed their social interests to other people. This means that as retirees you and I have to develop several meaningful new friendships each year. This may not be as easy for some of us as we first assumed.

Contributing to a community organization and associating with others enables many a retiree to feel that he becomes an interesting person to others again.

2. *"I feel that I am useful in ways new to me."* One of the rewards of the retiree who volunteers his services is the discovery that his leisure time can be given to rewarding work, new to him. Statements such as the following are made by many volunteers of community services:

> I retired three years ago, but it seems to me that I am much busier now than when I was working full time. My most interesting work is that of organizing and directing a male volunteer group in our local Home Hospital. At present we have 16 volunteers who work at various jobs in the Hospital, such as Physical Therapy, Foods, Printing, Pharmacy, Storeroom, Gift Shop, and Visitation. We have just finished printing our new Red Coat Handbook. We are called the "Red Coats" because we wear bright red coats or shirts at work. As for myself, at present, I am working two mornings a week in the Hospital Pharmacy where I have quite a variety of minor duties but do not

fill prescriptions. Working as a hospital volunteer is a very rewarding work, somewhat new to me.

A retiree likes to see evidence of the value of his contributions. Bert Kruger Smith, Assistant to the Director of Mental Health Education, Hogg Foundation of Mental Health, University of Texas, has offered examples of the benefits to people who were encouraged to find purpose for living and a goal in life:

> In a White House Conference on Aging, it was said, "medical science knows that people can die when they feel that they have no purpose for living and no goal in life. . . ."
>
> This fact can be demonstrated dramatically by a study which went on in a state hospital. Eighty-two patients in a back ward were chosen for the study. The control ward was left as it had been for years, while the experimental ward had added to it only the ingredient of friendship. Women came in and visited with these older women. They talked with them about interesting ideas. They exhibited concern about the women as people. Do you know what happened? Some of the older patients began to get out of bed. For the first time in many months they had a reason to get out of bed. One of them started playing the piano. Before long there was a singing group. Women took pride in their appearance. At the end of the study, it was demonstrated that not only had the women in the experimental ward been activated in remarkable ways, but fewer of them actually had died! . . .
>
> Let us look for a moment at some of the ways in which we promote growth in overall responsibility. In a center for the mentally retarded, skinny little Tommy, age 9 wouldn't walk or eat. He wouldn't, that is, until a "foster grandparent" came to visit with him, to help feed him, to encourage him to walk. Now Tommy runs around like the other children and has a regular boy appetite. Twenty-five such organizations as Foster Grandparent are now jointly sponsored by the Office of Economic Opportunity and the Administration of Aging. In this group older persons work twenty hours a week for $1.50 per hour. Interviews show that not only is the work a great help for the retarded and other needy young people, but the health and happiness of the senior citizens have improved remarkably. I know one person who lives alone and has no family and who says that she spends every Sunday sitting through any double feature that there is simply because she hates to be at home alone. It is painful to think of any woman's "killing time" in that fashion when many of the mentally ill

or mentally retarded or persons in nursing homes would wait the entire week for the privileges of having an hour or two of her time on a Sunday afternoon.[2]

However interesting, these descriptive findings from researches are less gratifying to a volunteer than the more meaningful responses of specific individuals who appreciate what the volunteer does for them. No reward equals that of the change of expression in the eyes of a frightened child who has found a friend whom he can trust, the tone of voice of a needy student who thanks the donor for a book that he wanted but could not afford, or for the lilt in the laughter of an aging person who has found a new purpose in his life as the result of what a healthy, concerned retiree did for him.

3. *"When I associate with others whose problems are more severe than mine, my problems become less severe."* Numerous community agencies serve people who are handicapped. An outstanding example is Goodwill Industries.

*Goodwill Industries* are nonprofit, locally autonomous agencies organized to provide vocational rehabilitation services; on-the-job training; employment; and opportunities for personal growth. Goodwill's main goal is to place into or return to the competitive labor market people who are handicapped.

Through the skillful use of recognized techniques, rehabilitation, social work, life guidance, evaluation, training, and useful employment, Goodwill seeks to assist the physically handicapped, mentally disturbed, and socially disadvantaged to attain the fullest personal development of which they are capable.

The principal work function in a Goodwill organization is the repair and renovation of clothing and household articles. Usable materials for these purposes are contributed by the public. Growing numbers of businesses and industries are contributing surplus inventories and cash gifts to advance the cause of Goodwill programs.

Because the basic workshop program of a Goodwill Industries is an industrial-type operation and produces a large percentage of earned income in relationship to its operating costs, it has many characteristics of a business, with one major exception. Instead of a profit motivation, Goodwill's aim is to serve the greatest number of handicapped people. Therefore, it is essentially a health and social welfare organization.

The first Goodwill was started in Boston in 1902 by Dr. E. J. Helms, a clergyman, who applied his personal philosophy to a humanitarian need. To help the handicapped people of his community he conceived a plan of "Not Charity But a Chance" . . . a chance to work.

Since then the Goodwill Industries program has grown until it is the nation's largest network of certificated sheltered workshops serving many types of handicapped men and women, regardless of religion or ethnic origin. There are 136 Goodwill Industries in the United States and in a number of foreign countries, including Canada, South America, Mexico, Australia, India and Pakistan.

Each Goodwill Industries is headed by an executive director and governed by a board of directors. Among the many staff members employed in Goodwill Industries, some of those usually serving in technical and professional positions are: director of personnel and rehabilitation, operations director, public relations director, sales manager, controller, contracts manager, transportation and security director, occupational therapist, physical therapist, nurse, social worker, psychologist, chaplain, and accountant.

Auxiliaries to Goodwill Industries utilize the volunteer services of men and women of all ages in supplementing the work of the staff.

Goodwill Industries of America, Inc., 9200 Wisconsin Avenue, N.W., Washington, D.C. 20014, is the national organization of which the local units are voluntary members. Governed by a board of directors, it provides a variety of services to the local units— national leadership, stature and recognition, program counsel, recruitment and training of executives, public relations materials, workshops and conferences, legal and legislative assistance, accreditation, publications, and records and reports.

*Opportunity Note for Retirees:* The need for Goodwill Industries in the United States alone, however, remains only partly met. More than 200 requests for assistance in developing a Goodwill Industries Center are currently on file in the office of Goodwill Industries of America, Inc.

*Senior citizens' centers.* One of the most frequently met community facilities for socializing by retirees is the senior citizens' center, found in many population areas. These centers are likely to appeal to those aging individuals who seek help or want more social life. However, some centers appeal also to those who want to give help.

Many senior centers emphasize social affairs: dances, card games, discussions on topics of interest, money-raising ventures, and similar opportunities for the retirees to meet and associate with others. In these ways, senior centers help older people who have difficulties in meeting strangers and developing friendships with peers. Those who need this kind of senior center can develop their social skills and raise their self-esteem.

Unfortunately, some older people cannot adapt themselves to the most simple requirements for socializing. They do not want to participate but they do want to watch others enjoying themselves. Generally, interpersonal relations with contemporaries are desirable but individual differences and preferences should be respected. Indeed, the healthier and alert retirees who enjoy varied interests of their own are interested in knowing about the senior centers that may be available, but they do not care to participate in the specially invented social affairs of centers planned for those who do not have their own well-established and satisfying social relationships.

A social, handicraft, or service club which meets weekly or less often will provide some of the needs of the older person, but companionship is needed not only on a Thursday or a Friday; it is a perpetual thing.

A senior center should be open at least five days a week and the activities should be as numerous and varied as the interests of the older citizens of the community. Such a facility can be the lifeline of the older citizens and an integral part of their community life.

A center should be and in a relatively few cases is a resource for information, counseling, and referral:

> Present day trends in our fast moving society as regards the role of Information and Referral Centers offer a challenge and point up the need for a re-evaluation of our health and welfare services to the

community in terms that are realistic and of practical value to the older person.

The many services at all levels, the lack of communication between agencies, combined with the failure of agencies to inform the public of their services, create a definite need for a well developed Information and Referral program particularly as it relates to the needs of older persons.

It has become increasingly more difficult for the average citizen to know, not only what services are available, but how and where to locate the particular service which is needed.

The question then is asked, "Where do older people turn when in trouble?" and "Are they getting the services needed?" All too frequently the answer is "nowhere" and "no service."

The answer to this is an Information and Referral Service which brings older persons with problems and unmet needs into contact with agencies and individuals who can help them.[3]

*Senior Citizens' Services, Inc.* (SCS), Clearwater, Florida, is outstanding in the range of services offered and its stimulating leadership in enlisting the participation of retirees.

A small city, Springfield, Illinois, has twenty organized citizens' clubs meeting regularly. Some individual members of these over-sixty clubs belong to as many as fourteen different clubs!

The activities of centers vary from art appreciation and fashion shows to sports and town meetings on the progress of legislation and services for the elderly, but socializing without purpose appears to be the main emphasis of most of these clubs.

Too many of these clubs seem to be populated mostly by old men who feel sorry for themselves. Not only are they miserable but also they make others miserable by talking about their ailments, the degeneration of the younger generation, etc. When you find yourself in one of these gloomy atmospheres, you can do any of the following:

1. Feel miserable with them.

2. Get as far away as fast as you can, or

3. Give the bemoaners something to do that lifts them out of their morass of despair into a healthier air of usefulness.

*Junior Achievement,* 51 West 51st St., New York, N.Y. 10019. The Junior Achievement program, originally organized in 1919, gives high school students an opportunity to gain practical prebusiness experience by organizing and operating their own small-scale businesses with the guidance of volunteer advisors from business and industry.

The founders conceived the idea to provide a "learn-by-doing" experience in business for city youth comparable to the 4-H-club method of teaching fundamentals of farming to rural youth. It was incorporated as a nonprofit educational program in 1926.

Meeting one night a week during the school year, thousands of youngsters in the United States and foreign countries are increasing their knowledge of the American free-enterprise system through this unique youth program.

Each miniature company, composed of fifteen to twenty teenagers, is assisted by adult businessmen. These men, acting as advisers, are representatives of a local business concern or a civic or professional service group. Many are experts in the fields of production, business, and sales.

The aim of Junior Achievement is to help develop employers, employees, and citizens who understand the freedom, incentives, and opportunities which free enterprise and private ownership provide for the worker, owner-manager, and investor. The method used to accomplish these objectives is by providing a laboratory or workshop in which the social and economic concepts learned in the schoolroom acquire form and substance. Junior Achievement utilizes the tested method of "learning by doing." The following statistics for a recent year indicate the extent of participation:

| | |
|---|---|
| Achievers: 130,255 | Canadian provinces: 5 |
| Companies: 6,302 | Foreign countries: 6 |
| Advisers: 21,364 | Stockholders: 660,000 |
| Counseling firms: 4,500 | Companies making a profit: 80% |
| Centers: 506 | Contributors: 60,000 |
| Areas: 248 | Number of students who heard |
| States: 48 | J. A. message: 1,200,000 |

*Engineers and Scientists Committee, Inc.* (ESCI). The ESCI organization is engaged in the gathering and distribution of technical literature from engineers and scientists in the United States directly to universities and groups throughout the world for use by knowledge-hungry students, faculty members, and technical workers.

Briefly, the program is a good-will offering from sincere Americans to students, engineers and professors in underdeveloped nations, since in the developing countries a great shortage exists of basic engineering and scientific material. All too often students, and even professors, share what little they have, work around gaps in reference materials, or even do without. Thus, ESCI is knowledge by the ton as technical books and journals are shipped from several distribution points.

A basic tenet of the program is that, except where it is needed to fill gaps in the library, the technical materials sent must be placed on open tables and shelves, thus making it readily available and accessible. In most places this has represented an entirely new concept since technical material was so scarce that it was usual to have it kept under lock and key.

ESCI can usually make good use of technical books, but does not handle textbooks. This is because textbooks are required in large quantities, and recipients usually want only the latest ones.

ESCI supplies one important benefit to donors of books to people in foreign countries—its shipments are likely to reach the people and institutions addressed. This is contrary to my own experience as an individual. In past years I have sent mail shipments of books and other items to needy students of foreign countries. Unfortunately, the shipments to some countries never reached the people addressed. When I inquired about the failure, the answer I received was that in certain countries, some employees of the postal and customs services supplement their incomes by intercepting and selling books and other items shipped to their citizens.

A recent ESCI descriptive circular offers the following information:

> Literature Contributions: Offer New Life for Your Surplus Journals and Books
>
> If you possess and no longer have need for engineering, scientific, or technical literature, or possibly even a library, in any of the professions or technologies (mechanical or civil engineering, chemistry, electronics, physics, mining, or plastics—to name just a few diversified examples) or if your organization can contribute surplus printed

materials, write to one of the following individuals or organizations, telling what you have to offer:

Metropolitan New York Area:
Mr. Eric J. Sparling
124 Hilton Avenue
Garden City, N.Y. 11530

San Francisco Bay Area:
Mr. Melville W. Clark
6454 Estates Drive
Oakland, Calif. 94611

Los Angeles Area:
Mr. Harold S. Spaulding
2195 E. Mendicino Lane
Altadena, Calif. 91001

Detroit Area:
Mr. Charles Drake
c/o Detroit Edison Co.
2000 Second Avenue
Detroit, Mich. 48226

Houston Area:
Mr. George W. Laitkep
344 Chamber of Commerce Bldg.
P.O. Box 53600
Houston, Tex. 77052

Do not send any material prior to establishing contact with one of the preceding individuals; you will receive full instructions. Donors must send literature prepaid to the distribution center, unless close enough to bring the contribution personally. Literature must normally be in a good usable condition. While current material is desirable, older literature items, such as past transactions and papers, are normally also desirable. You may even know of an estate which has a technical library for disposal.

The fair market value of all material donated can be taken as a Federal tax deduction, if desired.

## Hobbies

Leisure can become terribly boresome once you have rested up. It is not the heaven that some men anticipate. Mark Twain learned this through Captain Eli Stormfield's experience in the Hereafter. He found out while sittin' on a cloud bank with a halo that got heavy, with wings he could not maneuver, and with a harp from which he could not coax more than a single tiresome tune. He discovered that such a heaven was no fit place for a grown man who requires oscillation between the opposites in his character.

Leisure alone cannot fill retirement to the full. Leisure can be made more pleasurable by means of endeavor. Even though you as a retiree have a right to some extra leisure you may benefit from what Justice Holmes emphasized in his statement about aging: "The riders in a race do not stop short when they reach the goal. There is a little finishing canter before coming to a standstill." As a retiree, some "cantering" in the form of self-rewarding work is essential before you reach the "standstill" stage.

To be psychologically beneficial, a hobby must be pursued by the individual as a challenge to him, not as a meaningless activity that merely fills time.

A hobby differs from most community volunteer activities of retirees in regard to the extent that other people are necessary to pursue the activity. A hobby is pursued for the pleasure it gives the individual hobbyist. He usually can pursue it alone, and the reactions of other people to his activity are unimportant to him. The task challenges him. It is more than "idle" pastime. It is a long-term interest that he follows because he enjoys it. It may be useful, as in building furniture for the home or houses for birds. It may be creative, as exemplified in some of the arts, or as ordinary as collecting sea shells.

A hobby, though enjoyable, does not usually provide a feeling that it is a purposeful and useful activity. To some hobbyists, purpose is not important. Nonetheless it should be noted that several studies have shown the beneficial effects on older people of doing work that is purposeful and remunerative—their well-being improves. A study at the Moosehaven, Florida, home for elderly people included control of the health factor. Measurements were made of the attitudes and adjustments of one group of participants (104 men aged sixty-five to eighty-nine) and a group of nonparticipants (67 men aged sixty-five to ninety-four).

The results indicated that participation in the meaningful work program was a definite factor in the better adjustments of the participants—the purposeful workers felt better, healthier, happier, and more useful than the nonworkers.[4] Even though these patients were not hobbyists, the study suggests that purposefulness adds benefit to the effects of the activity.

A few hobbies can have a special purpose that ties into another interest of the individual. Examples are building a walkie-talkie of one's own for use in field sports or building a tape recorder to record bird calls. Fashioning jewelry for self-adornment is also common with many women who have the jewelry-making hobby.

In some cases the attempts to find and follow new hobbies are made by an individual to overcome his own boredom. The relatively recent retiree who discovers that boredom is one of his worst problems is likely to think of turning to a hobby. A survey of the aging by Janet R. MacLean who studied a 100-people random sample of residents of Bartholomew County, Indiana, who had lived ten years or more past life expectancy at birth, showed that the greatest problems indicated by the individuals themselves were four: loneliness, boredom, financial security, and health.[5] Individuals who have these problems have been retired so long that they are not likely to turn to a hobby.

When the leisure-time activities are surveyed of representative samplings of all the aging, not just specific selected groupings such as upper-income or well-educated men, the activities pursued by most of the aging are watching television, reading (mostly newspaper), visiting and being visited by telephone or in person, gardening, and church work. Hobbies are relatively few, particularly among the aged of rural areas.

Nor do very many members of the general population develop new interests—they just continue to pursue the same old activities. Small wonder that so many retirees are unhappy. They live through too many blank days. They learn nothing new and have nothing to excite them. Many do not even read a newspaper or get mad at what somebody in Congress or the rest of the world is doing or not doing.

As a new retiree from a responsible job, you may need appreciation of the psychological benefits of a hobby. It might help to keep you from losing interest in the world and becoming a member of the "rocking-chair brigade."

An important psychological benefit of a hobby is that it can help you maintain your morale under the stress of forced boredom by keeping you interested in at least one satisfying activity. When the going really gets tough, a hobby can protect a man's mental life:

> There is the case of a fighter pilot who was grievously injured and badly burned in the crash of his plane. He spent two years in Walter Reed, the first year of which he had to remain flat on his back, scarcely permitted to lift his head from the pillow. During this time he underwent surgery to restore his features and was given extensive skin grafts all over his body. Life presented a grim prospect for that young man because in addition to the great damage done to his body and his appearance he was without relatives and had no acquaintances in the vicinity of Washington. But from the outset, with the aid of nurses and attendants, he devoted himself to hobbies. He bought a Leica camera with which he took pictures of everyone who came into his room. He set up and maintained an elaborate aquarium in which he raised tropical fish. He learned to typewrite with one hand. Every waking moment when he was not undergoing treatment he was occupied with his hobbies or in reading hobby literature. Strangers became interested in him because of his hobbies. At the end of his two years he walked out of that hospital a whole man in body and spirits. Courage, fostered and aided by his interests in life, had sustained him through a very dark period and, coupled with the friendly associations of all who helped him, salvaged a life which had seemed without hope.[6]

Some retirees flit from one hobby to another in the hope of finding one that is satisfying enough to continue over the years. Only a few of these experimenters are successful. To be meaningful, a hobby should answer a psychological need. The need is likely to be a buried yearning or a quiescent talent that has not been given sufficient opportunity of expression and development. A study of a group of men who had succeeded in developing hobbies indicated that the hobby interest had appeared earlier in life but had been pushed aside for many busy years. As often stated: "In childhood we took or did what was assigned to us, in youth we sought to make something of ourselves, in adulthood we did what our work responsibilities required, but in our maturity we are free to release our gifts without pressures from others." If creative tendencies have been deferred, retirement allows them to be expressed in ways that often enrich the personality.

Generally, one does not choose a hobby, the hobby chooses the man.

Hobbies and similar activities are likely to have little or no appeal to you at the time of your retirement unless you have had them for years before you retired. No one can pick a hobby for you and hand it to you. If you have an established interest, you will know it and turn to it as soon as you can.

Judson T. Landis, the noted sociologist, in his study of older people in Iowa, found that the unhappy retirees were three times as numerous among those without hobbies as among those with hobbies. Most of the hobbies had been developed in earlier years. Few had new hobbies.[7]

Though few persons start a hobby wholly new to them at the time of retirement, some individuals do have longstanding interests which they do not appreciate fully until they retire. You may, for example, have had a long-term curiosity about why some stars blink and others do not, how birds follow directions in migrations, how lipreaders read lips, why stocks rise and fall in price, how various religions have affected cultures, or any one of thousands of other things we see and know to a limited extent.

When we look around us and see how many people kill time by useless, inane activities such as gossiping, walking on a beach, playing canasta, and visiting night clubs, we realize that many of the young as well as the old are in need of interests that give meaning to living. Killing time and loafing have their place in the life of everyone but the healthy retiree who has no other means to enjoy his waking hours is leading too sterile a life.

Curiosity, the quest for answers to a question, a project that adds to more meaningful living should last as long as health and energy permit. If, at the time before your death, you have worked on a project that is not completed, consider yourself fortunate. Any hobby that you pursue in the spirit of the artist or the creative craftsman should enable you to function happily all the years of your life.

Ideally, an activity for retirement is one that can be made as creative, as profitable, and as purposeful as the retiree wishes. A few men have a hobby such as raising a specific variety of fruit tree or breeding a strain of domestic animal. They start their hobby program a decade or two before they expect to retire and gradually move into the desired stage planned for retirement.

Unfortunately few business and professional men can do this because their recreational activities are influenced by their main occupation—they must defer the satisfaction of their personal urges in order to do the things that give them essential social relations with clients, customers, and managerial superiors.

Genealogy is one of the most popular hobbies among retirees. Its study seems to be especially popular with individuals who have had a long-term emotional need to prove their own self-worth to themselves or to others. No doubt other deep-seated needs are involved. At any rate, the subject is so popular that adult education courses are offered by the public schools. The titles are likely to be "Your Family Tree." A helpful pamphlet, "Is That Lineage Right?" is available from the National Society of the DAR, 1776 D Street, N.W., Washington 6, D.C. The Superintendent of Documents in Washington can also advise you of printed materials.

Information on how to trace birth and death records of United States citizens who were born or died outside of the United States and birth certifications for alien children adopted by citizens may be obtained from the Government Printing Office, Washington, D.C. 20025. Ask for Catalog No. FS 2.22:N 21/4/965. Cost is nominal.

A great deal of the work involved in this hobby is done by correspondence. It is the kind of hobby that renews old ties with relatives and develops new ones. If you do not care to study your family tree as a hobby, you should at least collect all the old family photographs stored in trunks or boxes of your own attic and in the homes of relatives. Write the names and genealogical relationships on the backs of the pictures. If this is not done by you or some other older member of the family, the pictures will probably be discarded as junk. This could be unfortunate for later members of the family.

If you have no hobby, look over the available books and magazines on the subject. If you are bored with the world, you may be able to find a hobby that is meaningful to you by reviewing past activities that you enjoyed. Your examination of your own history should suggest some hobbies or similar activities that you can pursue with zest.

Certainly, an absorbing hobby can be very helpful, but for most men, its main value is in rounding out the individual's life; not in providing the one central theme or core activity in his living.

## REFERENCES

1. Study reported by Doctors Duncan Macmillan and Patricia Shaw and summarized in *Geriatric Focus,* a publication of Knoll Pharmaceutical Company, vol. 6, no. 1, p. 2.
2. Bert Kruger Smith, "How Do We Grow From Here?" Governor's Committee on Aging, Annual Conference, April 7, 1967.
3. *Design for Action: Manual for Councils on Aging,* Massachusetts Commission on Aging, 19 Milk St., Boston, Mass. 02109, p. 10.
4. Robert W. Kleemier, "The Effects of a Work Program on Adjustment Attitudes in an Aged Population," in *Second Annual Report of the Director of the Moosehaven Research Laboratory,* Moosehaven, Fla., 1951, pp. 56–64.
5. Janet R. MacLean, *Aging in Indiana: Recreation and Leisure Time,* The Indiana State Commission on the Aging and the Aged, 1962, p. 39.
6. Prepared by a Committee of Retired Army, Navy, and Air Force Officers, *Retirement from the Armed Forces,* Harrisburg, Pa.: Stackpole Books, 1957, p. 202.
7. See Harold Geist, *The Psychological Aspects of Retirement,* Springfield, Ill.: Charles C Thomas, 1968, p. 28.

# PART THREE

# A Challenging Theme—
# Growth Toward
# A Personal Philosophy

## CHAPTER ELEVEN

# Your Life Review —
# An Aid to Self-discovery

*"Make it thy business to know thyself,*
*which is the most difficult lesson in*
*the world."*
　　　　　—CERVANTES: *Don Quixote*

WHEN YOU ASSOCIATE with older retirees you will notice that some spend a lot of time sitting and thinking. They are in reminiscent postures and moods. Many are reviewing their past. If they tell you their thoughts, you will realize that their emphases are on the past rather than the future. They dwell on the past as it was and not on what the past may offer as a guide to a satisfying future.

Whenever I have discussed the life-review process with retirees, certain ones have stated: "I don't think of the past—only the future. The life-review idea offers no benefit to me." My answer is "Congratulations to a limited extent only. Many fine men whom I know review their past in order to see what it may signify for the future. The reviewing can be either a 'bottleneck' or an 'open door' to happier retirement years."

When men of varied work backgrounds and psychological patterns review their past with you, you will be surprised to find that certain individuals who should look with pride on what they have done, particularly the values they chose to live by, may be deeply depressed about themselves. You as an old friend who knows that they really led very worthy lives may try to convince them of their self-worth only to arouse their antagonism toward you. This happened when I was talking with a relative who had been retired about eight years.

I knew Henry H. throughout childhood, youth, and adulthood. As a child he was reared in an orphanage, where he missed terribly the emotional security of a happy home environment. Accordingly, when he married, he became one of the finest husbands and fathers I have ever known. He gave his family so much attention that he never took time to capitalize on his potentials for personal advancement in the business world—he was too busy with the wife, children, and friends. I esteemed him for his devotion to his family because I felt guilty about the many occasions when I should have given companionship to my family but, instead, I remained in my study to improve my professional abilities. And so when he and I were talking about his retirement, I said: "Henry, I've often thought of the splendid attention you gave your family through the years. You devoted yourself to them and their happiness. In contrast, I gave relatively more time to my career at some expense to my family life. Now that I look back and compare our choices, I think that you may have chosen the better of the two emphases." I elaborated on my statement because I meant it. The longer I talked, the more he bristled in facial expression, even though I pointed out evidence to back up my appraisal. Finally, he could contain himself no longer and burst out in angry protestations: he had made no money, gained no social prestige, and worst of all, his grandchildren had grown away from him.

Of course the grandchildren had become adolescents and adults who had interests of their own. Henry had not adapted his thinking and attention to fit their new interests. He had failed to appreciate the *distinguishing quality* that characterized his life as a person— the devotion to his family. He should have been proud of that personal quality and realized that it should be continued in his retirement but adapted to fit the new situation.

I was too late in my efforts to help Henry view his own past with proper appreciation for its distinguishing quality and the need for new self-direction in the application of the one outstanding quality in his life. In his retirement he had failed to move ahead to learn to use the one outstanding talent of his life history. He had fixated his thinking. His evaluation of his life was derogatory and wholly unfair to himself. I could not help him, but he might have helped himself earlier if he had, when still in an open-minded mental state, realized that a review of one's past can lead to a brighter later life rather than the murkiness in which he lived.

Admittedly, use of the life-review idea will not give a delightful picture to the relatively few men who have been negative-minded or maladjusted during all the years before retirement. As thoughtful individuals, we cannot expect magic to solve our retirement problems, but we can try to maintain the good patterns we learned years ago and supplement those with a few new ones. Perhaps we may even achieve the kind of enriching old age the philosophers talk about.

The benefits depend upon whether the individual in the years past, developed the strength of character and objectivity that enable him to evaluate his past life reasonably honestly. Unfortunately, far too many retirees evaluate their life in terms of only one or two criteria, such as material wealth or health. People who are happy in retirement vary tremendously in regard to their possession of things such as money. Some successful retirees are poor, some are wealthy. Some are in poor health, some are in near-perfect health. The important factor is their life style, the adjustment patterns they developed. The happy retirees have developed many behavioral patterns which enable them to cope with life's problems, whatever the problems may be. They know that retirement is mainly what a man makes it.

The life review, when made intelligently and objectively, can and often does aid in growth toward wisdom and inner strength. Unfortunately, the individual does not make his life reviews by any orderly systematic procedures. His reviews are characterized by haphazard procedures which at times have certain themes or repeated feelings of remorse, fears, and doubts as well as positive feelings of pleasure, triumph, and discovery. When he reviews his past life without use of a systematic procedure, he is too likely to merely churn over his same old ideas without gaining greater insight or improved direction in his retirement.

Systematic directed-to-the-positive reviews of one's life are possible.[1] One purpose of this chapter is to offer you constructive approaches to the making of your own reviews before you become adamantly set in your thinking about your past and its possibilities for your future.

### Benefits of thinking in terms of the adjustment concept [2]

The review of one's life can be studied systematically by means of the adjustment concept. Simply stated, this means that we use a psychological approach to understanding the individual by noting his emotional problems and the behavioral patterns he developed in adjusting to the problems. Henry H., as an example, might have understood himself more clearly if he had been aware of his orphanhood as a child and his later behavioral patterns which stemmed from those earlier problems. In retirement, he failed to recognize his one distinguishing talent as a person, a quality that he had expressed so admirably that he should have continued to live by it in his later years. Had he appreciated his own history and the potentials for enjoyable living that developed, he would have learned how to adapt his earlier familial devotion to the adult needs of his grandchildren.

The benefits from the life review as sought in this chapter are:

1. To enable you to see the good in your own life, particularly your distinguishing qualities that might be continued advantageously in your retirement. You should realize with certainty that you can continue to utilize your established personal characteristics as sources of happiness in your retirement. Most people enjoy doing what comes naturally. The possibility of having to make some

adaptations to the doing of what comes naturally should be relatively easy.

2. Concurrently, a knowledge of the dynamics of adjustment as applied to others around you will enable you to live more pleasantly with certain retirees who are difficult to live with. Of course, you and I like to think that it is easy for others to live with us, but they may not think so! At any rate, each one of us will have to associate with some aging individuals who can be very trying. The more clearly we objectify their behavior, the easier it becomes to accept them and the better our relationships can become. As a result, we can concentrate more of our thinking on how they got that way and less on the way they are. Sometimes, too, when we understand an individual, we can help him identify distinguishing qualities about himself that can lead to more happiness for him.

3. In addition to accepting others, we have to accept ourselves. This often becomes more important than accepting others. It may be harder for you to accept the recognition of the fact that you have accomplished less with your potentials than someone else accomplished with his seemingly poorer potentials. As a result, the review of your life may be too negative. This is the stage where many unhappy retirees fixate their thinking about their past history. The retirees whom you see in their meditative postures are, in more instances than we realize, trying to give their life a better evaluation than they perceived in the past. Some work very hard mentally in their effort to think of praiseworthy ways out of their denigrating appraisals of themselves.

The answer could be simple and easy for them. It becomes easy just as soon as the life reviewer can make the great discovery that he became what he is as a natural way of dealing with his problems when they arose in his situations. From all the psychological influences that enable a man to adapt himself to a situation, he chose those that were natural for him at the time. *In a beneficent life review, a man's expectations from himself are reconciled with what he did and became. He accepts himself. Then he can move forward to another stage of development.*

### Begin your thinking about a person by noting his problems

A human being, whether young or old, has problems. He is a living organism and can be understood when we visualize him as an active organism who is adjusting to his problems. It is through adjustments that his personality evolves over a period of years. This means specifically that we can gain little help from statements such as "He has an inferiority complex," or "That's a defense mechanism." Such terms are convenient for discussion purposes, but they should be used only as points of departure for our thinking about the individual's past problems and the ways he characteristically deals with them. Start your thinking with the individual's problems stemming from his home life, parents, siblings, school, work, health, spouse, or other known difficulties involved in his development as a human being in his environment.

One of the most significant lessons we learn about people and their reactions to problems is that they do not solve every problem by directly overcoming the problem—they do something else to get around it. They adjust by means of a substitute activity. This is often necessary. As an example, let us consider Bill S. (page vi). In his early childhood, he was unable to meet his parents' expectations of him. They treated him in ways which to him meant that they thought he ought to be smarter than he knew how to be. He felt that he was a failure, even though he may not have stated that feeling to his parents at the time. Actually, he was very intelligent, as proven by his later academic record, but he did not feel that way about himself in childhood. To make life more bearable for himself, he turned to others to gain their goodwill and their words of praise. In adulthood, his kindness to foreign-born students was a carry-over from his childhood. He had learned that when he could not get the goodwill he wanted from certain people, he could get it from others who needed him.

A *substitute act of positive value,* such as Bill's behavior exemplifies, may be a more logical adjustment than a direct approach. As a child, Bill could not perceive himself as a mature adult would. He did not know how to gain the goodwill of his parents by means of direct approaches to the solution of his problem.

Whenever a person cannot solve a serious problem as such, he is likely to put extra energy into a substitute activity. Not every student who fails in his school work and decides to go into business works harder in business than he did in school, but many do. A sense of failure in one field is likely to stimulate the individual to put forth extra effort in another field. This is the usual psychological source of what we call "good motivation." Here are several examples of positive substitute adjustments.

## COMPENSATORY MECHANISMS

When we study the lives of famous men and women, we are likely to find that some of their psychological assets were their positive adjustments to severe handicaps. The important point for us to keep in mind is not that a man has problems or failures but how he adjusts to his problems to gain personal adequacy and whether his adjustments have value for others as well as satisfaction for himself.

The great men of the world have had all kinds of personal problems—some severe, some minor. Many factors entered into their success—too many for us to try to unravel here. The nature of their handicaps is less important than the direction of the effort which took place in the adjustments to their handicaps. Certainly, many of life's biggest prizes go to those who have been challenged by physical or mental handicaps, real or imaginary.

Every person has some defects and deficiencies, and so we expect him to have an urge to feel superior or at least adequate in one or more respects. Most men attain the satisfaction of these psychological needs through their work as we see it exemplified in the lives of the many happy employees, employers, executives, professional men, and other workers whom we meet every day.

Each man seeks to feel worthwhile in his estimation of himself. If he is frustrated in the attainment of his goals by direct action regarding the barriers in his way, he will attack his problem in indirect ways. Inferiority is difficult to endure. Superiority, or at least a sense of adequacy, must be achieved. A sense of failure, guilt, or shame is hard to accept, in youth and in old age.

Boys who cannot attain satisfaction in scholarship may do so on the athletic field. Girls who do not find their personal appearance attractive may become good students. The employee who feels disgraced because his father has been convicted as a criminal may achieve satisfaction by taking up art, athletics, church work, stamp collecting, or by inventing new machinery.

The man who goes into the business world and finds that he is not a good businessman can substitute for that lack of attainment the satisfactions of church work and fraternal activities. Of course, the normal individual takes some interest in his community, his home, and other phases of good citizenship but, if he remains in business and makes his outside activities a heavy sideline, a digression from the use of his best potentials and opportunities, he shows that he is not really well-adjusted to his job. He is seeking compensation for some lack that he feels within himself. If he enjoys the compensatory activity and views it as worthy of his potentials, he will view his life happily when he reaches retirement. And he will continue the activity either as an employee or as a volunteer in a service organization. (See Chapter 10.)

### AN "IMPROVE-THE-WORLD" TENDENCY

This may be considered as an aspect of compensatory behavior or as having a distinct pattern of its own. At any rate, a person who finds himself in a predicament because his life is unsatisfying is likely to try to deal with his own problem by attempting to alleviate the predicaments of others. The student who plans to become a research scientist and then later finds that he cannot do so may adjust himself by helping others who are in a difficulty similar to his. This type of adjustment is, perhaps, one of the most common psychological origins of the professional adviser. Teachers and executives who find their work unsatisfying or difficult often enter the advisory field as counselors, college deans, assistants to principals, welfare workers, or personnel men. This kind of adjustment is both psychologically sound and socially desirable. When people make comments about a psychologist or a personnel man to the effect that he is trying to help others make better adjustments because he really is trying to help himself make better adjustments, the comments are complimentary. The adjustment is beneficial to both the advised and the adviser. Growth as a person should be reciprocal in a man's relations with others.

Of course the urge to improve the situations of others may be carried too far. If the person who makes such an adjustment has had an intensely unpleasant experience in connection with his problem, he may develop an extreme form of the Messiah complex—the radical reformer's tendency. The radical's driving wishes are to destroy all people and features connected with the hated situation. He wants a new educational system, or a new economic order, or a new religion, or even an entirely new civilization, and he wants it immediately!

As a result of his insistence on immediate revolution rather than constructive evolution, he lives a life of unhappy frustrations. He differs psychologically from the majority of retirees who are essentially constructively inclined and willing to work and wait for improvements. However, if you will study very many life reviews of the elderly, you will find some individuals whose inner emotional life is dominated by hatreds that originated in childhood. Do not be surprised, therefore, when you find yourself listening to an eighty-five-year-old who recounts with bitterness the mistreatment he suffered when he was ten years of age. The intervening seventy-five years may or may not have brought feelings of forgiveness toward the offenders.

Interestingly, too, an elderly person may recount with intense feelings a misdeed of his own for which he has not as yet forgiven himself. In some cases, the feelings have been directed against institutions or persons who somehow symbolize the detested characteristic of the hater. This kind of person is likely to demand quick reforms of the institutions or people involved in the adjustment mechanism. The more you study the fanatical reformers, the more you are likely to discover that most of their hatreds really stemmed from their abhorrence of inadmissible characteristics and tendencies within and concerning themselves. (Is it any wonder that we have many unhappy protesters today who want to destroy rather than build?)

Happily, too, you will find many examples of truly mature men and women, those who earned their serenity through the kind of insight about themselves which George Bernard Shaw stated so well: "The world's best reformers are those who begin with themselves."

Fanatical reformers who have been analyzed are likely to reveal origins of fanaticism that occurred in childhood. They never learned that the problem of an unhappy childhood is not especially unusual nor very serious, but the method of adjustment may be very serious in its effects on happiness in adulthood and aging.

**IDENTIFICATION**

Identification means that the individual *feels* that temporarily "he becomes another person" and behaves as if he were the person with whom he has this tie. In some cases, he feels that he is part of the purpose of a person or an institution. The process is one of feeling rather than of intellect. (It should not be confused with "identity," the individual's psychological definition of himself.)

The retiree who watches a typical western play on television identifies himself with the hero, fights his battles, endures his hardships, conquers the villain, and finally marries the heroine. He is not, for the time being, a mere observer or onlooker but is the admired character in the picture or the play, psychologically speaking. Such a person makes many incipient movements that give reality to his imaginary acting. To note incipient movements during identification, observe the sports fan who watches a football game—he gives the player who is carrying the ball many a vigorous "shove" from his seat. For the moment the spectator carries the ball. He has identified himself with one of the teams and is mentally doing the same things that "his" team is trying to do.

An individual may also identify himself with his material possessions, as exemplified by the housewife who cleans and protects her home so well that it becomes uncomfortable to others. The older the person, the more likely he is to identify with possessions such as the house, clothing, automobile, and office desk. When he fusses over them and their care needlessly, he may be gaining feelings of security or superiority.

Many retirees cling to objects that symbolize superiority. If they cannot feel superior as a result of recognized achievements, they may collect around themselves objects that symbolize achievement.

Positive identification is one of human nature's most valuable means of making wholesome adjustments. It is present in the life of every well-balanced personality, and it occurs more often than you realize.

Identification is the important fundamental of a happy married life. Ideally and typically, two people marry, not mainly for sexual gratification, but for more complete identification of their personalities. In the course of history, society has developed many institutions in order to enable its members to identify themselves with satisfying personalities. In addition to marriage, we have the church, which aims to have the individual identify himself with the Cosmic Power.

The good citizen identifies himself with his community and his nation. The well-adjusted retiree identifies himself with other retirees, adapts himself to them, and learns from them—he knows that the more he resents the company of retirees, the greater his difficulties in adjusting to his own retirement.

The father image is a common form of identification. You very probably are or have been a father image to certain children and young people who know you. This image that you have to them may be unrecognized by you, but it is probably more influential to several individuals than you suspect. You can accentuate it, of course, by associating with children and young people, by trying to understand them, and by exchanging ideas of interest to them. (See Chapter 6.)

The way a retiree adjusts to retirement is important to his children. A man's children project themselves into their own future role of retirement as exemplified by their parent who has retired.

## Substitute activities that are usually
## of negative value

As you have undoubtedly observed in the life history of individuals, a person does not always adjust to a problem by doing something that has positive values, such as learning how to gain the goodwill of others. It may be easier for him to adopt a substitute activity of negative value.

The person who chooses to make a negative value or other *evasive* adjustment weakens himself for the next problem. His ability has been lessened. The evasive experience has weakened his personality.

Obviously, no person makes direct intelligent adjustments to *every* problem. Everyone uses evasion and retreat at times, but the strong personality tends to use the positive forms habitually, and the poorly adjusted man tends to use the negative or evasive forms in dealing with his problems.

If a given adjustment pattern is once firmly established, it is easily repeated in dealing with the same or related problems. Adjustments begin very early in life and are made every day until the end of life. Each time we deal with a problem, great or small, we tend to contribute toward or detract from our effectiveness in dealing with new problems. This means that the adaptable man is more likely to enjoy retirement than the individual who fixates his ways of living by clinging to the use of too many evasive forms of adjustment.

An example in business of adjustment by evasion is the cashier who steals money from the cash register. Fundamentally, stealing is wrong; not because of the laws against it, but because it weakens the individual psychologically for dealing with future situations. This is a major criterion of the positive or negative values of an act of adjustment: Does it strengthen or weaken the individual for dealing with future problems? Brief descriptions of weakening adjustments, all of which are found among retirees, follow.

## DEFENSE MECHANISM

The individual who has failed to develop adjustment habits that enable him to feel at home in his social situations may resort to excessively aggressive conduct and make himself a nuisance to others. More typically, however, he acquires habits of social inferiority. He reacts with pronounced fear responses to many social situations. His mannerisms of inferiority enable him to avoid much competition and criticism. The pattern of overt behavior of social inferiority is indicated by the usual symptoms: a tendency to derogate others, to rationalize inadequacies, seclusiveness, and over-susceptibility to flattery.

The defensive man is a lonely person and can be "reached" only when he is in circumstances where he feels secure from criticism. In previous generations, many of these dignified gentlemen held executive jobs. Today, if circumstances push them into executive positions, they are likely to be poor leaders. Modern business requires the ability to give and take criticism without excessive defensiveness. Modern retirement also requires the same kind of emotional maturity.

## REGRESSION

We occasionally meet the man who acts and dresses in the manner of several decades ago. We have also known the type of adult who talks of the "good old days when boys were gentlemanly and girls were virtuous." Such expressions may mean that he is simply giving evidence of having partly outlived his era. The problems of his present are too great for him to solve satisfactorily, and he regresses mentally to a former happier state when life was easier for him.

The employee who once had a good job but lost it may make an adjustment by mentally living in that former happy state, or he may react to his present situation in an aggressive manner and look toward the future rather than the past. *Psychologically, old age sets in just as soon as the past appears to be more pleasant than the present and the future.* (The only time when a man is justified in talking about the good old days is at his fiftieth class reunion!) An easy way to test the extent of your tendency toward regression is to ask yourself whether you admire the young people of today or whether you would prefer them to be as they were when you were young, say fifty years ago. A survey made by Judson T. Landis of the aged in Iowa showed that those who thought the world was better off fifty years before they were questioned were not as well adjusted as those who felt that the country was better off at the time they were interviewed.[3]

Children as well as adults regress. A child, for example, who must adjust to the arrival of a new infant in the home may regress by losing previously well-established toilet habits or by crying a great deal. Parents who do not recognize the meaning of the regressions are apt to scold or punish the child. Instead, the understanding parents will show the child that he is wanted and loved.

Regression to childish mannerisms, *infantilism*, is exceedingly common. The average grown-up shows some infantilism by behavior such as temper tantrums, pouting, dawdling, clowning to attract attention, making grimaces, or having noisy nasal and throat habits. These childish mannerisms are so common and meaningful that we can often recognize what a maladjusted person's behavior means if we say to ourselves: "What would the person's behavior signify if it were performed by a four-year-old child?"

Ever notice how some old people expect others to wait on them hand and foot, to cater to their wishes, to care for them? They have regressed toward infancy.

## RIGIDITY

Rigidity can be defined as a pervasive personality trait that restricts the range of behavior. It is protective. The rigid individual avoids many problems, particularly conflicts, by ignoring them—he lives in a world of "blacks" and "whites," no "grays." He holds strictly to one philosophy, set of ethical principles, or dogma. His behavior is usually quite predictable, but he is likely to have little leadership ability, is socially introverted, lacking in social skills, anxious, and unoriginal.[4]

In the case of retirees, to cope successfully with the problems of retirement usually calls for flexibility in action patterns. However, some individuals with rigid styles of life get along rather well in retirement, but they do it by avoiding situations that require flexibility. If life forces them to deal with very unpleasant situations, situations to which a less rigid person might adapt himself, the rigidly patterned person is likely to suffer some kind of mental breakdown.

The aging individual who has had an accident while driving may have his license taken away. If he is well-adjusted and objective he accepts the decision of the examiner who withholds the license. He uses buses and taxis. If, however, he cannot change his fixed ideas, he gripes to others about it, seeks their pity, and exploits their goodwill by expecting them to inconvenience themselves in order to transport him when he happens to expect their adaptation to his wishes.

An adaptable, well-adjusted man is willing to admit his failures and does not feel that he has compromised his own integrity or worth. It is the emotionally immature fellow who cannot accept anything less than complete surrender from others. It is well, therefore, to try to help the rigid man to feel pleased with himself by showing him that you admire him for certain qualities and that he really does not need the concession he insists upon having—you like him as he is.

Most of the persons who develop these fixed ideas lead so routine or narrow a life that they lack practice in making the little daily adjustments which we learn to make when we have learned how to interpret deviant behavior. Retirees who withdraw into a smaller world of their own become quite inflexible. Any effort on their part to become more flexible is likely to be a rather feeble attempt, as exemplified in a report of a speaker who recommended to an afternoon group of golden-agers how they might keep themselves flexible. After her speech one timid little woman came up and said: "Just for the devil of it, I'm going to cook my potato in a different pot tonight!" [5]

Rigidities and fixed ideas among retirees are quite common. Perhaps it would be well for us to organize a number of old men's clubs similar to the one in London which proclaims as its motto: "Older and bolder." The rules of the club require that every year all members above the age of fifty shall undertake some enterprise in which their life, their fortune, or their reputation is at stake! [6]

## PROJECTION

The process of ascribing to another person or institution the burden of our own repressions is commonly referred to as projection. The person who perceives in other people the traits and motives which he cannot admit in himself is probably using the mechanism of projection.

The fanatical reformer and chronic accuser are often unpopular among intelligent people. If one has a normal desire to improve the world, he will do it in a quiet and tactful manner rather than by beating his chest and crying his aims from the housetops.

Business men, too, exhibit adjustments by projection. The man who fails in business does not, as a rule, blame himself, but imputes his losses to "powerful competitors" or governmental interference.

The retiree whose old work habits have been broken may develop a tendency to blame a person incidental to the problem situation, such as his wife. If, before retirement, he rushed to work at a specific time each workday morning, he may find that he gets jittery each morning at that time. Somebody or something must be blamed for his emotional disturbance. The wife is usually a handy target for the feelings of such mild aggressions.

## HOSTILITY AND AGGRESSION

The hostile person is one who expresses aggressive behavior or attitudes toward others and reacts to minor frustration, social restrictions, and other people with spiteful anger.[7]

Feelings of hostility have many forms. Examples are resentment, suspicion, negativism, assault, verbal hostility, and guilt. Some of these are attitudinal, others have a "motor" component.[8]

The self-righteous person who has refused to yield to temptation is likely to be especially severe in his reactions to those who have yielded.

In the case of certain retirees, hostilities and attention-getting urges are satisfied by arrogance and by an authoritative manner toward everyone within range of the voice. Actually, the typical hostile man suffers from ego-weakness and makes unrealistic self-appraisals. We even see instances where the individual cannot select a suitable target for his hostility and then turns his aggressions against himself.

## ISOLATION, WITHDRAWAL, ESCAPE

Of course, one of the universally used methods of adjustment to unpleasant situations is withdrawal or escape. The individual simply refuses to deal with the problem directly. He treats it as though it did not exist. Or, if that is not possible, he may escape from it temporarily by concentrating his thinking on some other activity such as reading "escape" literature. If that kind of activity is not attractive to him, he can resort to the use of tranquilizing drugs.

The fact that so large a proportion of people turn to these avoidance types of adjustment indicates that some need release from their problems even though the respite may be for short periods of time only. Then too, those who have developed the tendency toward using the strengthening adjustments of the positive variety may find that their occasional *escape from* one kind of situation leads to an *escape into* a new and developmental interest. Certainly, not all adjustments by fantasy are detrimental to mental health. Daydreaming is a helpful, universally used mental activity employed by people of all ages to explore a wide variety of perspectives and courses of action. Fantasy also helps us deal with problems which cannot be solved directly, as exemplified by a study of marital dissatisfaction. Some marriage partners deal with their dissatisfactions by fantasy rather than real involvement.[9]

## Utilizing the adjustment concept

*Psychological insight and skill are applied whenever* an insightful friend feels with, thinks with, and works with associates who have disturbing emotional problems. The discerning friend may not be able to give a technical psychological name to a person's inappropriate adjustment, but if he recognizes the influence of a bothersome problem, notes the kind of evasive adjustment being made, and then instills confidence in the friend by showing him the possible direct-intelligent methods, the individual may be able to improve his behavior.

If you should happen to associate with or meet a very aged person whose mind wanders and who talks as though he were in a dream, listen for clues to what the talk may signify about the difficulties and pleasures in his life history. As an alert listener you can learn much from the ramblings of a person. That is how physicians and psychiatrists often learn how to be helpful to a patient. If you yourself have achieved a high level of maturity, you will be able to perceive many aging people with insight and helpful understanding.

Bear in mind that the unusual and troublesome behavior of certain older people should arouse in us a desire to become to them a source of strength and reassurance. To an older person who is confused, you can give much protective understanding by your voice and manner.

The adjustment concept causes us to recognize that we should not think of a person as *being* this or that—as, for example, being mean, conceited, or sarcastic when he deals with others. He *is not* mean, conceited, or sarcastic, but he *uses* meanness, conceit, or sarcasm when dealing with another person. He acquired these habit patterns because he did not learn to use more positive adjustment patterns when dealing with other people.

## CAN WE MODIFY OUR OWN ADJUSTMENT PATTERNS IN THE LATER YEARS?

Of course the patterns developed in the early years tend to persist into old age but that does not mean we cannot in our mature years change or improve the established patterns. Many individuals do bring about significant modifications.

The adjustment concept can be an important working tool in dealing with ourselves as well as with others. When, for example, a friend threatens to express his hostilities in overt action against someone whom he hates, you may say: "Sure, you can give him hell, and you'll feel better right after you've done it, but what is the effect going to be on you as a man? I've done that kind of thing, too, but the after-effects on me were bad—I decided I hadn't really handled it in a way that made me feel better as a man. So, think it over before you act, not afterward—then it will be too late." In this instance as well as in many others, you and I are counseling ourselves, aren't we?

Many men have attained the kind of growth characterized by the intelligently directed adjustments even though they have never studied academic psychology. The psychologists do not bring about good adjustments—they can only clarify for others the kinds of adjustments that have been made and, sometimes, they can suggest more suitable behavior for others as well as for themselves.

## To make the reviews of your life beneficial

As an adult of the retirement level of maturity you have developed a lot of insight into why individuals do what they do. You also understand yourself better than you did in your youth. You now understand why you just had to express certain urges that led to important activities. You can see how you happened to follow your work career. You can recognize how you developed certain values.

Let's refer to Bill and Henry as mentioned on pages 196 and 200 and to their use as examples 1 and 2 of the table on page 214. How much happier they might have been in retirement if they had objectified the choices they had made and how they happened to make them. Each should have recognized the distinguishing qualities of his life and continued to use those splendid adjustment tendencies. Each should have adapted himself to the new requirements at the time of retirement. Bill should have appreciated the friendliness of the hundreds of men and women scattered throughout the world and corresponded with them. He might have been an "ambassador of goodwill" instead of an embittered old man. Henry should have continued to express his interest in his grandchildren, even though it would have been necessary to learn the grown-up emotional needs of the young people.

**EXAMPLES OF THE THINKING IN SEVEN LIFE REVIEWS**

| The problem the individual had | The good adjustment that was made | (A poor adjustment that might have been made) | Distinguishing qualities as aids to a happy retirement |
|---|---|---|---|
| 1. Example of Bill S., p. vi. Was unable to meet the expectations of certain persons whose good will he very much wanted. | Gave friendship and inspiration to others who were friendless in a land that was strange to them | (Might have adopted an air of superiority to the persons whose good will he could not gain to the extent he desired) | Hundreds of men and women of other countries think kindly of Bill and wish that he would write to them. He should. |
| 2. Example of Henry H., p. 196. Reared in orphanage, he missed terribly the emotional security of a normal home environment. | He gave his family so much attention that he had little desire or time for advancement in his work. | (Might have become a delinquent who hated other people, particularly those who were enjoying a good home environment) | All his children and grandchildren became fine adults—millions of fathers wish they had done as well. Henry should have continued his fine relationships. |
| 3. "My health has been poor for years." | "I just endured the pain— rarely mentioned it except to the family physician." | (Might have become a chronic invalid, a burdensome whiner who felt sorry for himself) | People treat him in a normal manner. He inspires others who are ill to endure their illnesses with less suffering. |
| 4. "I do not hear well." | "I simply ask friends to speak louder, and I developed interests that do not require good hearing." | (Might have become very suspicious and sensitive as found on the part of some deaf people) | His partial deafness has stimulated him to enjoy the world of sight. He teaches others how to observe more intelligently. |

| | | | |
|---|---|---|---|
| 5. "I never was a good student, but I had to associate with good students of my family." | "I got pleasure from associating with people, became a salesman, and later an executive in marketing." | (Might have felt very inferior, become defensive by finding fault with others to build up his ego) | He discovered that developing men offers rewards as great as academic knowledge. Men who worked for him know him as a fine coach and return for his counsel in his retirement. |
| 6. "I was unable to make friends easily." | "I studied the social sciences and business— became a personnel man." | (Might have developed show-off behavior or withdrawn to avoid social contacts) | He represented employees to management, as well as management to employees. He is still sought as an adviser. |
| 7. "I became a good engineer, I hope, but never became a member of management or had a title." | "I studied the technologies involved in my work and learned to enjoy life through the sciences." | (Might have become very agreeable and ingratiating or an office politician to gain personal popularity) | He became an authority in his field and earned the profound respect of his associates—to them, he is above the need of a title. They still come to him for scientific counsel. |

The table on pages 214 to 215 lists briefly the adjustment history of two unhappy retirees and five whose retirement became happy because they continued to function in the commendable ways they knew best.

When you discuss with individual retirees their life histories you will find that the things of which they are most proud vary with the occupational level. Business executives talk about their achievements in improving organizational structures, reducing costs, and increasing profits. Employees of the factory talk about their job accomplishments and particularly the number of companies that were anxious to hire them when they retired. Professional workers talk about their innovations and contributions. Surprisingly, however, the more mature of all categories also express pride in what might be called by-product or character-quality satisfactions as indicated in these examples:

"I remained loyal to fundamentally sound principles in certain situations when others vacillated or surrendered to expedience."

"I was loyal to the men and the company for whom I worked—I always treated them as I would have wanted to be treated."

"I gave to others lifts in their morale when they needed emotional support."

"I encouraged some young people when they were in doubt as to their potentials, and they proved themselves later."

"I was a member of a team that had heavy responsibilities, and I performed my part in the team effort in ways that pleased me as well as others."

The man who underrates his record and himself in reviewing his past can invariably discover, in an objective life review, that many of the by-product satisfactions that come to him are more delightful than the ways of living he previously imagined he should have chosen. Pride in self is more important than conventional success. If he appreciates the pleasant by-product satisfactions, he can gain much benefit, especially increased pride, from his reviews of his life history as indicated in the last column of the table.

A man's life review deals with his past. Its purpose is to help him gain release from fixed ideas that may handicap his thinking and to have him recognize his resources for happiness in retirement. A life review should lead to the kind of objectivity needed in the development of a personal philosophy.

A personal philosophy must grow out of the individual's past reactions, mostly feelings, toward his everyday experiences. In the next chapter we shall present examples of everyday experiences that can contribute to meanings for living in the present and the future.

Of course the examples and the points of view presented in the remaining chapters of this book are not the only ones that can provide a frame of reference of the larger whole of which a man can perceive himself a part. As Otto Pollak [10] and other observers have noted, the larger whole may be a charitable enterprise, service to a category of people, an educational movement, or the interpreting of significant aspects of the universe. The specific frame of reference is not important—the extent of the individual's *engrossment*,[11] as some researchers call it, is very important.

# REFERENCES

1. The life review as a mental process of the aging has been studied by several researchers in the clinical fields. An especially illuminating description of its importance has been published in an article by Robert N. Butler, "The Life Review: An Interpretation of Reminiscence in the Aged," *Psychiatry*, Vol. 26, pp. 65–76, 1963. Another good reference for the reader who wishes to study the life review is Robert R. Kastenbaum, *New Thoughts on Old Age*, New York: Springer Publishing Company, Inc., 1964, chap. 20 and references at end of that chapter.

2. The adjustment concept has been treated in numerous books and articles. If you would like to read a more comprehensive treatment of the topic as mentioned in this chapter, you can do so in Harry W. Hepner, *Psychology Applied to Life and Work*, 4th ed., Englewood Cliffs, N.J.: Prentice-Hall, Inc., 1966, chaps. 2–8.

3. See Elon H. Moore and Gordon F. Streib (eds.), *The Nature of Retirement*, New York: The Macmillan Company, 1959, p. 86.

4. K. Warner Schaie, "Differences in Some Personal Characteristics of 'Rigid' and 'Flexible' Individuals," *Journal of Clinical Psychology*, vol. 14, 1958, pp. 11–14.

5. "The Added Years—A Major Challenge of Our Time," Report of the New

York State Committee of One Hundred for the 1961 White House Conference on Aging, Nov. 1, 1960. Reported by Belle Boone Beard.

6. See A. L. Vischer, *On Growing Old,* translated from the German by Gerald Onn, Boston: Houghton Mifflin Company, 1967, p. 111.

7. K. Edward Renner, Brendan A. Maher and Donald T. Campbell, "The Validity of a Method for Scoring Sentence Completion Responses for Anxiety, Dependency, and Hostility," *Journal of Applied Psychology,* August, 1962, p. 286.

8. Arnold H. Buss and Ann Durkee, "An Inventory for Assessing Different Kinds of Hostility," *Journal of Consulting Psychology,* vol. 21, 1957, pp. 343–349.

9. See Gerhard Neubeck and Vera M. Schletzer, "A Study of Extramarital Relationships," *Marriage and Family Living,* vol. 24, no. 3, pp. 279–281, 1962.

10. Otto Pollak, *Positive Experience in Retirement* (monograph), Homewood, Ill.: Richard D. Irwin, Inc., 1957, p. 2.

11. See report on researches by Robert Kastenbaum, "Life Perspective Difficult with Aging," *Aging in Michigan,* Newsletter of the Michigan Commission on Aging, Sept., 1968, p. 7.

## CHAPTER TWELVE

# New Meanings from Everyday Experiences

*"I pray that we may never be so blind*
*that our small world is all the world we see;*
*Or so supremely satisfied that what we are*
*Is all we feel we ever want to be."*
—BIRDSALL OTIS EDEY [1]

As THE RETIREMENT YEARS move you onward, the more likely you are to wake up each morning and say to yourself: "Ah, a gift from heaven! How fortunate to have another day to enjoy!" Men who reach an age when they feel they belong to those who are especially privileged to be among the living; "living on borrowed time," they tend to acquire a special inner self-confidence and perspective.[2] But the full benefits of this self-confidence and per-spective, so freely available to the mentally alert retiree, will not come automatically with increased age—receptivity must be de-veloped. And when you study the older people whom you meet, you will note that those who are attaining self-fulfillment have developed extra receptivity to receive these benefits.

This supernal privilege puts a good deal of responsibility on you as you grow older. If you want to gain optimum benefit from the daily opportunity before you, you will need some preparation for it.

Some of the preparation needed may have been achieved in the distinguishing qualities you developed before retirement, as described in the preceding chapter. The use of these special qualities will give you much satisfaction, but their full use is not usually feasible for most men whose work life took place in a modern corporation. As stated in Chapter 1, page 14, "In the years on his job a man becomes a member of a network of pleasant human relations in an organization." And, as mentioned in the quotation from Harold R. Hall, the employee "is a respected and honored member of his business group" before retirement.

As soon as a man retires from a corporation he is no longer a member of a network of work relations in an organizational structure of an important group. This means that even though he developed some worthy distinguishing qualities before retirement, after retirement he is not a member of an active functional network in which he can express his distinguishing qualities. To appreciate the problem more clearly, look at the work history and unique personal quality listed for each of the men numbered 5, 6, and 7 of the table on page 215. Each one can function only as a nonmember and then only a fraction of his time. This means that too much spare time is available to most retirees of ability who have become accustomed to the tempo of modern business. In addition to those from business, many retirees from other occupational fields have an equally troublesome spare-time problem.

As you may have observed, it is necessary for many able retirees to utilize a large share of their time by means of a new interest, preferably one of a creative nature. The reason for recommending a creative interest is that most high-grade retirees want to continue their growth as a person after they retire. And growth as a person can come about only when a man adds to what he already knows and can do. New ways of perceiving and thinking, practiced every day, are just as essential to psychological expansion in retirement as in the work years.

This does not imply that every retiree should take formal educational courses or read a lot of books in the hope of becoming a so-called creative thinker. Rather, it should be recognized that many growth-minded men devote some of the thinking of their later years to their interpretation of what life is all about. Each man wants to decide for himself life's significant meanings. In retirement, some of his available time can be productively invested in the quest for a personal philosophy. For the intelligent retiree, an appropriate way to begin the quest is to look to the immediate environment for stimulation.

The environment offers you much fruitful stimulation, even though you have been living in it for many years. It probably gives you pleasant feelings of comfort and security. But it also offers you unappreciated stimuli for imagination. As the philosopher Santayana and others have pointed out: "In the human being, imagination is more fundamental than perception."

Now that your retirement has given you extra time to observe objects and events and to think about them, you realize more fully that objects and events of today can have meanings which they did not have for you in the earlier years. Let us take a very simple example—you observe a woman who is knitting. In the earlier years, you probably said to yourself that her knitting required considerable rhythmic accuracy and skill and that the activity seemed to give her the kind of satisfaction that a man gets from golfing or sailing. In the later years, you are more likely to think that her activity will enable her to give a token of her esteem to someone whom she loves —that her urge to do something for others is an age-old inner drive of womanhood at its best.

The important recognition in your maturity is that objects and activities can have meanings more important than or in addition to those of self-satisfaction, recreation, or usefulness. They can be perceived in terms of greater values as indicated by their *agelessness,* their reappearance in generation after generation. You appreciate more fully that you can perceive ordinary objects and events in the same ways some artists and philosophers perceive them.

People in ages past enjoyed many of the same kinds of experiences that you now enjoy and which people in ages to come will also enjoy. Those individuals of past eras who noted the patterns in the behavior of people and in nature asked themselves questions of the kinds that you ask yourself. This recognition of the ongoingness in your life and in the lives of other thoughtful men will give exaltation to your feelings, especially when you feel that you have learned to live in the spirit of meditative men at their very best.

In the practice of this process, you will also sense that you are attaining a satisfying inner growth that leads to the serenity and wisdom which men have had to earn for themselves throughout the history of civilized man. You will realize that this enrichment to your living is not something that has happened to you alone, nor have you been set aside from other men. Instead, you will think of this inner growth as that which comes to all men everywhere when they search for interpretations of daily experiences.

They ask themselves numerous questions about what they see and experience. Their self-questioning brings forth interpretations which do not usually occur in the early years of adulthood. Now that you have reached the retirement stage, you have a background of experiences that enable you to ask yourself more thought-provoking questions than you could have asked years ago. This is one of the best assets of maturity, because it enables you to gain richer meanings from current and future experiences.

## REFERENCES

1. From "My Prayer" reprinted by permission from *Builders*, Poems by Birdsall Otis Edey (published 1940 by Girl Scouts of America). The poem, written in 1936, was dedicated to Lou Henry (Mrs. Herbert) Hoover, who had succeeded Mrs. Edey as President of the Girl Scouts.
2. Harold Dwight Lasswell, *Power and Personality*, New York: W. W. Norton & Company, Inc., 1948, p. 52. Dr. Lasswell, trained in psychoanalysis and now a professor of law and political science at Yale University, described, in part, the effects of infantile paralysis on Franklin D. Roosevelt: "Like many men who escape death, he achieved the inner self-confidence and perspective of one who lives 'on borrowed time.'"

# Ageless Experiences

The examples that follow will suggest how an individual can develop significant perspectives and interpretations from everyday objects and events, meanings he may not have had time to appreciate before retirement. Of course the aspects and thoughts presented here are not the only ones appropriate to the described experiences that follow. You will add to and improve on these examples in ways that are especially meaningful to you.

These examples have not been arranged in any specific order but rather as a sequence of simple experiences that might be common to the lives of many retirees. Any one or more of the described experiences could be noted in the course of any day, depending upon the mood of the individual and his attitude toward stimuli at the moment.

The events and the locale chosen are incidental —the kinds of meanings perceived and the questions asked are the significant parts of the experience.

*You walk to a dock on a misty morning. The fog intrigues you by the mysteries which it seems to hide from you. When it lifts, the world may be revealed to you in some new ways, and you may find yourself beckoned to enjoy a new adventure. Perhaps new knowledge and clearer insights may be yours, and you will gain a new hope for the future? Through the ages men have waited for fogs to lift from within their minds, and they have felt upsurges of hope for the greater insight that somehow seems to be hidden from them. Would they be happier if they had complete knowledge of everything they hoped to know? Or is the quest more exciting than the completed achievement?*

Frederic Lewis

When you walk on a beach, you note that the windblown sands are arranged in wave-like formations. You imagine that men of past centuries have walked over similar patterns but never noticed them nor wondered how they came about. You suspect that others in centuries to come will be equally unobserving. And then you wonder what basic intelligence in the universe arranges the patterns so beautifully. What universal influence and physical forces produce these definite patterns? Why do some men walk over these formations and never see any significance in the patterns or wonder what they may signify for the observer?

H. Armstrong Roberts

*A cobweb in the morning dew catches your attention. The pattern before you traces a finery more delicate than that of the laces made by men. How beautiful! As patterns that reveal a Greater Mind in the universe, they have a significance that enriches the day. And then you think of the housewife who notes cobwebs, but she is likely to think of them as added chores. That realization causes you to wonder whether almost every boring task we perform really offers us special meanings to enjoy if only we bring to the task a mind that is sufficiently alert to note the significance in patterns around us. Do you think it is true, as some claim, that to the mentally alert there are no routines? To what extent can a person learn to perform boring tasks by perceiving larger meanings?*

Philip Gendreau

*A flight of birds passes overhead. You note their patterned flying formations, characteristic of the species. The orderliness and gracefulness are beautiful to see. You think also of their patterns in yearly migrations. Men have observed these patterns for centuries and wondered what intelligence has provided the guiding mechanisms that direct them on thousand-mile courses, courses which man has been able to chart only in part?*

Philip Gendreau

Some leaves on the ground attract your attention.
They have patterns that are characteristic of
their species, just as characteristic as the flights
of various species of birds. As you examine
the numerous patterns in nature around you,
new meanings come to you from the simple
experiences. You wonder how many other men
perceive the same patterns and ask themselves
the same questions that you ask yourself?
You think of the many generations of men and
women who have cut an apple in two, but noted
no characteristic arrangement of the seeds.
If only men will see them, meaningful patterns
are everywhere. Would increased perceptiveness
of the patterns in the world around a person
increase his sense of awe of the universe?

You doubtless have noticed trees and other plants of your area. Perhaps gardening is one of your spare-time interests. If you will paste a leaf or two of a favorite species in this space, you can study the pattern at your leisure. Specimens of the leaves of two favorite varieties of the same species will enable you to note the differences for future identification.

*A wind-tossed tree on a hill shows by its shape
that it has weathered fierce winds. Somehow
it has adapted to adverse conditions. Then you
realize that strength of character achieved
through adversities seems to be an attribute of
plants as well as of human beings. The tree's firm
roots were important in its survival. Perhaps
you think that if we as individuals cling to firmly
rooted values through adversities, we too can
survive the storms of life more easily. And the
next time you see an old man with gnarled
hands, deep furrows in the brow, wrinkles that
portray resolute purpose, and the light of
inner pride in the eyes, you increase your
admiration for the enduring powers of the
human spirit. You may wonder to yourself: "How
many and what kinds of adversities do men
need to achieve strength of character?"*

H. Armstrong Roberts

*Soliloquy from the top of a hill. When you view the houses and the people and their activities from the top of a hill, you wonder how others live their lives. What does each individual desire for himself? How is he trying to attain it? How do the hopes of the younger people differ from those who are mature?*

*You do not know—nor can you answer—your own questions, but you gain some new perspectives for yourself when you compare your own life with the imaginings you attribute to others. You recognize the limitations in your thinking because your observations and assumptions are limited to only their outward behavior. The dreams and hopes of others are hidden from you even more than your own.*

*Perhaps you conclude that some men devote so much time to thinking about themselves that their lives become self-centered and they fail to live as fully as they might. What lessons does man's experience through the ages teach us in regard to the proper balance between self-centered and other-directed thinking?*

H. Armstrong Roberts

*You see a skilled craftsman at his workbench repairing a product to increase the pleasure of the person who uses it. He is obviously so intent that he must be getting gratifying self-expression from his work. You hope that he enjoys his work so much that he suffers few frustrations of any kind. May he have none of the ailments found among those who are unhappy, those who never learned to enjoy anything that involves self-fulfilling learning or skill. Why is it that some men never do learn to enjoy constructive effort, but find pleasure in destroying what others have or do?*

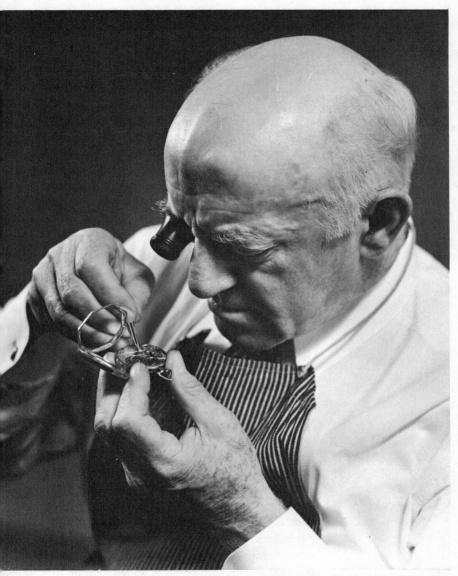

Photographed by Harold M. Lambert

*You watch children with a caterpillar. They are studying it and perhaps wondering how it will look after metamorphosis. They are exploring their world. You hope that their childhood curiosity will continue to make the experiences of each day so interesting that they will practice their lively curiosity through all their adult years. If they do, their old age should be as delightful as their childhood. You wonder why curiosity decreases for many children as they grow older. Will future generations deal more intelligently with this problem?*

Herbert Lanks from A. Devaney, N.Y.

*You see a boy talking with his dog. The two are somehow communicating with each other. He is explaining some of his important thoughts to his friend. The dog does not understand the words, but the two seem to be sharing mutually understood feelings. The boy will continue to try to explain and the dog will try to understand, for such has been the relationship of a boy to his dog for many centuries. Why do some children and animals come to understand each other? What are the factors in their abilities to communicate?*

*A grandfather and his grandson are engaged in discussing a mutually shared interest. His sincere interest in the small boy's enthusiasms are a manifestation of his love for the child. He knows that he cannot guide the child into intelligent adulthood by means of words only. Instead, he guides his growth into manhood through love, expressed in acts the child can appreciate. As the boy grows older, he will realize that his grandfather's love was dependable—he understood and loved him as a child. How can grandparents who wish to reach their grandchildren do so, when they did not understand each other years ago? What are the variables involved in this age-old question?*

Photographed by Harold M. Lambert

*Do you remember the last time you took a drive
over one of our country's mountainous highways?
Did you notice the great patterns formed by
the mountains, and the valleys that revealed
themselves to you from the top of a hill?
Next time you take a drive, stop on a high
summit and look around you. Think of the many
people in years gone by who have seen the
same sight and the many others to follow who
will also gaze with awe and admiration on
the patterns formed by the hills and valleys.
The hills you see now will change their contours,
but there will always be other hills and other
people to see and admire them. As a result, you
increase your feelings of kinship with
thoughtful men of the past and the future.*

Brown Brothers, N.Y.

*In the evening, you watch the setting sun. You think of the many orderly patterns of the universe which the sun exemplifies as it rises and sets, making the days longer or shorter. This pattern has been a continuous one since our universe began. To you and others, it has symbolized to men of all the past ages a reassuring beauty that eases troubles of the day and enables one to look forward to new tomorrows.*

H. Armstrong Roberts

## CHAPTER THIRTEEN

# Great Perspectives

*"The great use of life is to spend it*
*for something that will outlast it."*
—WILLIAM JAMES

AS YOU LOOK BACK over your life and the things which are especially meaningful to you, you realize that you would like to feel that
the "good" in your life will continue after you are gone. Women,
particularly, though they do not often talk about it, have this feeling
about their children. It is natural for a woman who is the mother of
sons and daughters to take pride in her children. The pleasures she
enjoys as she continues to live through their personal qualities and
achievements make her own life supremely satisfying. She feels
that her life and the things in which she believes will continue
through her offspring long after she has gone. A father, too, has
this same parental feeling in regard to his sons and/or daughters,
particularly when the sons and/or daughters develop as the father
hoped at the time when he saw each child for the first time.

Fortunate, indeed, the father who feels that he will continue to
live more fully through his children. If his own offspring are developing in the hoped-for directions, his satisfactions can be deeply
gratifying. Of course, every sensible parent does not expect his
children to become duplicates of himself, nor to live exactly as he

does. He does, however, expect them to develop into adults who live their life intelligently.

In the case of the man who has no children or whose children have developed in directions that he does not admire, the father is especially likely to turn to other young men or to institutions and principles that he can admire. He may not feel about these "psychological adoptions" in quite the same way he could toward his own descendants, but his hopes for the continuity of his own selfhood are likely to be centered in psychological substitutes: human, institutional, or idealistic. And some men are so fortunate as to have both the admired type of blood-related descendants and those whose kinship is expressed in a psychological relationship only. Most men have to settle for one of these rather than both. But each one or all can contribute to what he feels is worthy of continuity into the future. Horace (65–8 B.C.) phrased the feeling well: "I shall not wholly die. What's best of me shall 'scape the tomb."

## *What parts of your life do you consider worthy of continuity?*

Much of your thinking as to what parts of your life are worthy of continuity is governed by your basic attitudes toward others and yourself, by certain criteria of success, by concepts of personal responsibility, and by meanings of life as you perceive them. These constitute a "value system." Even though you have never formulated a personal philosophy—a conscious design for living—you have functioned in terms of patterns of things worthwhile to you.[1] Obviously, this question requires considerable contemplation on your part. It takes up much of the time of thoughtful men as they grow older.

As a man grows older, his concern with the inner life is likely to increase. You can often note this in the kinds of books that many older men read and the lectures they attend. David L. Gutmann, a research psychologist, has made several studies in this field and found, for example, in a study of 145 men aged forty to seventy-one that: ". . . older men fall off markedly in active participation with the outer world, shifting their attention to intrapsychic events.

Whereas the forty-year-old man tends to ignore the inner life and strives to dominate the outer world, older respondents seem to deploy their energy inward in the attempt to master the psychic life." [2]

When you are released from the old work responsibilities that tied down very much of your thinking, you will have the best opportunities of your lifetime to explore new meanings of life for you. To find the new meanings you have the benefit of your perspectives gained from years of experience. With those as a basis for thinking you can differentiate things which are really worthwhile from those which are only trivial. But this will have to be an active search, not a mere sitting around the house with the expectation that great ideas will come to you—they will come to you only if you actively seek them as definite objectives.

### AN ACTIVE MENTAL LIFE IS ESSENTIAL

Looking for meanings in life to some people suggests a withdrawing from the world, a sitting back and becoming inactive. They think of it as some vague procedure, such as the one practiced by certain ancient philosophers who put themselves into a state of *umbilicocity* (sitting under a shade tree, head bowed with chin on chest, and staring at the navel while meditating). Instead it must be a lively activity, a reexamination of what is observed, a searching and evaluative mental process similar to that of the scientist who conducts an experiment. He constantly reviews the findings and looks for the significant in the seemingly trivial.

One of the first tasks of the man who tries to clarify his personal philosophy is to decide for himself whether he lives in and is part of a capricious universe or whether he is a member of a universe that operates in terms of dependable patterns. If his universe is not dependable, there can be little hope for any continuity. He knows that he is in the midst of changes constantly taking place, but do the changes occur in accordance with recognizable patterns?

## *Dependable patterns in nature*

If you want to justify your hopes for the continuity of the best within your own life and the lives of others, you will have to sense the orderly functioning of the universe. You can acquire this perspective in several ways. Some men acquire it from their observation of a mechanical device or appliance such as a radio, television receiver, automobile, or a machine in a factory.

Other men acquire it when they stand on an upper floor of a towering building and look out over a great city where they see ships coming and going, automobiles and trains running in numerous directions, and people hurrying to and fro. The observer in the skyscraper notes the all-and-sundry activities, apparently without order but actually highly organized. He realizes that the seemingly random activities of people take place in an orderly manner.

Some women sense the orderliness of the universe by noting the rhythms in life and nature, as exemplified in the birth, growth, maturity, and death of human beings and the life cycles of the flowers of the field and garden.

The order and vastness of the universe, even if only feebly perceived, lift a person to a higher, nobler level. When his perspectives include time and space, he enriches his imagination and removes himself from much pettiness.

Great patterns in valleys, mountains, and unique rock formations have certainly been observed for many ages. Likewise the cycles of the seasons, the waxings and wanings of the moon, and the risings and the settings of the sun. Patterns of the Carboniferous period, reproduced on frosty window panes, have probably entranced children from the time when man first learned to make glass and use it in cold climates.

These and infinite numbers of other patterns have been seen by peoples of the earth long before the scientific methods of observation were developed. Now that we have the instruments of science we know that individual snow crystals are flat and six-sided. Within those limits, however, they show many variations; all have a characteristic pattern and belong to the hexagonal crystal system.

The modern scientist finds that many substances form crystals as orderly as those of the snowflake. All materials that crystallize can be classified into six natural systems. Each of the systems is characterized by definite patterns of crystal shape, one of which is hexagonal. The same patterns appear regardless of whether the crystal is 10 feet in length or microscopic in size. Most forms of matter crystallize and hence have distinguishing patterns. Interestingly, however, crystals never have the fivefold symmetry found in many biological forms such as in the five-armed starfish.

In the physical and biological sciences, the modern student sees countless examples of patterns which are indisputable evidence of the orderly functioning of the universe. In fact, the whole edifice of science is built upon the foundation of predictable patterns in the behavior of substances. Much of the scientist's daily activity is concerned with studying these recurrent patterns, so that he may discover the immutable principles which govern them. Generalizing from these observations permits him ultimately to formulate the natural laws of the universe—knowledge which is basic to human progress in every sector of life.

And yet, in spite of the fact that innumerable patterns are all around us every day, we seldom notice them or appreciate their significance. We fail to realize that patterns in nature indicate the functioning of mind or "Something" that has the attributes of mind as we know it. Without the influence of mind in the universe, there would be only chaos, instead of cosmos. Without mind, there could be no orderly relationships such as are found in the snowflake, the flower, the rhythmical ebb and flow of the tides, the life cycle of plants and animals, or the "birth" and disappearance of rocks and mountains. All these patterns, within limits, are orderly and stable.

At first thought, you may imagine that the most enduring things of the world are the rocks and mountains. Actually, as scientists have learned, the things that live are more nearly immortal than the so-called "everlasting hills." Seaweeds and jellyfish, as examples, are far older than the mountains.

The scientist of today studies the continuity of mountains, seaweeds, plants, and animals, as well as the behavior of atoms or light waves, in order that he may extend his knowledge of the natural laws their patterns illustrate. An appreciation of his findings opens up to us a cumulative revelation of the functioning of mind in our universe. As Galileo Galilei said: "With regard to objective certainty,

# Empathy

Can you feel the movement of a bird in flight
which this earthbound sculpture so beautifully
exemplifies? If you can, you are experiencing
empathy. This is the mental process of "feeling
oneself" into a situation, particularly into action
that is depicted by an artist. You experienced
this feeling when you watched a waterfall and
felt as though you were cascading over the
falls with the water.

Empathy is especially important in the life of
retirees. It is involved in the frequently made
recommendation to the retiree: "Stay in the
mainstream of life when you retire."

The retiree who continues to function in the
mainstream of activities reacts to the objects
and activities around him. Usually he is not
physically able to participate in the same work
and sports he enjoyed in his earlier years,
but empathy can more than make up for his
inability to participate in the physical sense. He
participates mentally and emotionally by
reading about news events, watching television,
and talking to others about the events in the
fields of his interest. He finds new mainstream
meanings every day. And he can enhance the old
meanings by turning to the messages
of the artists.

"Bird in Space" by Constantin Brancusi.
Collection, The Museum of Modern Art,
New York.

the few verities known by the human mind are known as perfectly by man as they are by God." [3]

Religion can gain far more through the findings of science than science can ever take away from religion, for, as Sir James Jeans has written: "The universe seems to be nearer to a great thought than to a great machine." Great scientists, sooner or later, have tended to become philosophically religious as they grew older and became more keenly aware of the infinite wisdom shown in nature's orderly processes. "There is always triumph: not of earth's physical force but of man's superb intelligence." [4]

Isn't it a pity that so many of us fail to use our intelligence to appreciate the significance of patterns in nature? We are like the animal in that we limit our view to the immediate situation only and fail to see it in its larger meanings. We keep our visions small and get bogged down in dealing with the trivial. And yet, the intelligent view of the immediate and the simple might enlarge our perspectives to appreciate the sublime and the magnificent.

When you have the larger perspectives you note the windblown sands that form wave-like formations, the silken finery of the cobweb, the orderly arrangement of the leaves and flowers of a plant, the flight pattern of a species of birds and, seeing these patterns, you *feel* yourself a part of the orderly continuing processes they represent.

As you watch birds in flight, you not only note the patterns in their movement, but you also feel yourself into their movement. If you have watched gulls soaring through the air, you experienced the movement, balance, and poise of the soaring bird, and you derived pleasure from it. This feeling oneself into and losing one's identity in a situation or object is called *empathy*.

Empathy is exemplified by the small boy who watches a galloping horse and then gallops in imitation of the horse's movement or by the man who watches the water cascading over falls and feels himself carried along in the leaping flow and spray.

Surely, you too have sensed these and other movements and patterns in nature. Why not appreciate that they represent eternal verities, truths that are timeless? Men in centuries past recognized them and countless men in centuries to come will also recognize and feel themselves a part of them. These empathic experiences offer you the privilege of enjoying a kind of immortality that transcends all ages known or yet to be imagined.

If you grasp this perspective, you will feel more secure because you will realize that you can put your trust in the dependability of the universe. As Justice Oliver Wendell Holmes so wisely stated: "It is enough for us that the universe has produced us and has within it, as less than it, all that we believe and love." If we can see our own life as part of a larger whole and think of ourselves as members of a cosmic team, the order and beauty inherent in nature offer us daily reasons for appreciation that we were born. What a privilege for one to live and experience the grandeurs in living! Why should anyone, particularly a retiree, cease to learn about the universe and all things that are in it? Retirement should be a most privileged opportunity to develop new insights and deeper meanings. The length of a man's life is, after all, not especially important —its breadth and depth are.

## Benefits of scientific advancement

Have you ever stopped to consider what a triumph the mere existence of life on this planet represents, how impossible it would have been for life to develop if the solar system were at all capricious, if its physical and chemical forces were not held in so nice a balance? The maintenance of life-supporting temperature, for example, depends on the constancy of the earth's distance from the sun, which is our primary source of heat and light. On earth, life occurs where the average—as distinct from the range—of the annual temperature is between 32 and 104 degrees Fahrenheit. A drop of 40 degrees in the average and another Ice Age would freeze us; a further 40 degrees drop, and life would be completely extinguished! A similar change in temperature in the opposite direction, lifting the average to, say, 160 degrees, would make life on the earth equally impossible. Fortunately for us, the orbit of the earth is unchanging. The universe functions in a remarkably reliable manner, so unvarying that astronomers can set their watches by the surface markings visible on the planet Mars during its rotations.[5]

You and I can have increased hope for the future of man when we have confidence in the fundamental dependability of our world. This confidence sustains and encourages us, especially when events in our own little lives turn out different from what we had hoped.

At first thought, a sublime perspective of the scheme of things might be construed as an invitation to "live among the stars" and ignore the ordinary, earthly events of our lives. Not at all. Rather, the opposite. The fact that our universe behaves in predictable patterns means that there are dependable natural laws that we can utilize for our benefit. We do this through science. As scientists widen their knowledge of the world about us and the laws that govern the behavior of its substance, we are able to devise new uses for resources and new ways to improve our living conditions.

Scientific progress, given practical application by technologists and industrialists, is responsible for our comfortable homes, our improved health, our short working day, our rapid transportation and communication systems, and our trained and informed citizenry. Science is more than merely the key to our material progress; it is the important link between man and his universe. It adds not only to his physical well-being and cultural development, but also—if he will see its larger significance—to his peace of mind. Only with a great perspective that shows man his relationship to the universe about him can there be inner peace and security.

In contrast with the more primitive peoples, the civilized human being of today is an expert in adapting nature to his needs and in adapting himself to nature's conditions. "No other vertebrate can live as can he on Antarctic ice cap, in Amazonian jungle, beneath the surface of the sea, or high in the air. Furthermore, man is the world's foremost specialist in transforming environments to bring them within the range of his powers. Far more efficient than the beaver or the mound-building ant, he drains the swamp, irrigates the desert, tunnels the mountain, bridges the river, digs the canal, conditions the air in home, factory, and office." [6]

For the group as well as for the individual, scientific advancement has brought great benefits, at times solving problems of social organization that otherwise would have required slow, costly experimentation. Generations ago, for example, social theorists were greatly perturbed by the loneliness of life in rural areas, and set up committees and organizations to devise ways of improving the situation, so as to give farm families a more varied, normal social life. While the sociologists talked, the scientists, engineers, and businessmen were developing the automobile and the radio, thereby overcoming the isolation of rural life and giving these people a better social life than the theorists could have conceived. The same kinds of solutions will probably be found for many of our social problems of today. Sometimes the bad will be corrected as by-products of the applications of science to other problems.

Fortunately, the opportunities for greater quality in living are increasing. As scientists push back the frontiers of knowledge, as the engineers, technicians, and industrialists learn how to utilize this newly· won knowledge, as modern means of communication bring a more rapid exchange of ideas, we may expect men to find new causes of conflict but also to rise to greater heights of understanding. Much has already been accomplished in the relatively short time that civilized man has been on earth, and future progress will take place at an even faster pace. The fact that it is scientific achievement that is revealing new facets of man's relationship to his universe and to his fellow men is immaterial; the important thing is that these developments open new avenues through which man may grow toward ultimate greatness of spirit. Certainly, many problems in life require the benefits not only of science but of every resource at our command.

These higher perspectives give a man poise in handling the everyday incidentals in life and, at the same time, enable him to live in quest of those values that are intrinsically worthwhile.

To summarize and apply these principles:

1. When you see patterns in nature, as in a cloud formation, striations of rocks, arrangement of plant leaves, and coloration of birds, let them represent to you the fact that the universe operates in an orderly, dependable manner. Your world should, therefore, be to you as an adult who is reaching for full maturity, just as secure and dependable as it was to you as a child when you trusted a dependable parent or other adult. In childhood, you felt secure because of some stronger person. Now that you are grown up, you are learning to understand and trust the cosmos more fully.

2. When you see an automobile on a street, an x-ray machine in a hospital, a great dam in a river, or similar man-made devices, think of them as examples of the ways in which men have utilized the dependable laws of nature for man's benefit. Assuredly, you can expect scientists, technical men, and businessmen to make further improvements for man's welfare in the years to come. The fact that we still have earthquakes, droughts, floods, wars, and various kinds of conflicts only means that we have not as yet learned how to understand, apply, or adapt ourselves to the forces available in our lives.

3. These greater perspectives should add to your search for the larger meanings in living. The motor operating in an automobile and the fact that 2 and 2 always make 4 should represent the orderly functioning of the universe and help you grow toward philosophic maturity. Inner strength to meet adversities comes to those who have attained this kind of personal growth.

4. When you strive toward the attainment of great perspectives, you find the daily commonplaces of life more meaningful. As you note additional examples of nature's patterns, such as the characteristic marks that a caterpillar makes in the dust of a garden path or a river makes through a mountain-range, your interests widen and your emotional satisfactions become intensified.

5. Your alertness to the patterns in nature and human affairs will increase your capacity for active responsive wonder. The most mature and creative adults have an openness of mind that enables them to find new facets in every experience. The lives of such persons are never dull nor are they bored. There is so much to explore that excites their interest and fires their imagination. They do not

make the statement, "So what?" characteristic of the individual who has closed his mind to a perceptive study of the world around him.

6. The best things in life can be enjoyed wherever you are: the home town, the big city, the living room, and among people you already know. These offer just as much opportunity to appreciate enduring truths as the academic hall, the mountain cabin, or the scientist's laboratory. It's the person doing the thinking that counts; not the place where he thinks.

7. When you attain great perspectives you are not overwhelmed by threats from modern-day rebels who, as one writer stated, advocate "sex without involvement, life without commitment, and freedom without purpose." The news services that feature the advocates of self-indulgence without self-discipline, the writers and artists who believe in nothingness or perversion, and a vapid world without appreciation of enduring values will not frighten you. Such emanations come from individuals who have not learned to see the great wonders of the universe, nor have they learned how intelligently directed approaches might be utilized more effectively. These unhappy people are confused and uncertain about themselves and the nature of the universe. They failed to continue in their quest to understand life a bit more fully each day.

Clearly, your perspectives, great or small, can be a major inner resource in the years of your maturity. If your perspectives are based in the things that have endured through the ages and you have added your own interpretations to the heritages from the past, you will have lived your life "for something that will outlast it." And you as a person will have advanced well on the road to the development of a personal philosophy, appropriate to your time and place.

## REFERENCES

1. See book by the staff of Rohrer, Hibler & Replogle, Charles D. Flory (ed.), *Managers for Tomorrow,* New York: Mentor Executive Library Books, published by The New American Library, Inc., 1967, chap. 16, "The Manager Is a Philosopher."
2. Bernice L. Neugarten, "Personality and the Aging Process," in Richard H.

Williams et al. (eds.), *Processes of Aging*, New York: Atherton Press, 1963, vol. 1, p. 330.

3. See Ernst Cassirer, "Galileo: A New Science and a New Spirit," *The American Scholar*, vol. 12, no. 1, p. 8.

4. Quoted from a letter, dated January 10, 1941, by Edward Ellery, National President of the Society of the Sigma Xi, in welcome to new members and associates.

5. See Waldemar Kaempffert, "Life: Vast Riddle of the Planets," *The New York Times Magazine*, June 26, 1932, p. 11.

6. For more complete explanation, see Kirtley F. Mather, "The Future of Man as an Inhabitant of the Earth," *Sigma Xi Quarterly*, vol. 28, no. 1, p. 7.

## CHAPTER FOURTEEN

# Further Thoughts for Developing a Personal Philosophy

*"For age is opportunity no less*
*Than youth itself, though in another dress,*
*And as the evening twilight fades away*
*The sky is filled with stars, invisible by day."*
— HENRY WADSWORTH LONGFELLOW,
"Morituri Salutamus"


SOME MEMBERS of every generation have imagined that they lived on the brink of destruction of their civilization. They believed they had somehow been assigned the responsibility of saving their civilization because, to them, it represented stability. They were concerned about political instabilities. These political instabilities have been with us so long and so often that we ought to recognize what Clarence Day pointed out: that only the hearts of men have remained essentially the same through all the various cataclysmic changes. To find the stability that we retirees want in our later years, we have to seek it in nature and in the life of individuals, not in the turbulent histories of nations. Nor can we find it featured in the daily newspaper or the television news program. The mass media feature the exceptional: the bizarre, the criminal, and the destroyers. They seldom find newsworthy the normal, the honest, or the build-

# THE WORLD OF BOOKS

Is the most remarkable creation of man
Nothing else that he builds ever lasts
Monuments fall
Nations perish
Civilizations grow old and die out
And after an era of darkness
New races build others
But in the world of books are volumes
That have seen this happen again and again
And yet live on
Still young
Still as fresh as the day they were written
Still telling men's hearts
Of the hearts of men centuries dead

—CLARENCE DAY

Reproduced by permission from *The Story of the Yale University Press Told by a Friend*—Clarence Day.

As an example of Clarence Day's statement about books that are "Still telling men's hearts/Of the hearts of men centuries dead," you may wish to read Hecuba's lament over her dead grandson in Euripides' *The Trojan Women:*

Poor little one. How savagely our ancient walls,
Apollo's towers, have torn away the curls
Your mother's fingers wound and where she pressed
her kisses—here where the broken bone grins white—
Oh no—I cannot—
Dear hands, the same dear shape your father's had,
how loosely now they fall. And dear proud lips
forever closed. False words you spoke to me
when you would jump into my bed, call me sweet
    names
and tell me, Grandmother, when you are dead,
I'll cut off a great lock of hair and lead my soldiers
    all
to ride out past your tomb.
Not you, but I, old, homeless, childless,
must lay you in your grave, so young,
so miserably dead.
Dear God. How you would run to greet me.
And I would nurse you in my arms, and oh,
so sweet to watch you sleep. All gone. . . .

Come, bring such covering for the pitiful dead body
as we still have. God has not left us much
to make a show with. Everything I have
I give you, child.

This was written 400 years before the birth of Christ.

*Source:* W. W. Norton & Company, Inc., an excerpt from *THREE GREEK PLAYS: Prometheus Bound, Agamemnon, The Trojan Women.* Translated with Introductions by Edith Hamilton. By permission of W. W. Norton & Company, Inc. Copyright renewed 1965 by Doris Fielding Reid.

ers of their age. You must find and observe these on your own initiative.

The basic hopes and fears, the delights and despairs, and the problems and frustrations that are the lot of mankind today have been described by great minds for the past thirty centuries. And yet to each of us in our time, the experience of recognizing age-old human characteristics appears to be as new as though we were their first discoverers. We as individuals need this experience of discovery, for that is the way we learn to appreciate the age-old truths.

## The eternal verities

From your present knowledge of the Bible, the works of Shakespeare, Aesop's *Fables* and other books, as well as your own observations, it becomes obvious to you, as you reflect on it, that there is one essential concept common to most great writing and art. The essence or recurrent theme, the message presented by the greatest minds of all time, is: *appreciate the events and principles in human experience that are timeless, the eternal verities, those that have lasting values in all ages.*

This is not so difficult as, at first thought, you may imagine. You now appreciate enduring values when you note an event or act that is significant for human growth and survival; you enjoy its emotional satisfactions. Whenever you, in your own situation, have an ennobling experience that others, too, have had in their time, you enjoy a perpetually recurrent phase of life. You have it when you discover a significant truth for yourself and say: "This principle is fundamental to human life; it always was so and always will be so. It is enduring, perpetual, ageless." Sometimes you have this kind of appreciation emotionally rather than intellectually, especially when you see a kind act, look into the eyes of a trusting child, listen to great music, see a fine painting, admire good dancing, attend the theater, or take part in a service of worship. You respond to affirmations that have meanings far above the content of the immediate situation.

All of us have experiences in our daily lives that reveal enduring truths, even though we may fail to recognize them or appreciate their significance. Each one of us has, for example, watched a craftsman at work and noted that he enjoyed it as a challenging task rather than for the reward obtained at its completion. At another time, we have seen a mother sacrifice her own comfort in order to give pleasure to her child. Or, we watched a father chide his son, and we realized that he was seeking emotional compensation for his own failures by urging his child to succeed. Or, we talked with a great man and we discovered that, being great, he had no need to emphasize his greatness. Or, we met a happy man and found that he had learned to live modestly, without desire for riches or fear of poverty. Truly, daily experiences whether you are rich or poor, old or young, educated or untutored, offer numerous opportunities to appreciate significant truths and events that appear generation after generation.

"There should be windows in heaven and skylights in hell" was the humorous way one man expressed this idea. He was using the old concept of a heaven located above the earth and hell below it. Imagine, then, a person who has lived a full life, died, and gone to either heaven or hell. From his window or skylight he could note the events beyond his own lifetime. His perspective would include, let us imagine, the time previous to his life, his own life, and the time beyond. From such a vantage point, an imagined person could note those phases of human experience that are important and those that are unimportant. Undoubtedly, he would think of some of his own lifetime experiences that worried him severely but were really trivial when viewed in long-term perspective. And he would think also of the pleasures that might have enriched his life if his friendships had been warmer, if his enjoyment of the fine arts had been keener, if his emphasis on money and status had been lessened. He would have defined the satisfactions to be sought in life on the basis of their values beyond the sorrows or joys of the immediate day.

The man who seeks for himself these finer appreciations of the timeless in human experience realizes that each person has, in the course of his physical life, one fundamental unit, namely, the experience of the moment. In the time sense, that is all that anyone can ever have. In terms of perspective, however, each moment may have rich memories of the past, splendid hopes for the future, and meanings with great value. Why not, then, live each moment to the full?

The man whose goal in life is the attainment of great perspectives and the enjoyment of the enduring truths lives across a greater span of time than his own years. As Socrates said, "The true end of life is to know the life that never ends," to know it here and now. Furthermore, such a man attains happiness for himself and contributes to the happiness of others. His goal of finding for himself and others the repeated fundamentals in human experience is so stimulating and satisfying that almost every waking hour adds a bit to his stature as a man. Such a man seeks the unfolding of his own fundamental nature and that of other human beings and therefore attains genuine happiness. He lives life at its best. Most of the greatest minds of all time have appreciated and taught this message in their writings. The things that mattered most to them were not the detached events of the day but the whole pattern of life as viewed in long-range perspective.

When we study the books of men whose writings have lived through the centuries, we are likely to conclude that many of them tried to answer for themselves and others the question: *When has a man lived life at its best?* Perhaps you have asked that same question when you looked at a tombstone in an old cemetery. As you looked at the name of the man buried there, you may have said to yourself: *"John Doe! I wonder, when he was alive, did he merely exist for a certain number of years or did he live life at its best, in the manner of a truly mature man?"*

And then also you probably said to yourself: *"When some stranger, a hundred years hence, looks at my name, will he ask the same question? Whether he does or not is incidental. Let me live the answer for myself in the here and now."*

To develop your own personal philosophy, one of the first requirements for attaining the full life is to feel at home, secure, in your universe. You have to know how to enjoy the things that stand the tests of time and last through the ages. As Seneca said 2,000 years ago: "Wisdom allows nothing to be good that will not be so forever; no man to be happy but he that needs no other happiness than what he has within himself; no man to be great or powerful that is not master of himself."

## The search for a personal philosophy usually begins with a personal problem

The benefits that you can derive from a personal philosophy are mainly these two: aid in adversity and a perspective for continuous intelligent living.

A few individuals seemingly develop their philosophies without the stimulus of tragedy or harsh misfortune in their earlier years. Motivated only by their desire to have the best that life can give, these few strive toward the attainment of a high level of maturity in their living. They learn to enjoy the beauty of a world of ordered intelligence through systematic thinking that brings about increased recognition of timeless patterns in nature and life. Certainly, a great philosophy should be just as important, perhaps more important, to the healthy, unperturbed individual as to the person who is undergoing some adversity.

Unfortunately, most persons are not motivated so as to make their discoveries of the great realities until burdens overwhelm them, and it is necessary to seek meanings for a life that is all but unendurable. This fact has caused someone to coin the witticism, "A philosopher is a fellow who, in adversity, consoles himself with maxims." The witticism has considerable truth insofar as it indicates the initiating stage in the development of most personal philosophies. This has been indicated time and again when I have asked persons untrained in philosophy the question, "What is your philosophy of life, especially in time of adversity?" The most common answer I received was, "I think of someone else who is in a predicament even worse than mine." They paraphrase the old Arabian proverb, "I had no

# Foreboding

*The artist, a German, painted this in 1936, a time when his nation was undergoing ominous changes. The darkness ahead was portrayed by an empty landscape under a lowering sky.*

*Individuals, in times of peace as well as during impending war, find it difficult to cope with the darkness of impending cataclysmic change. Some, in their despair, give up all hope of achieving peace with their world. As a result, the most despairing look toward an ending of their world as they know it.*

*This is a very old form of adjustment to all kinds of adversity—if the present appears to be completely hopeless, why not destroy the world? Many religious sects, cults, and individual theorists of every age have sought answers by this stance. If you want to estimate how often movements of this kind have occurred over the centuries, start with the Apocalypse and list recorded religious dogmas and movements that have predicted specific dates for the ending of the world.*

*For our own time, you might consider certain extremists, protester groups, who offer nothing constructive, only destruction of everything and everybody except themselves. By contrast, philosophers rarely lead political or mass movements to change the world. Instead, they try to improve themselves as individuals. They know that when individuals rise to the best within themselves, faith and hope still persist, whatever the temporary chaos in the world without.*

"Expectation" by Richard Oelze. Collection,
The Museum of Modern Art, New York.

shoes and complained, until I met a man who had no feet." This kind of answer indicates, of course, that the individual has not as yet learned to appreciate the positive aid in life of the enduring values.

Various kinds of answers to my questions have been given, but in many of them it is apparent that unhappiness or misfortune has provided the original impetus to philosophic thinking. The following replies illustrate the stimulating influence of problems in finding answers that result in the appreciation of meaningful values:

"When the problems of life weigh heavily on me, my first resort is what might be termed 'The continuity of life.' I think of all the great minds that have existed down through history. The great poets, musicians, philosophers, scientists, and men of letters parade by my eyes, and as I consider the tremendous contributions they have made to man's happiness, I realize how insignificant and trivial my worries really are. This process of reevaluating the present in terms of the much greater past seems to restore values to their proper place."

"When I get a feeling of depression because something has caused my life to go haywire, I like to sit down at a piano and play great music. Then the depressed feeling leaves. I think music is a good outlet for one's emotions, particularly classical music, for there is something good and beautiful about it which makes you forget all troubles."

"When I come up against a certain problem which seems to have no solution, I know that, whether the problem comes out good or bad, I'll always have friends and music and good books and nature to make life worthwhile. These are things which will always be comforting and give life a brighter outlook, even though life has become a complicated problem."

"I have discovered many beautiful and natural phenomena in life —things that cannot be soiled or hurt by the human touch—and I feel that these things surmount human problems, human mistakes. Such things are the stars, the sky, nature in general, and, especially, good music."

Quite rightly, the personal problem is often present as a motivating influence in the search for meanings, meanings that dwarf the pains and sorrows of the moment.

## Benefits of a personal philosophy

A personal philosophy should be of direct practical aid in dealing with life's most difficult problems. It should enable one to make more adequate adjustment to accident, ill health, old age, and death. To be worthy of its function, a philosophy should be useful when a man breaks a leg, is victimized by someone to whom he was kind, or finds that he must adapt himself to a new way of earning a living after he has retired. And many of those who suffer from severe catastrophes do develop for themselves a meaningful philosophy, an understanding of life that not only makes their problems endurable, but also lifts them to new strengths of character. To the casual observer, such persons appear to have had an unfortunate life; actually, their inner peace and strength are likely to be cause for admiration rather than pity.

I have known men who had developed a personal philosophy that stood up under the severest of tests.

One was a philosopher and a brilliant writer, a faculty colleague at Syracuse University, T. V. Smith, who reported in his autobiography an incident of how he met what appeared to be imminent death. The incident happened years ago, before airline pilots had adequate communication with the ground, as he was in a small plane flying over Boston. Lost in a heavy snowstorm and the gas almost gone, the copilot told the three male passengers "It's time to say your prayers." The gas supply was so low that a crash landing had to be made. While waiting for what might well be the end, Smith wrote an epitaph for his death on the portable typewriter that was on his lap:

> If in some midnight quietness, some roseate burst of dawn,
> Some noon-day's foggy frightfulness, these wings should happily
>     fawn to earth;
> And the friendly feverishness of life surrender its quick charms
> To the final dreamlessness of death, enfolding nescient arms,
> Say this, and only this you say
> On that not too unwelcomed day:

"He loved his life but recked it not,
And gladly died while the blood was hot."

Then scatter these ashes from a safer plane,
While the motors drone this last refrain:

"He loved life, loved it all—
Loved this, too, this last quick fall!" [1]

Men such as T. V. Smith are examples of the truly mature, those whose perspectives on life give them the ability to face serenely the final adversity. A personal philosophy should not only enable a retiree to face the end of his life but, more importantly, live his last years in happiness and fulfillment.

Charlotte Buhler has made studies of meaningful living in mature years and has given us descriptions of characteristics of persons who have achieved this level of maturity:

> The meaningful living person is seldom overactive in too many directions. Usually he concentrates on certain activities which are important to him.
>
> Very impressive for me was the interview with a 75-year old man I met as a bell man in a resort hotel. His name was Basil and he had emigrated some 50 years before from Yugoslavia. He was a retired railroad worker and lived as a widower on his social security, except for occasional odd jobs in resorts, which he loved.
>
> This man was a perfectly happy old man who in between his little duties enjoyed looking at the beautiful lake and the mountains, who occasionally liked to read a book about history or nature, and who said he liked to please and to help people as much as he could—in a casual way as well as through his lodges. He also liked to visit occasionally with his daughter and her children, about whose development he felt great satisfaction. With these few activities this man was perfectly content, because he was completely at peace with himself his God, and the world. His life had been meaningful to him and so was his old age . . .
>
> Study of the lives of persons who live their later years with the same zest as their life before gives insight into some important facts. One is that at all times, even if retired from employment, these individuals assign themselves self-chosen tasks and live on in a *rhythm between assignments and recreation and rest*. A second fact is that even for their leisure activities these individuals *choose occupations that have some fulfillment value*. The planning of activity programs

for people who have lost or perhaps never developed the concept of a meaningful living and fulfillment, is not a true solution of the problem of old-age.

In a culture of "progress" in which action represents the supreme value, the less active participant is apt to feel useless and worthless. The aging individual on whom more inactivity than desired is often enforced, is most in need of a *philosophy of life*. He should be assisted in re-establishing the *integrity of his inner life* and in the understanding of what he owes to himself as a human being.[2]

## To evaluate the significant experiences of your past

Those persons who have learned to deal intelligently with their earlier problems achieve the inner strength and happiness which make for worthy living in the later years. Everyday problems and seemingly unbearable situations stimulate them to acquire insights that eventually enable them to enjoy the experiences that contribute to genuine inner growth. They attain great perspectives. Fortunately for the person who has reached the retirement age, he can look back on the events in his personal history to evaluate the significant experiences in his past as well as in the present. He can apply three basic criteria to any experience:

1. Is it timeless—that is, did it probably occur in the experiences of individuals in the year, say, 200 B.C., and is it likely to occur also in the lives of those who will be living in A.D. 2200?

2. Does it have enduring human values—that is, does it contribute to the positive development and happier living of those who experience it? (Crime, vice, ignorance, greed, and pain are found in every age, but they do not contribute positively to enduring human values.)

3. Does it offer the person who experiences the situation a greater appreciation of some fundamental pattern that reveals the Basic Mind of the universe?

For, as we study the stages in the development of man on the earth, we note that the lower the scale of human development, the more man tends to adjust on the plane of his physical senses. As he rises in his growth, he responds more and more to things intellectual, aesthetic, and spiritual. He becomes aware of the enduring nature of these higher responses. He gradually realizes that he represents the timeless and significant elements in all human experience.

He attains his highest levels when he is sustained by a personal philosophy that enables him to say to himself: "I have learned to survey life in terms of its finest perspectives. I have learned how to appreciate the simplest everyday events so that I have continuously experienced the eternal. Each moment is timeless, ageless, and, for me, endowed with order, beauty, and peace."

Such a man has grappled with the age-old question, "When has a man lived life at its best?" The answer is: "A man lives life at its best when he has learned to enjoy most fully the timeless truths."

### Contributions of the fine arts

Scientific analysis and invention are generous aids to those of us who seek to understand our living more fully, but the fact that an engineer invents a cardiograph does not mean that he has an educated heart. The laboratory expert in plant anatomy does not necessarily see the beauty of the flowers, nor does every structural geologist experience the grandeur that is in the mountains. These greater discernments are matters of feeling in which the senses as well as the intellect participate. Science alone can never teach us the art of living. That can be sought best through philosophy, the fine arts, and religion. The function of these is to open up our sensitiveness to the best in all human experience—to reveal to us the great enduring truths in the life of man. Philosophy and the fine arts are more than descriptive or instructive—they help us to choose and to clarify our values and to redirect our baser emotions toward noble ends.

Through them, we learn to discern and interpret the more significant relationships in daily experiences, to know what to love and what to ignore. Through them, we learn to "feel" the patterns in mountain ridges, shadows on the lawn, the dewy cobwebs of a summer morning, leaves of oak trees, waves in the blown sands, the spire-like formations of an old canyon, the colorful rose, or the patterns in the behavior of children. They enable us to feel the rhythm and beat of human life as portrayed in the painting, the poem, the statue, the dance, and the symphony.

The universe in all its immensity and infinite mystery is a stage upon which, each moment, is offered to every man the privilege of feeling the things that are greater than man himself, but great only because of man. The patterns of cycles and rhythms in the larger universe are constantly epitomized in the cycles and rhythms of the individual life. Every man begins as a microcosm whose origin is hidden in the biological ages. He is born into a world that is to him a strange and 'uncertain place; he becomes the exploring toddler who learns what is pleasant and what is harmful, and passes on to awkward adolescence when he tries to adapt himself to an unyielding society. His passions and ambitions drive him to learn and to control the urges within him as well as the conditions around him. He goes on into middle life, becomes either more cynical or more tolerant, more blind in his fixed habits or more discerning in his judgments. Eventually, his body declines in vigor, though his mind may achieve a peace and wisdom that transcends the knowledge and ambitions of youth. These are the age-old truths which the fine arts portray, the universal human experiences they seek to explain.

Beauty arouses lively associations that enable us to interpret our idealizations through measure and symmetry. Insight into the beauties of life's rhythms and patterns is heightened through the fine arts, such as the symphony with its strains of conflict and eventual victory or consolation. The artist is usually concerned with a single experience and from that he distills the essential quality, universally applicable and worthy of preservation in color, form, sound, or motion. His art symbols depict for us the whole creation and order of the illimitable universe. The great artist does not ignore the ugliness in life. Rather, he endeavors to look beyond the squalor or desolation of the scene, finding the patterns of form or color which give beauty to every aspect of life. In the hands of an artist, even a dreary landscape can become a part of the larger beauty of nature, symbolizing its power and grandeur.

Alinari—Art Reference Bureau

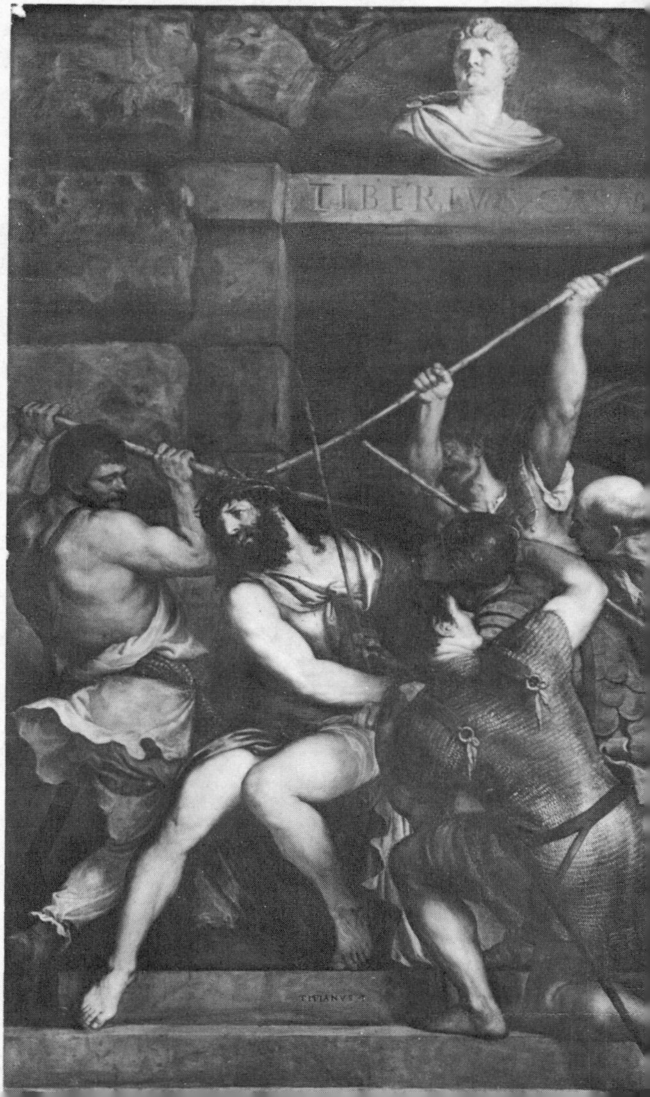

Bruckmann—Art Reference Bureau

## How Has the Artist Matured as an Artist through the Years?

*If you want to see the effects of psychological maturity in the works of great artists, you can do so by comparing the works of their youth with those of their later years. The painting in the Louvre by Titian (Tiziano Vecellio, 1477–1576) of "Christ and the Crown of Thorns," was done in 1542. Note the attention to details in the costumes and the facial expressions of the guards.*

*Here the facial expression of Christ shows the pathetic sadness of a victim of cruelty.*

*In Titian's later painting, done in his ninety-fifth year, there is less detail and less portrayal of action, but the total presentation to the viewer is a timeless image of suffering endured by a man of great character, a man to whom pain is incidental—his superior character and the kingly purpose in his mind enable him to rise above the effects of pain.*

*Generally, when you study the differences between earlier and later works of the same artist, you are likely to find that the earlier paintings have more emphases on externals, more naturalistic beauty, and more literal reproduction. In later works, there is likely to be more visionary beauty, more signs of inward harmony, more evidence of character, and more concern about enduring values.*

## How Has the Retiree Matured as a Retiree through the Years?

*People who associate with a retiree view him in ways similar to those of a knowledgeable person who studies the early and later works of an artist. They, too, apply their standards of judgment concerning the retiree's changes in personality and behavior through the years. When he is a prospective or recent retiree, they expect him to be oriented toward the usual retirement pattern: talkativeness about what and where he eats, recitals about his health, detailed descriptions of his chore routines, anger over insults by others, dependence on restricted social contacts, and participation in recreations of the old folks variety—the static way of life of the stereotyped retiree.*

*As he moves through the retirement years, a retiree's associates note whether he has settled permanently into a static, perhaps regressive, way of life or moved forward into a new stage of active self-fulfillment. Is he reaching out for ways to live anew: taking interest in problems new to him, people new to him, and previously unexplored means of enjoying the days added to his years? If his mental life is dynamic in tone, many of his reachings are likely to be related to his interpretations of what life is about.*

The fine arts give us freshness of vision and emotional glamour, insight beyond the cold realities. Music gives us sentiment without words, while poetry uses words to give us truth with sentiment. Literature and the theater recreate significant pictures of life. Painting and sculpture give color and form. Each medium offers new facets of life and leads us to venture into the mysteries that pervade and outlast life itself. The fine arts take the everyday experiences of the ordinary individual and illuminate them to produce meaning for him.

The enduring lessons of the fine arts are also necessary for the people of a nation to achieve growth and unity. The only way we can have an enduring nation is by means of well-developed arts. History shows that those nations which had developed the arts never perished from the earth, even though their political and economic achievements are forgotten. Only the artist can bring together the related parts in the life of the nation and the individual and thus reveal the deeper patterns.

He deals with that which is universal in human experience, and uses this common language to point the way toward achievement of man's greater goals. You and I, in our day, can continue to live in our established ways, but our lives will be richer if, to the earning of our daily bread, we can add the satisfactions of the artist and the philosopher, derived from a constant search for a better understanding of the universe, an appreciation of the enduring principles in human experience and the sources of inner strength of character, and a clearer insight into the nature of reality. We can expand our own horizons if we listen to music, see plays and paintings, and read literature with genuine artistic understanding.

Many of us, of course, have not as yet learned how to enjoy classical music, fine paintings, or great literature. But any one of us can develop the ability to use them for philosophic thinking. The first requirement is that you recognize the universality of the experiences which the great artist is depicting. The mighty thoughts, splendid designs, and great perspectives of artists and philosophers will have no meaning for you unless you have encountered them before, either consciously or through the inner awakening of a dream.

Undoubtedly, you have already observed the physical patterns in nature as well as those in human experience such as joys and sorrows, periods of peace and conflict, and the failures and triumphs of your own life and the lives of other men and women. As you observed and experienced them, you may have thought also of others whose lives had followed similar cycles in the past, and of those who will have like experiences in the future. If you have meditated on the perpetually recurrent patterns that have taken place in human life through the centuries, you have found the symbolisms of some of the arts both soothing and stimulating. The arts have some meanings for you, even though you cannot express them in words that are adequate. The power to *feel* their meanings and through your feelings to rise to a higher level of strength and insight is the main objective for yourself.

To the great artist and philosopher, the commonplace may represent or at least lead to the meaningful and the sublime. What you bring to the experience and the interpretations you make and feel determine the level of your understanding of the artistic.

Obviously, when you find that you have risen to a slightly higher level of appreciation of one or more of the fine arts, you will want to develop your appreciation further. You may still listen to some of the same kinds of television drama, read the same kinds of fiction, and attend the same grades of moving pictures that you enjoyed in your earlier years. But when you have learned to feel secure because of the orderliness in the universe, to sense the designs in nature, to note the patterns in human behavior, to seek inner strength for yourself, and to think of your daily experiences as having enduring values, you will find yourself interpreting even poor drama and fiction in worthy ways.

Fortunately, each one of us becomes, to some extent, his own artist. He needs the stimulus and example of the great artists, but each man also makes his own art. He makes it when he looks out of his shop window and notes the graceful flight of a bird, when he glances at his work and feels the pride of craftsmanship, or when he directs his child's developing character toward the things he believes to be timeless in human life. His modesty may not allow him to say that he has learned the art of living, but the wise artists of the ages know that he is truly cultured, for the truly cultured man may not be erudite—he feels the right things. As Quintilian expressed it 2,000 years ago: "The learned understand the reason of art; the unlearned feel the pleasure."

Surely art is not limited to the few people who make it their profession by painting pictures, molding clay, or writing plays. Many persons do, indeed, practice the fine art of living, and this is the greatest of all the arts. They do it by giving their lives meaning and beauty, and they do it regardless of the era in which they live, whether in an ancient bow-and-arrow or in a modern atomic age.

### "In          We Trust"

In a recent graphics contest in which the problem centered about the typographic illustration of "words we live with," first prize went to a white rectangle with bold black letters stating "In          We Trust." The point, as explained by Janet Horner, a 20-year-old student at Pratt Institute of Art School, is that "people today—rightly or wrongly—put their trust in many things besides God and I felt my design would have greater impact with the word removed."

Aside from getting into the theological or denominational ambiguity of the familiar "In God we trust" declaration—after all, which religion's God do "we" really trust in?—the prize poster painfully clarifies the difficulty of pinpointing something in which modern man does indeed trust. While many people have managed to maintain their various faiths, there is a widespread questioning of values both spiritual and secular.

Give it a try: Art, Science, Psychiatry, the Corporation, the State, LSD, Love, Diplomacy, Logic, Power? Any one or even a combination of these somehow seems inadequate in the face of frustrations in Vietnam, racial disorders at home or a creeping vulgarity on practically a world-wide basis.

One of the most disturbing elements in some of the social and moral upheavals in contemporary life—and there are and have been many—is the all too frequent assault on a traditional base or belief with apparently nothing in the offing to fill in the subsequent gap.

Perhaps out of that very need will in time come a general restoration of belief. We do not profess to know; we merely note a mark of the age: An increasing unease among all types and classes of people that can usually only be described vaguely as a feeling of emptiness.

And it is this sad state, this emptiness, that Miss Horner has graphically—even if unintentionally—illustrated.[3]

## Religion, the greatest of all the arts

Regardless of what religion may or may not mean to you, when you think of the phases in your life that have occurred in the lives of other human beings throughout the centuries, you realize that religion has survived because of the values it has given many people of all races and eras. Through religion, millions of individuals have attained a sense of personal worth, trust in the ultimate victory of good over evil, membership in a communal fellowship, confession and forgiveness, principles for the guiding of youth along approved paths, a disciplined way of life, and aspirations toward a better selfhood.

Through religion, many of those who suffered from guilt, found a healing forgiveness. Those suffering from sorrow had their grief eased. Those suffering from fear obtained a dependable faith. And those suffering from hostility found a comforting love. When we think of these contributions of religion, whatever the unique form of its dogma for any one person, we can understand why it has offered and will continue to offer benefits that many persons need. From it, certain persons gain a sense of security for themselves in time of trouble because their religion makes extremely difficult events appear reasonable rather than the effects of an evil influence.

Sooner or later, every man has a personal problem which he cannot solve. Nor can any other human being solve it for him. He knows that all hopes for aid from earthly resources are completely gone. And so, in the midst of his need, he turns for help to the Power which is back of all the resources of the universe. He discovers his God. The individual's relation to his God is always a personal one— a fact which explains why hymns are written in the first person.

Sometimes his God comes to his rescue or at least appears to do so. At other times, the individual finds that his problem is not solved directly, but he discovers previously unrealized resources within himself, and these resources enable him to rise above his problem.

He finds that the unsolved problem which he did not want to bear forced him to become a stronger and wiser man. Eventually, he finds that the supposedly unendurable problem was necessary for him in order that he might discover not only the will of his God, but also the laws and loves of his mind. Many a person not only has found his God, but also learned how to live on a higher spiritual plane as a result of coming to grips with an intense fear such as the imminence of death in battle or disease.

Religion is essential to the individual who has mild problems as well as to him who has grievous, insuperable problems. Every person has so many difficulties and uncertainties in life that he feels lonesome and afraid. His little problems often accumulate into a burdensome emotional load. He does not quite understand or fully appreciate his own impulsions. Nor do other people realize the weight and extent of his burdens, his inferiorities and his inadequacies. Only with his God can he find satisfying fellowship. The inner freedom he gains must be attained by keeping the struggle on a high spiritual basis, not as an attempt to bargain with God. Any other approach to man's freedom would be merely a political, economic, or social one and essentially unworthy of a man's highest respect.

The individual deals with many moral problems of his own. His animal urges are constantly with him. Primitive impulsions beset him. Conflicts disturb him. However, his religion offers certain standards of conduct that help him solve many dilemmas as to right and wrong. Furthermore, he realizes that even though his religion may not always answer his particular ethical questions, it does help to uphold certain moral standards which he believes to be good for himself and his fellow men.

Religion, at its best, is far more than a keeper of morals for others. It becomes a challenge when it offers the individual an incentive to stand for the best human values, such as kindness to the weak, loyalty to truth, and consideration for the needy at sacrifice of personal comfort.

Religion is not a device for getting more things for ourselves. Nor is one's God to be commanded to have the wind blow from the south when we travel from the south—unmindful of the sailor who is traveling from the north toward the south. Prayer for the privilege of having our own way is less challenging than prayer for personal integrity. It should be directed toward the desire to live each day fully, with strength to do the task before us and do it well, not asking that it be made easier. It should lead toward strength of character as well as insight into the patterns and laws of truth.

Every thoughtful man knows that he is a participant in many patterns of activity in the universe. His birth, life, and death are obviously parts of some larger pattern of human development. Every activity of every moment of the day is a phase of some larger pattern of reality. He senses that all these patterns are orderly because there is some orderly control or universally intelligent "Mind" at work. Of those who recognize the influence of a universal mind, some prefer to call it the Cosmic Intelligence; others personify it and think of "God" as a fellow being.

Great truths in life and in religion can be expressed best by means of the arts. Jesus was an artist who taught timeless truths by means of artistic speech. When He wanted to offer His hearers a fundamental concept for their living, He usually presented a picture, a story, or a drama. A spoiled son leaves home; a man is robbed and beaten and lies by the side of the road where self-righteous men pass him by; the kingdom of heaven is like unto a small child; the meek shall inherit the earth; and the God-given array of the wild lily outshines the glory of Solomon.

Jesus spoke the fundamental language of religion, the language of the picturesque, the symbolical, the dramatic. He knew that the lasting messages of religion are attained through the personal experiences of the individual and the individual's interpretations of his experience. He knew that logic alone does not answer many of the individual's most important questions and personal problems.

As with all arts, religion has endured because it has offered interpretive experiences, satisfying for their own sake; because it is the greatest of the arts for most people. It offers courage to deal with personal problems of daily life, to enjoy life more fully, and to appreciate the timeless truths that have enduring spiritual values.

People at present are adrift because their intellectual leaders have broken with the old beliefs but have not taken the time to master the elements of a conception of life that does full justice to science, philosophy, and the moral nature. When we appreciate the fact that all material things are primarily values and interest us only as such, we are ready to advance to the demonstrable conclusion that the utlimate power expressed in these values is an Intelligence with whom we have to do when we deal with nature and life. This is a bedrock on which one can build a conception of life's meaning that sets free the religious impulses. For religion is a response of our whole nature to our fundamental beliefs. The theology on which the old-time religion was based had its origin in the science and philosophy of long ago, when modern scientific concepts had not yet been worked out, and when man's life on earth was so uncomfortable that he had to look to an afterlife for pleasure. A vastly better theology is now possible, largely as the result of the productive work of scientists, philosophers, and religionists. It is in an evolutionary process of development.

Fortunately, sublime living is not measured by the number of years before death nor by an expected existence after death. Completeness of living in terms of the appreciation of timeless truths and experiences may be felt in childhood, intelligently recognized in early adulthood, and enjoyed in maturity rather than after death. It is in the here and now.

It is a constant exercise of the intellect and the spirit that reaches eagerly for quality in daily living. The search for quality leads to a reverent quest for that which is best in human experience. As Maxwell Anderson has stated:

> The dream of the race is that it may make itself better and wiser than it is, and every philosopher or artist who has ever appeared among us has turned his face away from what man is toward whatever seems to him most godlike that man may become.[4]

The individual who has accepted himself and led what he believes to have been a good life adjusts easily to aging. He enjoys a life of inner serenity in his later years because his daily living is worthwhile. He who has learned to live in terms of great values that are meaningful to him has no fear of death. For when he comes to the end, he sees death as the completion of a pattern that is natural and wholly acceptable.

In the meantime, as a retiree, you can enjoy the privileges of old age, delightfully affirmed by T. V. Smith when he retired from academic life at Syracuse University. At that time he read a witty and moving essay, taken from his *Retrospect and Prospect,* a volume published in his honor by his colleagues and reprinted by popular demand for those facing the philosophical adjustment to the unaccustomed leisure of retirement. You may find especially helpful the following extracts:

> I think I see a way, with the aid of the philosophers, not unassisted by the poets, of reconciling us in retirement to the gradual deprivation of deference, meantime prudently availing ourselves to all that is in sight, properly rationed. The philosopher has been whimsically but cannily described as a man who, when he meets a difficulty, makes a distinction. We ourselves have now met the greatest of all difficulties: namely, that we cannot evaluate life merely in terms of life, as is our American wont, without surrendering life to credulity or making death a tragic thing. Let us, then, try evaluating life in terms of a category larger than life, large enough to accommodate both growth and decay, to house both life and death. "Reverence for life" is great; reverence for *being* is greater. . . .
>
> As Carl Becker so well puts it: "Apart from man, the universe knows nothing at all—nothing of itself or of infinite spaces, nothing of man or of his frustrated aspirations, nothing of beginnings and endings, of progress or retrogression, of life or death, of good or evil fortune. The cosmic view of the universe and of man's ultimate fate within it, is man's achievement . . . man's most ingenious invention, his supreme work of art."

Smith recognized very well the fact that the definitions of the great truths of human experience always will be topics of continued discussion and that the final answer for the individual can be put into words only by the poet, whose descriptions of truth are in the realm of the fanciful:

> To all hastening men and especially to the argumentative ones, my doorplate shall hereafter proclaim the dear primacy of fancy:

"Do not come and look for me, I shall be gone;
My bed will be empty, my door standing open—
I have a pilgrimage to make before the dawn!

There is a hill against the far horizon,
Where the heavens dip down, and at last disappear.
If I climb to the top, when the stars are just setting,
I know I can reach them, they will be so near!

Knee-deep in flowers, with the night winds about me,
I shall stand where the sky and the hill crest meet,
And here a star, and there a star, I'll gather for a garland
Which I shall bring at dawning to lay before your feet."

—JAMIE SEXTON HOLME [5]

# REFERENCES

1. T. V. Smith, *A Non-existent Man,* Austin, Texas: University of Texas Press, 1962, p. 33. Copyright by T. V. Smith, 1962.
2. Charlotte Buhler, "Meaningful Living in the Mature Years," chap. 12 in Robert W. Kleemeier, *Aging and Leisure,* New York: Oxford University Press, 1961, pp. 383–386.
3. Courtesy of *The Wall Street Journal,* Aug. 2, 1967, p. 10.
4. Maxwell Anderson, *The Essence of Tragedy and Other Footnotes and Papers,* Anderson House, 1939, Reprinted by permission of Maxwell Anderson.
5. T. V. Smith, *On Being Retired,* Syracuse, N.Y.: Syracuse University Press, pp. 24, 32, 35. Copyright 1956 Syracuse University Press. The poem by Jamie Sexton Holme was quoted from this source. The original publication and copyright owner of the poem are unknown to the author of this book. The best possible conjecture is that it may have been published by H. H. Harrison and that the publication rights passed to A. S. Barnes & Company, Inc.

# Index